# About Richard Estep

**Richard Estep** is the author of more than twenty books, including Visible Ink Press's *Serial Killers: The Minds, Methods, and Mayhem of History's Most Notorious Murderers*, *The Serial Killer Next Door: The Double Lives of Notorious Murderers*, and *The Handy Armed Forces Answer Book*. Additionally, he has written numerous paranormal nonfiction titles, including *The Horrors of Fox Hollow Farm: Unraveling the History & Hauntings of a Serial Killer's Home* and *The Haunting of Asylum 49: Chilling Tales of Aggressive Spirits, Phantom Doctors, and the Secret of Room 666*. He is a regular columnist for *Haunted Magazine* and has also written for the *Journal of Emergency Medical Services*. Richard appears regularly on the TV shows *Haunted Case Files*, *Haunted Hospitals*, *Paranormal 911*, and *Paranormal Night Shift*. He has had a lifelong fascination for true crime, the military, and ghosts. British by birth, Richard now makes his home in Colorado a few miles north of Denver, where he serves as a paramedic and lives with his wife and a menagerie of adopted animals.

# Also from Visible Ink Press

*Alien Mysteries: Conspiracies and Cover-Ups*
by Kevin D. Randle
ISBN: 978-1-57859-418-4

*American Cults: Cabals, Corruption, and Charismatic Leaders*
by Jim Willis
ISBN: 978-1-57859-800-7

*American Murder: Criminals, Crime, and the Media*
by Mike Mayo
ISBN: 978-1-57859-191-6

*Area 51: The Revealing Truth of UFOs, Secret Aircraft, Cover-Ups & Conspiracies*
by Nick Redfern
ISBN: 978-1-57859-679-9

*Assassinations: The Plots, Politics, and Powers behind History-Changing Murders*
by Nick Redfern
ISBN: 978-1-57859-690-4

*Celebrity Ghosts and Notorious Hauntings*
by Marie D. Jones
ISBN: 978-1-57859-689-8

*Conspiracies and Secret Societies: The Complete Dossier of Hidden Plots and Schemes*
by Brad Steiger and Sherry Hansen Steiger
ISBN: 978-1-57859-767-3

*Control: MKUltra, Chemtrails, and the Conspiracy to Suppress the Masses*
by Nick Redfern
ISBN: 978-1-57859-614-0

*Cover-Ups and Secrets: The Complete Guide to Government Conspiracies, Manipulations & Deceptions*
by Nick Redfern
ISBN: 978-1-57859-638-6

*The Government UFO Files: The Conspiracy of Cover-Up*
by Kevin D. Randle
ISBN: 978-1-57859-477-1

*The Handy Armed Forces Answer Book*
by Richard Estep
ISBN: 978-1-57859-743-7

*The Handy Forensic Science Answer Book: Reading Clues at the Crime Scene, Crime Lab, and in Court*
by Patricia Barnes-Svarney and Thomas E. Svarney
ISBN: 978-1-57859-621-8

*Hidden History: Ancient Aliens and the Suppressed Origins of Civilization*
by Jim Willis
ISBN: 978-1-57859-710-9

*The Illuminati: The Secret Society That Hijacked the World*
by Jim Marrs
ISBN: 978-1-57859-619-5

*The New World Order Book*
by Nick Redfern
ISBN: 978-1-57859-615-7

*Runaway Science: True Stories of Raging
Robots and Hi-Tech Horrors*
by Nick Redfern
ISBN: 978-1-57859-801-4

*Secret History: Conspiracies from Ancient
Aliens to the New World Order*
by Nick Redfern
ISBN: 978-1-57859-479-5

*Secret Societies: The Complete Guide to Histo-
ries, Rites, and Rituals*
by Nick Redfern
ISBN: 978-1-57859-483-2

*The Serial Killer Next Door: The Double Lives
of Notorious Murderers*
by Richard Estep
ISBN: 978-1-57859-768-0

*Serial Killers: The Minds, Methods, and May-
hem of History's Notorious Murderers*
by Richard Estep
ISBN: 978-1-57859-707-9

*Time Travel: The Science and Science Fiction*
by Nick Redfern
ISBN: 978-1-57859-723-9

*Toxin Nation: The Poisoning of Our Air,
Water, Food, and Bodies*
by Marie D. Jones
ISBN: 978-1-57859-709-3

*The UFO Dossier: 100 Year of Government
Secrets, Conspiracies, and Cover-Ups*
by Kevin D. Randle
ISBN: 978-1-57859-564-8

**Please visit us at VisibleInkPress.com**

# GRIFTERS, FRAUDS, AND CROOKS

## TRUE STORIES OF AMERICAN CORRUPTION

### RICHARD ESTEP

DETROIT

# Grifters, Frauds, and Crooks: True Stories of American Corruption

Visible Ink Press®
43311 Joy Rd., #414
Canton, MI 48187-2075

Visible Ink Press is a registered trademark of Visible Ink Press LLC.

Most Visible Ink Press books are available at special quantity discounts when purchased in bulk by corporations, organizations, or groups. Customized printings, special imprints, messages, and excerpts can be produced to meet your needs. For more information, contact Special Markets Director, Visible Ink Press, www.visibleink.com, or 734-667-3211.

Managing Editor: Christa Gainor
Art Director: Alessandro Cinelli, Cinelli Design
Cover Design: John Gouin, Graphikitchen, LLC
Typesetting: Lumina Datamatics
Image Editor: Gregory Hayes
Proofreader: Larry Baker
Indexer: Shoshana Hurwitz

ISBN: 978-1-57859-796-3 (paperback)
ISBN: 978-1-57859-827-4 (hardcover)
ISBN: 978-1-57859-828-1 (eBook)

Cataloging-in-Publication Data is on file at the Library of Congress.

10 9 8 7 6 5 4 3 2 1

# Contents

Introduction ... ix

# Introduction

At its inception in 1776, the United States was founded on the notion that it would be a fair and equal nation, a society free from corruption—as far as this could reasonably be achieved. The Founding Fathers found little to celebrate in the British systems and customs of government. At the seat of the British Empire, a person's success depended mostly on who their father was, their social standing, and the circumstances of their birth.

Although it was widely regarded (at least among its own elite) as one of the greatest forms of government in the world, the British system was clearly bloated and corrupt. Many accused it of being little more than a boys' club—one in which privilege, status, and material wealth were of prime importance. After the Battle of Waterloo in 1815, the Duke of Wellington famously remarked that the battle had been "won on the playing fields of Eton," the elite private school attended by many of his officers.

The United States, it was hoped, was going to be different. The new nation was conceived as a meritocracy, a place of opportunity in which hard work, diligence, and no small amount of luck could see men such as George Washington and John Adams rise to hold the highest office in the land. In this great democratic experiment, there was no place for a king, wielding supreme power over his subjects; instead, there was to be a presidency, an office that would share power with a congress. This would provide checks and balances, reducing the possibility of a tyrant, such as the one they had overthrown, from gaining control. The leaders of the United States were intended to be the servants of the people, not their masters.

There would be growing pains, but there would also be much for Americans to be proud of in their new country. If the course of human history teaches us anything, however, it is that scandal and corruption are never far from the source of power, no matter which system of governance is in place. The likelihood of there being corruption should never be in doubt; it is simply a question of the degree to which it infiltrates the rooms and corridors of power.

Saying the name "George Washington" conjures up an image of trustworthiness, honest, and decency in the minds of most Americans. It is therefore all the more ironic that the city named after him, the very capital of the nation he helped found, has become a byword for corruption and dishonesty.

Our notions surrounding the character of the first president of the United States are mostly correct. Washington was revered as the man who had beaten the British army, the world's preeminent military machine, to secure the new nation's freedom and independence. As such, he rode a tidal wave of good will into office that few presidents since have enjoyed.

It is important for us to remember that Washington and his peers were being judged by the standards of their times, and the American public of the late 18th century was far less tolerant of what they perceived to be corrupt behavior than they are today. In the United States of the 21st century, not a single day goes by without fresh allegations and ironclad proof of political corruption being part of the 24-hour news cycle. It is so common and widespread that we have become inured to it. We are no longer surprised, let alone shocked, when the latest news story concerning corrupt behavior breaks.

Back in Washington's day, corruption and scandal were considered a much bigger deal than they are now. Citizens were less willing to cut their elected officials slack for their behavior. Politicians were expected to put service before self. By almost any measurable metric, George Washington's administration was among the least corrupt of any in U.S. history, yet that did not protect him from taking flak for some of his own actions and those of his associates. Even though he was about as clean as any president in history, as his time in office went on, the glow of Washington's hero status began to fade. Detractors slung mud in the hopes that at least some of it would stick. Inevitably, some did.

The Jay Treaty (1794), named after its architect, Chief Justice John Jay, was a prime focus of the American public's ire. In the aftermath of their Revolutionary War defeat, the British had abandoned a series of frontier forts. This abandonment was one of the conditions of their surrender, and when Redcoats reoccupied one of these installations, Washington deemed it unacceptable. There was still a strong British military presence in Canada, however, and despite the urging of his colleague Thomas Jefferson, the president knew that his fledgling nation was ill prepared for another war with the British.

The agreement Jay brokered would guarantee the British vacated the forts for good, but it bestowed trade benefits upon Britain in return. George Washington was stuck between a rock and a hard place. Sign the treaty, and he would be seen as being soft on Britain; refuse to sign and allow the British to reoccupy the forts, and he might spark a war that the United States was ill equipped to win. When the document went public, it was met with vitriol and hatred the intensity of which had not been seen since the outbreak of the War of Independence.

Making the president's life harder were accusations of pro-British corruption being part of the treaty negotiations. Copies of the treaty document were burned in the streets by angry crowds. Damned if he did, and damned if he didn't, Washington deliberated on the matter and ultimately chose to sign the treaty. Far from being corrupt, the president had done the right thing at the expense of his public standing. In doing so, he had endured false accusations intended to tarnish his image.

George Washington's presidency was arguably one of the least corrupt of them all, which meant that things could only get worse—and they did. Each changing of the guard in Washington brought new scandals, some large, some small, but they always came in one form or another. Today, the name of Washington (the center of government, not the man) brings up images of bureaucratic corruption and Machiavellian political intrigue. This begs the question: just how corrupt *is* the nation?

## Just How Corrupt Is the United States?

One source we might look to for answers is Transparency International (TI), a nonprofit organization based in Germany. Pertaining to information and analysis on corruption, TI is widely regarded as one of the least biased sources available. The organization tracks and reports on corruption in a multitude of countries around the world and publishes its findings on a regular basis. TI maintains the Corruption Perceptions Index, or CPI, ranking nations on the basis of corruption in its public (i.e., government) sector. To what degree, CPI asks, do the country's leaders and civil servants leverage their position of authority to line their pockets or further their own private agendas?

The CPI assesses each country it studies on a scale, with scores ranging from 100, which means there is minimal corruption, down to zero, which indicates that a country's governing hierarchy is riddled with corruption. The results make for illuminating reading.

In both 2020 and 2021, the United States scored 67 out of a possible 100, ranking as the 27th most corrupt nation out of the 180 countries that comprise the CPI. This constitutes an all-time low score for the United States. Americans may be alarmed to note that the score had been steadily slipping. In 2017, the United States scored 75. The following year, 2018, it had fallen to 71; in 2019, it was 69. If the numbers are to be believed (and there are those who question their validity), then the United States appears to be on a downward spiral into ever-deepening corruption.

The United States maintained a score of 67 through the final year of the Donald Trump administration, and it stayed there through the first year of Joseph Biden's presidency. Trump had campaigned on a promise of, among other things, "draining the swamp"—rooting out the corruption that is entrenched and widespread throughout the public sector. If the CPI score of the United States is a valid indicator, it would appear that he was unsuccessful. It remains to be seen whether Biden can do any better.

On June 3, 2021, the White House issued a memorandum declaring corruption to be a threat not just to national security but to democracy itself. President Biden stated that countering corruption would be a core national security interest of the U.S. government going forward and that his administration would "bring transparency to the United States and global finance systems; prevent and combat corruption at home and abroad; and make it increasingly difficult for corrupt actors to shield their activities."

The document outlined a broad strategy via which these goals would be approached. This would include modernizing and empowering governmental departments and agencies to more effectively fight corruption; combating money laundering and illegal finance operations, both domestically and offshore; freezing the assets of corrupt individuals and, where appropriate, seizing those assets; liaising with international partners to prevent corrupt interference in the U.S. democratic process—the list goes on.

Every administration since that of George Washington has tried to root out corruption from within, with varying degrees of success. The story of the United States is seen by many as one of triumph over adversity, but that history has been repeatedly marred by the tentacles of corruption infiltrating every aspect of life.

This book will examine some of those stories—episodes from American history in which corruption played a key role. This is not an attempt to identify the most corrupt people or organizations or to rank them in some kind of order; it is not a case of "America's most corrupt." The intent is to show the many ways in which corruption has impacted the lives of Americans at all levels, from one generation to another, and how some of those individuals were brought to justice.

Within these pages, we will meet men and women whose lives were at first enriched, and then usually ruined, by corruption, in one form or another. Some were simply greedy, seeking to make a fortune through the suffering of innocents. Others started out with the best of intentions, only to find themselves eventually up to their necks in trouble because of poor choices they made.

Beyond the age-old desire for money and power, corruption takes many forms. Sometimes, people are led astray by matters of the heart; some abuse their positions of authority to satisfy deviant sexual impulses and then try to cover it up by drawing others in to shield them. Some seek fame and influence, wanting to see their name in lights. Others fall in with poor company, throwing in their lot with an organization that possesses few scruples or ethics.

The many facets of corruption are as insidious as they are varied. This book seeks to put a human face to some of them; it also demonstrates just how badly human beings can behave when they are part of a group. And it presents those who have devoted their careers and lives to tackling corruption.

The first step in defeating corruption is to understand its nature. The book you are about to read is an attempt to do just that.

Richard Estep
Colorado
August 2022

# The Man, the Myth, the Rascal

M any different words could be used to describe Daniel Edgar Sickles: Lawyer. Soldier. Politician. Curmudgeon. Just as fitting, however, would be terms such as blowhard, thief, swindler, or scoundrel.

Sickles's life was a web of bluster, deceit, and scandal that would have been worthy of its own soap opera, had such a thing existed in the 19th century. Even the date of his birth has been contested; Sickles himself sometimes gave two different years when asked about his birthday. To some, he claimed to have been born in 1819, and to others, he said 1825. Little is known about his childhood, which was spent in New York. Despite his prominent position in society and the fame (many would say infamy) he would later gain at the Battle of Gettysburg in 1863, Sickles never wrote, or at least never published, a personal memoir. This is somewhat surprising for a man who loved to be the center of attention as much as Dan Sickles did.

The Sickles family was wealthy. His parents had the means to send him to college, where he studied the law. After graduation, Sickles set up his own private legal practice. It was here that his penchant for engaging in shady practices first arose, although, in a theme that would continue throughout the rest of his life, Dan Sickles had an almost miraculous way of walking between the raindrops. Troubles and controversy beset him often, but none of it ever seemed to soak through.

Sickles came to be known as a man who could not be trusted with the money of others, having a tendency to siphon it into his own pocket in a series of schemes and swindles. His laissez-faire approach to paying back debts also earned him the reputation as a person to whom it was unwise to loan money.

With his love of wheeling and dealing, Sickles was a natural fit for the corrupt brand of politics that prevailed in 1840s and 1850s New York. He became an affiliated Democrat and embroiled himself in the intrigues and machinations of the infamously corrupt Tammany Hall, which is covered in more detail later in this book. If somebody wanted to make it big in those cutthroat circles, it was advisable to possess few scruples and have blood as cold as ice running through one's veins. Dan Sickles was more than up to the task. He was always willing to fight in his corner, physically if the need arose, and got involved in multiple altercations with others that came to blows.

Daniel Edgar Sickles could rightly be described as a lawyer, soldier, politician, or curmudgeon. Just as fitting, however, would be terms such as blowhard, thief, swindler, or scoundrel.

This ruthless streak undoubtedly contributed to Sickles's fast rise through the political ranks throughout the 1850s, leading him to occupy a series of influential positions first in the state and later in the federal government. He was also instrumental in purchasing and developing what is today New York City's Central Park.

His star was in the ascendant, and Sickles, now in his thirties, made the most of the power and good fortune that his new positions brought him. He liked the best of everything—the finest food, drink, and to be surrounded by beautiful and sophisticated women. He wined, dined, and flirted with socialites, cutting a dash on the social scene.

Bachelors tend to be at a disadvantage in the political field. Recognizing that it was finally time for him to settle down, likely more for the benefit of his career than for love, the 33-year-old Sickles married a 16-year-old girl named Teresa Bagioli. Some have speculated that the reason Sickles sometimes claimed to have been born in

1825 was to appear closer in age to his teenage bride. He became not only a state senator but also a congressman for New York. Mr. and Mrs. Sickles duly relocated to a grand new residence in Washington, D.C., so that he could serve his term in Congress more conveniently.

The biggest scandal of his life up to that point occurred on February 24, 1859. In an event that shocked the nation, Dan Sickles committed murder—in public.

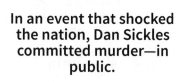

**In an event that shocked the nation, Dan Sickles committed murder—in public.**

Unbeknownst to him, his wife Teresa had been engaging in an extramarital affair with Philip Barton Key II. Key was himself an influential man—his father, Francis, was renowned for having written "The Star-Spangled Banner"—and much like Mr. and Mrs. Sickles, Key was a regular on the Washington, D.C., social scene. Key was also the district attorney for Washington. He had escorted Teresa Sickles to public functions on more than one occasion, though that in itself was not particularly scandalous. The fact that he was unmarried, however, did not help his standing in Dan Sickles's eyes when he learned that the pair were enjoying secret liaisons in a vacant house on 15th Street.

Everybody who knew him was aware that Sickles had a violent temper. Predictably, the next time he saw Key in public, the politician exploded. Drawing a pistol, Sickles stormed up to the unsuspecting Key and opened fire at close range. Key fell to the sidewalk, mortally wounded, and soon bled to death.

The resulting uproar made front-page headlines across the nation. Although marital infidelities in Washington political circles were hardly big news, cold-blooded murder certainly was. Sickles was arrested and charged. Unsurprisingly, given his boorish personality, he was completely unrepentant, insisting that Key had "dishonored" him and his family and that the dead man had simply gotten what was coming to him.

Sickles had the money to hire the finest lawyers available, and his legal representation was led by Edwin Stanton. The lawyer possessed a disciplined, razor-sharp legal mind, and after Abraham Lincoln's inauguration, Stanton would go on to become a crucial part of Lincoln's famous "team of rivals." Stanton and his fellow lawyers knew that their mercurial client would refuse to even consider pleading guilty. The defense they came up with was a stroke of genius: Sickles would plead not guilty by reason of temporary insanity.

The insanity defense was nothing new, but the claim that a defendant could experience circumstances so shocking that they were rendered *temporarily* insane—that was novel. Sickles's lawyers argued that their client had gone briefly out of his mind upon learning about his wife's infidelity and that Key, who had "led her astray," was directly responsible for that state of derangement—and, therefore, for his own death.

It was a bold move, and it paid off in court. Sickles was found not guilty, and he was allowed to walk free with his head held high. Many were sympathetic toward him, particularly the large number of husbands who declared that they would have done the same if they were in his shoes. Remarkably, he and Teresa remained together, which actually caused public opinion to turn against him in some quarters. It was also well known that Sickles had committed adultery himself, not just once but many times, but sexist double standards and hypocrisy were par for the course in those days.

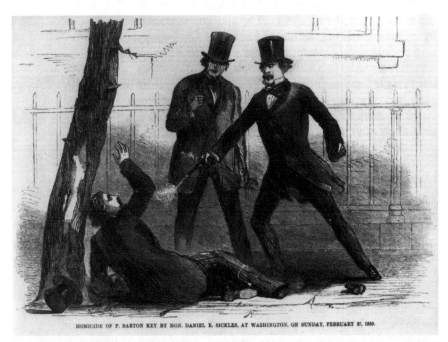

HOMICIDE OF P. BARTON KEY BY HON. DANIEL E. SICKLES, AT WASHINGTON, ON SUNDAY, FEBRUARY 27, 1859.

Soon after Sickles discovered his wife's affair with Philip Barton Key II, he encountered the adulterous man and publicly took his life.

The murder of Philip Barton Key and Sickles's subsequent acquittal due to temporary insanity might well have remained the totality of Dan Sickles's legacy were it not for the outbreak of the Civil War in 1861. Sickles threw himself into the business of raising troops from his home state, and he was awarded an officer's commission so he could lead them. Lest we make the mistake of thinking that he was acting out of altruism or a deep-rooted conviction for the Union cause, it should be borne in mind that blowback from the murder of Philip Barton Key effectively ended his career as a congressman. He was seen as too controversial a figure, too toxic, to represent his state.

In many ways, the onset of war was a godsend for Sickles. The North needed soldiers and officers. Thanks to his still-considerable political influence, he soon found himself promoted to the rank of general. To the great surprise of many who saw his appointment as being entirely politically motivated, Sickles performed competently on the battlefield, at least at first. He was by no means a stupid man, and his aggressive nature was not necessarily a bad thing, given the proper circumstances. The greater problem was that he had relatively little experience commanding large bodies of troops in combat and yet somehow found himself appointed to command first a division and then an entire corps, which was the role he filled at the Battle of Gettysburg on July 1, 1863.

Gettysburg began badly for the Union Army of the Potomac. On the first day of the battle, the blue-coated troops had been pushed back through the town by the assaulting Confederates, and they ended the day occupying defensive positions anchored upon Cemetery Hill. As the fighting intensified on the second day of the battle, July 2, it soon became apparent that Dan Sickles was in over his head. He found it difficult to process the vast quantity of information that a corps commander needed to take into account, and so he tried to compensate with bluster and aggressiveness. This was the "ready, fire, aim" mentality that had gotten him into trouble so many other times in his life. Posted at the southernmost end of the Union defensive line, Sickles found himself in a situation where he very nearly lost the entire battle for his side.

The commanding officer of the Army of the Potomac, General George Gordon Meade, had placed Sickles's corps at the extreme left of his defensive line, which was anchored upon two hills known as the Round Tops. General Meade was Sickles's direct superior and had a right to have his orders obeyed promptly and accurately. True to form, however, Sickles felt that he knew better. Rather than maintain the straight north-south alignment of troops that Meade wanted, Sickles instead chose to push some of his troops half a mile forward in front of the units on either side, forming a salient in his own line that was shaped like an inverted letter V.

Not only was Sickles's new line longer (and therefore weaker) than the one he had been ordered to form, but it was also so far out in front of the neighboring units that it was difficult for them to support it with gunfire. The anchor point of the Union's entire left flank was Little Round Top, which Sickles's corps had to abandon to move forward to their new positions. This made it feasible for the attacking Confederate forces to sweep around the hill to Sickles's left, gain control of Little Round Top, and perhaps even roll up the entire Union left in a north-facing attack.

The result was predictable: Sickles's troops were savaged by the Confederate assault, taking heavy casualties in their exposed position. To the credit of the Union soldiers, the Union line held, and despite his vilification for conducting an advance that directly countered the orders issued to him by Meade, there are still some historians who argue in Sickles's favor today.

Sickles lost his leg to a cannonball during the battle at Gettysburg, where he is here shown, photographed 20 years later.

The Union army would go on to win the battle, but things could easily have gone badly for Sickles in the aftermath. Disobedience is rarely seen as a desirable quality in a general. Fate intervened later that day, however, when Sickles took a severe cannon ball wound to his right leg. He was stretchered from the field and placed in the care of the surgeons, who amputated what was left of the mangled limb. Difficult as it may be to believe, the loss of his leg turned out to be a huge boon to Sickles's career. It is hard to publicly fault an officer who not only tackles the enemy head on but also loses a limb in the process. In the eyes of the public, Dan Sickles became the very definition of a wounded warrior, and he dined out on that reputation for the rest of his life. The fact that he was later awarded the Medal of Honor for his actions at Gettysburg didn't hurt his image one bit.

Dan Sickles regularly attended veterans' reunions, and whenever he was asked about his actions at Gettysburg, he stood resolutely by his decision to position his troops forward, ahead of the main line of defense. His personal narrative was built on the idea that it was Sickles, not Meade, who was responsible for winning the Battle of Gettysburg. Such were his powers of persuasion that there were those who fell for this story hook, line, and sinker.

Much as he had done with Central Park, Sickles worked hard to help sustain and preserve the Gettysburg battlefield for future generations to experience. He played a key part in placing many of the statues and memorial markers that dot the field today.

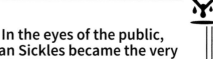

Dan Sickles returned to politics in 1892, becoming a congressman once more, and continued to enjoy the profligate lifestyle for which he had become so well known. He inherited, and then lost, millions of dollars during that time. Accusations of financial malfeasance never went away, and at the end of

**In the eyes of the public, Dan Sickles became the very definition of a wounded warrior, and he dined out on that reputation for the rest of his life.**

his life, when Sickles was head of the New York State Monuments Commission, he was removed from office when it was discovered that tens of thousands of dollars in funds had gone missing. (It should be pointed out that Sickles, then 92 years old, had probably lost the money due to his own incompetence rather than having actively purloined it.) He came perilously close to being imprisoned for the loss but, just as he had always done, was somehow able to avoid taking the fall.

As a man, Daniel Sickles had been by turns complex, corrupt, and colorful, and as such, he doesn't fit neatly into any particular pigeonhole. He died on May 3, 1914, having sustained a massive stroke, and is buried in Arlington National Cemetery.

# The Military-Industrial Complex

Not only was Dwight D. Eisenhower one of the most respected U.S. Army generals of World War II, but he was also highly regarded for his work as the 34th president of the United States. Eisenhower occupied the White House for two terms, from 1953 to 1961, and he knew war like few other presidents before or since.

As Supreme Commander of the Allied Forces, Eisenhower had been the ultimate authority behind Operation Overlord—the D-Day landings in Normandy, France, launched on June 5–6, 1944. It was one of the most complex, high-risk military operations of the entire war. Six years after victory had been declared, the general went on to assume command of the armed forces of the newly formed North Atlantic Treaty Organization, or NATO.

As president, Eisenhower—nicknamed "Ike" by those who liked him, of whom there were many—was a steady hand at the tiller of the United States as the country navigated the murky waters of the early Cold War. Even as World War II had been coming to a close, Eisenhower and many of his comrades viewed the rising specter of communism with disquiet and no small amount of distaste.

Where the Soviet Union was concerned, the newly elected President Eisenhower bore two key things in mind. First, appeasement would never work as a viable policy. The early days of World

War II had clearly demonstrated the fallacy of that approach. Soviet leader Joseph Stalin deplored weakness in all its forms. He respected only strength and the ability to apply force on a grand scale.

Second, the United States and its western allies did not want, and could not afford, to enter an all-out war with the Russians. The prospect of two nuclear superpowers locked in a shooting war held the potential for nothing less than global Armageddon and, by extension, the extinction of all life on Earth.

Based in no small measure on his experiences fighting the Axis Powers, Ike was a firm believer in the value of a strong military as the best deterrent to foreign aggression. The road to a lasting peace, he believed, was via mutual strength and respect between ideological adversaries. To this end, Eisenhower left office in 1961 with the armed forces numbering almost 2.5 million servicemen and women. In a farewell address that was broadcast to the American people on January 17 of that year, Ike told the nation: "Our arms must be mighty, ready for instant action, so that no potential aggressor may be tempted to risk his own destruction."

During his farewell address, President Eisenhower cautioned, "Only an alert and knowledgeable citizenry can compel the proper meshing of the huge industrial and military machinery of defense with our peaceful methods and goals, so that security and liberty may prosper together."

The potential aggressor Ike was speaking of indirectly was, of course, the Soviet Union. The viewing public found nothing surprising in Eisenhower's message thus far, but that was about to change when he issued a stark warning about something most of them had never heard of before: the military-industrial complex. He continued:

"We have been compelled to create a permanent annual armaments industry of vast proportions. Added to this, three and a half million men and women are directly engaged in the defense establishment. We annually spend on military security more than the net income of all United States corporations.

"The conjunction of an immense military establishment and a large armaments industry is new in the American experience. The total influence—economic, political, even spiritual—is felt in every city, every

State house, every office of the Federal government. We recognize the imperative need for this development. Yet we must not fail to comprehend its grave implications. Our toil, resources, and livelihood are all involved. So is the very structure of our society.

"In the councils of government, we must guard against the acquisition of unwarranted influence, whether sought or unsought, by the military-industrial complex. The potential for the disastrous rise of misplaced power exists and will persist.

"We must never let the weight of this combination endanger our liberties or democratic processes. We should take nothing for granted. Only an alert and knowledgeable citizenry can compel the proper meshing of the huge industrial and military machinery of defense with our peaceful methods and goals, so that security and liberty may prosper together."

In Ike's view, although the powerful manufacturing infrastructure for maintaining the military was essential to the nation's survival, it was also prone to abuse and corruption unless the American people were vigilant. He could envision the potential for spending so much money on armaments and defense that the public sector would suffer. Every dollar spent on preparing for war was unavailable for investment in infrastructure, scientific research, and the overall betterment of the American people.

Eisenhower's warning was both insightful and timely. It would also go unheeded. Throughout the 1950s and into the 1960s, government money poured into the coffers of defense contractors with gleeful abandon, all in the name of opposing the spread of communism. Taxpayer money went not just to equipping and training the Army, Navy, Air Force, Marine Corps, and Coast Guard but also to funding military research and development. Although some benefits of that scientific research did bleed over into the civilian realm, the majority was directed toward making better weaponry. The United States was caught up in an arms race, striving to develop better aircraft, tanks, ships, and missiles than the Soviets.

> **Eisenhower's warning was both insightful and timely. It would also go unheeded. Government money poured into the coffers of defense contractors with gleeful abandon.**

As the Cold War continued, maintaining a high level of defense spending was not a difficult concept to sell to either the American people or their representatives. The argument was made—by heads of the military and by the corporations that armed and supplied them—that the United States could never afford to be caught with relatively weakened and underprepared armed forces, a position it had found itself in at the onset of World War II.

When war broke out in Southeast Asia following an incident at the Gulf of Tonkin, the United States found itself embroiled in a conflict that would cost the lives of 58,200 of its military personnel and millions of Vietnamese civilians—the exact number will never be known—over the course of a decade. The Vietnam War also cost the country tens of billions of dollars, much of which fell into private hands. In 1969, the defense contractor Lockheed received $2 billion, which accounted for almost 2.5 percent of the entire national defense budget.

After the war ended, the United States continued to support its foreign policy by employing the military whenever Washington saw fit. The Cold War ostensibly ended in 1991, but despite the diminished threat from the so-called Red Bear, the military-industrial complex continued to prosper. Defense spending continued to climb even without a major national adversary to be fought.

Though the Cold War lost its teeth by 1991 in the face of an evolving world and through the concerted efforts of international leaders, the USA's war machine would not stop its dramatic growth.

**Grifters, Frauds, and Crooks: True Stories of American Corruption**

And the military-industrial complex continues to thrive. In 2020, the defense budget totaled $778.23 billion, up nearly 6 percent from the previous year. The great majority of the nation's most expensive weapons platforms, such as the F-35 Lightning II fighter jet and the Virginia-class attack submarine, are manufactured by a handful of corporations, such as Lockheed Martin and General Electric Boat (aided by partners and subcontractors). At such a high level of technological expertise and specialist manufacturing capacity, there can be little in the way of competition for these giants; very few companies have the capability of delivering a comparable product. That gives the handful of corporations that *are* capable of producing the latest and greatest weapons systems something very close to a monopoly. When the U.S. Department of Defense is in the market for a new fifth-generation fighter, it doesn't have much choice when putting the contract out to tender. The pool of eligible bidders is tiny.

The deep infiltration of political interests into the defense procurement process can sometimes make it extremely difficult for the government to cancel a project once it has gotten underway. Take the case of the F-22 Raptor, a state-of-the-art jet plane that was promoted as being the most advanced fighter in the world—"the definition of air dominance," according to its manufacturer, Lockheed Martin.

The Pentagon was impressed with Lockheed Martin's sales pitch, and it gave the Raptor program the green light. Factoring in the costs of research and development, the Raptor came with a price tag of approximately $350 million—*per plane.* (For perspective, a community hospital costs somewhere around $175 million to build.) The plane that will eventually take over most of the Raptor's role, the F-35, costs less than half that.

By the time the government put the brakes on the massively bloated program, 186 Raptors had already left the assembly line and had been delivered to the U.S. military. Intended to be the Air Force's primary fighter until the middle of the 21st century, it was instead cancelled in 2009. The program was seen by many defense pundits as a waste of time, effort, and money. The Raptor will remain in service until the early 2030s, but it will still be withdrawn at least 20 years earlier than the Pentagon had originally anticipated.

To halt the F-22 program, Defense Secretary Robert Gates had to invest a great deal of time and effort. One of the ways in which defense contractors seek to make their expensive programs "unkillable" is to spread the production of components across as many different states as they possibly can. Few senators or representatives will vote in favor of shutting down a program that would cost the jobs of voters in their home state; such a move can be political suicide. Fully aware of this, Lockheed Martin made sure that parts of the F-22 were manufactured, tested, and assembled in no fewer than 46 different states. The politicians representing each of those states had a vested interest in keeping the program alive and the Raptor flying for as long as possible.

Stopping a pork barrel project in its tracks is no mean feat. Not only did Gates lobby aggressively to bring the F-22 to an early end, but then-president Barack Obama stated he would veto the entire defense bill if it involved continuing to fund the Raptor. The threat worked; the Senate pulled the plug, although the vote was still close, with 58 for shutting down the program and 40 against.

In 2021, the United States spent 3.74 percent of its gross domestic product (GDP) on the military—some $754 billion, according to government sources. To put that figure in perspective, the United States spends more each year on defense than the next nine countries combined—China, India, the United Kingdom, Russia, France, Germany, Saudi Arabia, Japan, and South Korea—according to the Peter G. Peterson Foundation.

Each decade, trillions of dollars are funneled through the budget of the Department of Defense and into the accounts of private, for-profit corporations. In and of itself, this is not necessarily a bad thing; as the old saying goes, it's cheaper to pay for your own military than for somebody else's (i.e., that of an invading enemy). But more concerning is the military's seeming inability to account for exactly where those trillions of dollars go.

The sprawling headquarters of the U.S. Department of Defense, the Pentagon has become synonymous with both military might and excess.

The first time the Department of Defense was comprehensively audited was in 2017. There was good reason for concern as to how the Pentagon was spending its money. In 2016, *Washington Post* reporters Craig Whitlock and Bob Woodward wrote a story stating that the Pentagon swept under the carpet a report on how $125 billion of taxpayer money had been lost to administrative wastage by the Pentagon.

The authors of the report advanced several proposals for cutting back on wastage. Some of the recommendations contained in the report involved controlling the financial excesses of defense contractors. The report contained the worrisome fact that the military was paying almost as many support personnel and administrators (including a veritable army of civilian employees) as it was deploying personnel in the field. A million support staff members must be balanced against 1.3 million uniformed, active-duty troops. Throughout history, the leaders of armies have tried to keep the "teeth to tail" ratio low. The teeth are the combat forces themselves—the men and women who do the fighting and the dying. The tail is the logistical and support infrastructure required to get them there. The more tail there is in relation to the teeth, the more bloated and inefficient a military tends to be.

The study in question recommended numerous ways in which those tens of billions of wasted dollars could be recouped and funneled into the combat arms of the military—paying to support weapons systems and fighting personnel, rather than a sprawling bureaucratic tail. If this had been achieved, it would have constituted a big step forward for the defense of the nation and the efficiency of the armed forces. So why did the military leadership not only bury the study but also actively attempt to disavow its findings?

Put simply, accepting the findings of the report would have made the Pentagon look bad. Its senior chiefs had spent years calling out for more money, banging the drum to demand increased funding for their respective services. Each branch of the military competes for a share of the annual defense budget. Admitting that a huge chunk of that money had been misspent would have revealed gross inefficiency and ineptitude at the heart of the military establishment—and perhaps also have led to funding cuts. Those cuts would have bitten both the Pentagon and the civilian defense contractors in the pocketbook.

**Why did the military leadership not only bury the study but also actively attempt to disavow its findings?**

Implementing the recommended cost-saving practices would have been challenging, even if the military leadership had gotten on board with the report's proposals. One key obstacle would have been the many congressional politicians representing the states in which the Defense Department employed hundreds of thousands of people. We're back to the reason it is so difficult to cut a federal program that creates jobs in multiple states. The politicians would not simply stand by while the livelihoods of their constituents were dissolved in the name of cost savings. Whether such wastage cuts were for the good of the country would have taken a back seat to their own political interests.

Small wonder that many saw annual audits of the Pentagon as cause for deep concern. Those concerns were ultimately proven to be justified; the Pentagon failed its 2018, 2019, and 2020 audits dismally. By the most conservative of estimates, even with reforms of its internal administrative practices, it is unlikely to pass a comprehensive audit until 2027 at the earliest.

Until then, corruption and waste will continue to corrode the operations of what is arguably the world's preeminent military.

# An Ill Wind

**"** **I**t's an ill wind that blows no one any good." So says the old proverb. For the federal agents who staffed Operation Ill Wind, the corruption they uncovered within the upper levels of the U.S. government blew little good for anybody—particularly not for a high-level public official named Melvyn Paisley.

Born in Portland, Oregon, in 1924, Melvyn R. Paisley came from hardworking country stock. The son of a lumberjack, Paisley was commissioned into the U.S. Army and served as a fighter pilot during World War II. Lieutenant Paisley achieved the coveted status of ace, shooting down a total of eight enemy planes and earning the Distinguished Service Cross in the process.

After the war, Paisley returned to civilian life and embarked on a career dedicated to aviation engineering. His firsthand knowledge of piloting stood him in good stead when he took a job with the aircraft manufacturer Boeing, where he worked on a diverse range of aircraft programs and missile platforms.

Having proven himself as a solid hand with whom to entrust some of the nation's most important (and secret) defense programs, Melvyn Paisley climbed the Boeing career ladder all the way up to the level of director. Arguably his greatest professional achievement came in 1981, when he traded a career in the private sector for life in the public sector. Paisley was appointed to the post of assistant secretary of the Navy for research, engineering, and systems during the Ronald Reagan administration.

Unfortunately, those achievements are not what he is best remembered for today.

Paisley's time in government ran until the spring of 1987. Months later, it was revealed that he had been paid hundreds of thousands of dollars for his high-level role in a large-scale military procurement fraud scheme.

The process for bidding on military technology and equipment contracts is a lucrative and competitive one. At the top of the pyramid, billions of dollars are at stake. Entire business enterprises can stand or fall on the strength of a single contract award or refusal. Little wonder that the process has, at times, been a fertile breeding ground for corrupt insiders seeking to leverage their privileged position to line their own pockets on the side.

Among other examples of corruption, Operation Ill Wind uncovered Melvyn Paisley's role in procuring lucrative defense contracts in exchange for bribes.

In the summer of 1986, one such individual—John Marlowe, a consultant with numerous connections in the defense industry—offered up sensitive information to a small military contracting firm regarding one of its competitor companies. If the price was right, Marlowe promised, then the knowledge he was selling could give the company enough of an edge to win a major contract.

Rather than take the bait, the contractor did the right thing: the company reported the matter to the U.S. Navy. This started the ball rolling on an investigation that would draw in the Naval Criminal Investigative Service (today called the NCIS, but simply the NIS back then), the Federal Bureau of Investigation (FBI), the Defense Criminal Investigative Service (DCIS), and a host of other government agencies, all with an interest in uncovering and prosecuting corruption.

After confirming the validity of the complaint and confronting him with the evidence, agents were then able to get Marlowe to start cooperating with them, leading them to other similarly corrupt individuals within the defense establishment. As a growing body of evidence came to light, it became easier for the investigators to obtain warrants for wiretapping and other forms of surveillance. Each fresh lead then pointed the investigators toward another. The operation's focus became that of identifying employees and companies who had offered and accepted bribes to have contracts assigned to specific businesses.

In 1994, Beverly Hills–based defense contractor Litton Industries pleaded guilty to charges of purchasing sensitive

**Each fresh lead then pointed the investigators toward another.**

information pertaining to the bidding process on three separate government contracts. Litton had hired two corrupt consultants, who in turn had gotten the company confidential details pertaining to the bids of its competitors—all for the bargain price of $96,000.

In the end, Litton would end up paying out $3.9 million in fines. That paled in comparison to the $190 million payment agreed to by the Unisys Corporation as part of its own guilty plea; this was the largest settlement of its type ever to be recorded at that point in U.S. history. The company had been another of those that had bribed Melvyn Paisley to use his influence on its behalf.

Litton and Unisys were far from the only offending companies, however. United Technologies Corporation paid $6 million in fines for similar crimes. Grumman Aerospace Corporation, manufacturer of the F-14 Tomcat fighter jet used by the U.S. Navy to defend its carrier strike groups, refused to admit culpability but paid the government $20 million to settle the case out of court.

Of all the individuals who were investigated as part of Operation Ill Wind, Melvyn Paisley held the most senior government position. Indicted and tried in the summer of 1991 on a panoply of charges that included bribery and conspiracy, the then 66-year-old admitted his guilt. He had helped ensure that specific contracts went to bidders who had paid him off with kickbacks to the tune of more than half a million dollars. Most of the money was paid to him after he left office in 1987 and had retired from public life.

For his crimes, Paisley served four years in prison and paid back $50,000 to the government. He died at home on December 19, 2001, after a lengthy battle with cancer.

Other high-ranking government officials also paid a price for their corrupt practices as part of Operation Ill Wind. James E. Gaines, deputy assistant secretary of the Navy, was a subordinate of Melvyn Paisley. Just like his boss, he was found to have sold his influence to the highest bidder, accepting expensive gifts in return for manipulating the bidding process into favoring those who had bribed him. Because he did not rake in hundreds of thousands of dollars as Paisley had, Gaines was given the lesser sentence of six months in prison, two years' probation upon his release, and a fine of $5,000—one-tenth the amount of Paisley's.

Victor D. Cohen, deputy assistant secretary of the Air Force, pleaded guilty to charges of bribery and conspiracy. He had accepted thousands of dollars, and he had stayed in high-end hotel rooms on the corporate dime. At his sentencing, those bribes cost Cohen $10,000 and 33 months in jail.

By the time Operation Ill Wind concluded, it had secured 54 convictions in what Attorney General Janet Reno called "one of the most successful investigations and prosecutions ever undertaken by the Department of Justice against white collar crime."

There were broader legal ramifications in the aftermath of Ill Wind. As a direct consequence of the investigation, Congress passed the Procurement Integrity Act of 1988. Designed to prevent abuse and exploitation of the government contract bidding system, the act specifically forbids any bidder from intentionally obtaining information about bids from competitors. Hefty legal punishments can be levied against those who violate the act, and it is this piece of legislation that forms the true legacy of Operation Ill Wind.

# Fat Leonard

What's in a name? "Fat Leonard" evokes images of a cheerful, jolly sort of character, but it is, in fact, the nickname of the central character in the single most wide-ranging corruption and bribery scandal in the history of the U.S. Navy.

Leonard Glenn Francis was a Malaysian entrepreneur who, throughout the 2000s and 2010s, ran his own defense supply company, the Singapore-based Glenn Defense Marine Asia, also known as GDMA. Much of the organization's business was conducted with the U.S. Navy, which was by far its biggest customer.

Francis seemed to have an instinctive talent for wheeling and dealing, as evidenced by the company raking in more than $35 million from lucrative defense-related contracts. The catch: Fat Leonard (so called because he weighed 350 pounds) was using cash, the services of sex workers, and other material enticements to grease the palms of admirals and other naval officers. He invited some of them to lavish parties at which he provided gourmet catering and an unlimited supply of liquor. Some of the parties went on for days at a time. Other officers were gifted with fully paid vacations on which they stayed in luxury hotel suites on Leonard Francis's dime.

What did Fat Leonard get in return for his money? Primarily, insider information. Like many other government organizations, the

U.S. Navy has established a set of clear rules concerning the crimes of kickbacks and bribery. These rules are meant to ensure that a fair and equitable bidding process precedes the award of any contract to a private supplier. The naval officers whom Francis was paying off would let him in on the

> **What did Fat Leonard get in return for his money? Primarily, insider information.**

secrets of the contracting process, including the movements of specific U.S. warships. If an American naval vessel was going to dock in a certain port on a certain date, knowing about it in advance would give Francis and GDMA a significant advantage in the bidding process.

## U.S. MARSHALS
## WANTED
### REWARD: Up to $40,000

**WANTED FOR:**
**BRIBERY**

Date of photo: 2017

**LEONARD FRANCIS**

Aliases: Leonard Glenn Francis

WANTED SINCE:
**September 4, 2022**

IN:
**Southern District of California**

FOR:
**Bond Default - Bribery**

| | |
|---|---|
| DOB: **10/22/1964** | Race: **Asian** |
| Sex: **Male** | Hair: **Black** |
| Height: **6'02"** | Eyes: **Brown** |
| Weight: **350 lbs** | |
| Scars/Tattoos: **N/A** | |

Fugitive criminal Leonard Glenn Francis, wanted for bribery, appears on a U.S. Marshals wanted poster dated September 2022.

Once the vessel was moored in the dock, Francis would go to work. Thanks to his extravagant bribes, he had already scooped up the contracts to supply the Navy's warships and their crews with all manner of consumables. If the crew ate it or drank it, flushed it down the toilet, or used it to fuel or clean the ship, the odds were high that Fat Leonard had supplied it—and at a grossly inflated cost.

Francis's administrative staff turned in a steady stream of false invoices to the Navy for reimbursement. Some of these documents exaggerated the quantity of supplies that had been delivered, while other claims were entirely fictitious—no product had been supplied whatsoever. Some of the subcontractors listed on the GDMA invoices as suppliers didn't actually exist.

Why didn't anybody check up on these false invoices and vendors to verify their accuracy? Because many of those who signed off on those documents were officers who had been expertly schmoozed by Fat Leonard. Their compliance had already been bought and paid for with lavish bribes, which ensured that they would rubber-stamp the invoices without a second glance.

It's one thing for a relatively low-level officer such as a lieutenant or an enlisted petty officer to be caught taking a bribe, but one of the most shocking aspects of the Fat Leonard scandal was that it permeated even the highest echelons of the U.S. Navy. Admiral Robert Gilbeau was the first senior officer to be convicted once the real scope of the scandal began to unfold. Gilbeau had enjoyed a robust social life thanks to Francis's bribe money, enjoying the services of numerous call girls in exchange for facilitating Fat Leonard's abuse of the Navy's contracting system.

> **One of the most shocking aspects of the Fat Leonard scandal was that it permeated even the highest echelons of the U.S. Navy.**

After admitting that he had lied to Navy investigators, Gilbeau, a veteran of the war in Iraq, was given a relatively light sentence—18 months behind bars. When rumors of his connection to the fraudulent scheme began to emerge, Gilbeau illegally destroyed a batch of official documents in an attempt to cover his tracks. Unfortunately for him, it was too late.

Gilbeau may have been senior, but he was far from the only Navy leader to be found guilty of engaging in fraud at Fat Leonard's behest. Captains, chief petty officers, and other commissioned and non-commissioned ranks also took hundreds of thousands of dollars as part of the widespread bribery scheme. In addition to helping influence the passage of Navy ships into ports that were dominated by GDMA, they pulled confidential information on the company's competitors and slipped it to Francis. This gave him an almost unbeatable edge over his rivals when he was assembling bids for supply contracts.

The most senior uniformed position in the United States Navy is the chief of naval operations, or CNO. The admiral occupying this office reports directly to the secretary of the Navy. According to a July 23, 2021, report in the *Navy Times*, the outgoing CNO, Admiral Gary Roughead, turned over his office to Admiral Jonathan Greenert on September 23, 2011. The prestigious event took place at the United States Naval Academy in Annapolis, Maryland.

Such ceremonies are usually lavish affairs, attended by some of the most influential military officers and their civilian guests. In a turn of events that would shock many when it came to light, Admiral Roughead's list of personal VIP guests for the event included none other than Leonard Glenn Francis himself.

Quite how the most notorious con man in U.S. military history came to attend such a prestigious event remains problematic to this day. Admiral Roughead himself offered no clear answer when queried by reporters from the *Washington Post*. A close examination of his past showed that Leonard Francis was no stranger to black-tie Navy events, most of which were attended by scores of high-ranking civilians and admirals. The smiling fraudster never missed an opportunity to be photographed shaking hands with a member of the Navy top brass.

Chief of Naval Operations (CNO) Adm. Gary Roughead testifies in 2010 before the Senate Armed Services Committee during the Defense Authorization Request for Fiscal Year 2011 and the Future Years Defense Program for the Department of the Navy.

In 2017, *Post* reporters learned that the Naval Criminal Investigative Service, or NCIS, was investigating more than 450 potential suspects as part of the scandal—including 60 admirals, some of whom were on active duty at the time.

Leonard Francis pleaded guilty to multiple charges, including bribery and fraud. While in detention at his home in San Diego to await sentencing—and to receive medical treatment for kidney cancer—he cut off the ankle bracelet used to monitor his whereabouts and disappeared on September 4, 2022. Later that month he was found in Venezuela, from where he intended to fly to Russia. He was arrested at the airport in Caracas, however, and as of this writing remains in custody in Venezuela.

The investigation and subsequent legal case that arose from the unprecedented corruption scandal surrounding him is ongoing, and it has highlighted the need for the United States Navy to take a closer look at how it deals with supply contract bids.

# Dangerous Dave

The upper echelons of the United States Army are packed with high achievers. The selection process to reach the rank of general is extremely competitive. Unless an officer has punched the proper combination of assignment tickets, serving at various levels of command during their climb to the top of the ladder, they are unlikely to ever attain a position of high command.

David Petraeus was commissioned into the Army in 1974, just as the Vietnam War was coming to a close. The post-Vietnam U.S. Army was not a happy one. It was often said that the U.S. military won the battles but lost the war, and after the withdrawal from Vietnam, morale in the Army slumped to an all-time low. Disciplinary problems and drug use were rife. In some units, men assaulted their superiors without giving it a second thought. Stories abound of officers and non-commissioned officers being afraid to enter barracks unaccompanied or unarmed.

The 1970s were a difficult time to be an American soldier, but Petraeus not only survived the experience; he thrived. Ten years after joining the service, he was back at West Point, only this time as part of the instructional cadre, devoted to teaching the next generation of up-and-coming officers. More promotions followed. Petraeus punched ticket after ticket, always excelling no matter what assignment he was given.

In 1991, Petraeus assumed command of an airborne infantry battalion based at Fort Campbell, Kentucky. During a live fire exercise, one of his soldiers stumbled and accidentally pulled the trigger on his rifle. The stray round hit Petraeus in the chest, passed through his body, and exited through his back. Petraeus was lucky to survive the incident, which he did after a five-hour-long surgery.

After recovering, Petraeus rose from battalion to brigade command before taking charge of the 101st Airborne Division in the 2003 invasion of Iraq. An officer who was always rated very highly by his superiors during evaluations, Petraeus was a natural choice for the post of the Multi-National Force in Iraq (MNF-I) when the position opened up in 2007, and he was duly appointed by President George W. Bush. In this role, as in almost every other endeavor he had undertaken, the general exceeded expectations.

U.S. Army Gen. David H. Petraeus, the commander of Multi-National Force–Iraq, briefs reporters at the Pentagon on April 26, 2007, on the current military situation in Iraq.

Retiring from the Army in 2011, Petraeus was then nominated and unanimously confirmed for the role of director of the Central Intelligence Agency (CIA). He would serve in that position for just one year. In a bombshell revelation, it emerged in late 2012 that Petraeus had engaged in an extramarital affair with his biographer, the author Paula Broadwell. Both parties were married to other people at the time.

Broadwell had served as an Army officer herself. Her book, *All In: The Education of General David Petraeus*, was the result of extensive cooperation between herself and Petraeus. It covered the general's remarkable military career and summarized some of the hard-won lessons learned along the way. *All In* is an interesting and well-written book, which only makes it sadder that it gained publicity for all the wrong reasons.

David Petraeus was undeniably a smart and highly educated man, having earned a master's degree and a Ph.D. from Princeton University, both in the field of international relations. In addition to the affair between himself and Broadwell, whose nickname for him was "Dangerous Dave," further investigation revealed that the general was responsible for a breach in confidential data. Some of the documents that Petraeus provided for Broadwell's use as source material for her book contained classified information. She held no security clearance that would allow her to legitimately read it. Broadwell was, in effect, a civilian who was given official government secrets by her lover for use in writing a biography that would bolster his public image—and make her some money.

> **Broadwell was, in effect, a civilian who was given official government secrets by her lover for use in writing a biography that would bolster his public image—and make her some money.**

During the affair, the husband of Jill Kelley, who was a colleague of the general's, received an email from an unknown sender. The email told Scott Kelley to "rein in" his wife and claimed to have photographs of her fondling senior military officers and civilian officials. A similar message was sent to General John Allen.

Jill Kelley began to receive harassing emails herself. After contacting the FBI, which in turn opened an investigation, the messages were traced back to their source: Paula Broadwell. When agents accessed Broadwell's email account without her knowledge, they found evidence that she and Petraeus were romantically involved. She had also engaged in a personal vendetta against Jill Kelley, perhaps seeing her as a potential love rival for the affections of Petraeus. Jill Kelley, for her part, maintained that there was nothing between her and Petraeus other than the good-natured banter of colleagues who got on well with one another.

General David Petraeus poses with Paula Broadwell in July 2011, days before he would relinquish his command in Afghanistan.

FBI agents questioned both Petraeus and Broadwell at length. Both parties admitted to the affair. Seeing the writing on the wall, Petraeus tendered his resignation as CIA director to the newly reelected President Barack Obama. Informing CIA personnel of the situation, Petraeus wrote: "After being married for over 37 years, I showed extremely poor judgment by engaging in an extramarital affair. Such behavior is unacceptable, both as a husband and as the leader of an organization such as ours. This afternoon, the president graciously accepted my resignation."

The reality of it was that Petraeus had left himself with no other choice, not least because charges were soon heading his way. In 2015, after his lawyers negotiated a plea deal, he was charged with the mishandling of classified materials (the notebooks that he had loaned to Broadwell) and, upon pleading guilty, was fined $100,000 and sentenced to two years' probation. For her part, Paula Broadwell was charged with no wrongdoing.

Despite her steadfast insistence that she had not engaged in inappropriate behavior, either with Petraeus or anybody else, Jill Kelley's reputation was dragged through the mud. In 2016, she wrote and self-published a book that gave her side of the story. It was titled *Collateral Damage: Petraeus, Power, Politics, and the Abuse of Privacy*. Not only does the book contain some of the emails between herself and Petraeus, but it also outlines what Kelley believes to have been gross intrusions by the FBI into her personal life.

After leaving the CIA and the U.S. Army, the former general traded the military life for one spent in the realm of finance. As of 2022, David Petraeus is the chairman and also a partner of the KKR Global Institute, an investment company that he helped establish in 2013.

# Steal Big

"If you're going to steal," an old saying goes, "steal *big*."

This advice was taken firmly to heart by 53-year-old Kerry F. Khan, a former colonel in the U.S. Army Corps of Engineers, and his partner in crime, 55-year-old Michael A. Alexander.

When it finally fell down all around them in 2011, Khan and Alexander were responsible for a corrupt government contracting enterprise that left federal investigators stunned by its sheer size, scope, and audacity.

The premise behind their scheme was a simple one. Like all branches of the military, the Army Corps of Engineers contracts with a wide variety of civilian providers for many different products, services rendered, and consumable supplies. Khan, Alexander, and their co-conspirators were able to submit massively exaggerated reimbursement invoices for a range of contracts they oversaw.

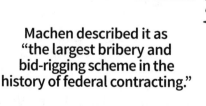

Machen described it as "the largest bribery and bid-rigging scheme in the history of federal contracting."

They were only able to get away with this brazen behavior because the system of procurement and repayment used by the Corps of Engineers was overly complicated and suffered little to no oversight. Khan and Alexander were both program managers for the corps and, as such, were in a position to help siphon off millions of dollars of Defense Department money. The two men were able to steer contracts to companies whose employees were already in their pocket, which in practice meant bribing members of the committees that were empowered to award those contracts.

Once the contract was assigned to their favored provider, it was then necessary to bribe key people within the company hierarchy with cash and gifts to keep them compliant. The bribed individuals went on to inflate the asked-for cost on the invoices they sent back to the Army by outrageous sums of money, sometimes asking for millions of dollars more than the true cost of the goods or services supplied.

The U.S. Army Corps of Engineers is renowned for its work on massive infrastructure projects both at home and abroad, including the Panama Canal. In 2011, the year Khan and Alexander were caught cooking up a $780 million scheme, the Corps's budget was just over $5 billion.

In all, the conspirators raked in around $30 million over a period of four years. They splashed out millions of dollars on condos, mansions, flashy cars, designer clothes, high-end watches, and mistresses. By the time they were apprehended by Army Criminal Investigation Division officers, Khan, Alexander, and their cronies were on the brink of bringing in their biggest haul yet: a $780 million contract that would put hundreds of millions of dollars into their pockets.

Michael Alexander was sentenced to 72 months' imprisonment. The sentence was relatively light when compared to that imposed upon Khan. Despite recommendations from the government prosecutors that he be given 15 years in prison, Kerry Khan was jailed for 19 years and 7 months. Khan was singled out as the operation's ringleader by U.S. Attorney Ronald C. Machen. The presiding judge took the view that embezzling the U.S. Treasury on such a grand scale—Machen described it as "the largest bribery and bid-rigging scheme in the history of federal contracting"—required that a strong example be made, and he felt that a harsher sentence than those imposed on Khan's 14 co-conspirators would be appropriate.

# The Windy City

For generations, Americans have debated the identity of the country's most corrupt city. The obvious choice would, of course, be the nation's capital, Washington, D.C. As a general rule, the greater the concentration of politicians in any given area, the higher the level of grift and corruption there tends to be.

According to a 2020 report published by the University of Illinois, however, the corruption capital of the United States is Chicago. This conclusion was based upon a careful analysis of the number of federal public corruption convictions in major U.S. cities over a period of 42 years, ending in 2018 (the last year for which data was available when the report was compiled). Chicago led the nation with 1,750 convictions for public corruption, beating the closest runner-up, Los Angeles, at 1,547; Manhattan followed at 1,360. Surprisingly, D.C. came in fifth, with 1,178 convictions.

When it comes to states, rather than cities, it's a slightly different story. The most corrupt state, district, or territory, based on the same corruption data viewed from a statewide perspective, is the District of Columbia, which had 1,178 convictions between 1976 and 2018. It is important to note that the researchers used per-capita data, meaning that the convictions are ranked in relation to the number of people living in that state. This yields 16.79 convictions per 10,000 citizens of D.C.

**Grifters, Frauds, and Crooks: True Stories of American Corruption**

In second place was Louisiana, with 1,223 convictions (2.62 per capita). Third was Illinois, at 2,120 and 1.66 per capita, respectively. It is important to note that the statistics only include *convictions*. Just how much corruption goes undetected, unreported, and therefore unprosecuted is impossible to determine.

Chicago has a long and storied history of institutional grift.

The corruption capital of the United States, Chicago has a long and storied history of institutional grift, which began long before Al Capone and the Mob cemented the Windy City in the public consciousness as America's crime central. The city was incorporated in 1837. Prior to that, much of the land was settled by entrepreneurs and hustlers. The United States was expanding westward, its population stretching out toward the Pacific, and there was a lot of money to be made in trading and commerce. Some of that profit was come by honestly. Most of it was not.

Thanks to its key location, the burgeoning city was a natural railroad hub, a situation that continues to this day. A constant tide of trade goods surged through Chicago from all directions, bringing with it dollars aplenty. It was inevitable that along with those dollars came both crime and corruption.

People enter public service for a variety of reasons. Looking back on those who occupied positions of civic responsibility in the Windy City throughout its storied history, it becomes apparent that many of them entered the business of government because that's exactly how they saw it: as a business rather than public service. As a means of making money, being in local government was much easier than working for a living—and it was often considerably less honest.

Throughout the 19th and 20th centuries, Chicago grew fast—almost explosively so—and crime and corruption grew right along with it. Along the way, thanks to the criminal factions that vied for control of the city's multitude of rackets, there were plenty of actual explosions too.

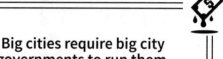

At the time of writing, Chicago is the country's third largest city, home to around 2.7 million Americans. To some degree, Chicago's level of corruption can be explained by its great degree of urbanization. Big cities require big city governments to run them, and the more political and administrative organizations are operating within a city, the more opportunities for grift and corruption arise.

**Big cities require big city governments to run them, and the more political and administrative organizations are operating within a city, the more opportunities for grift and corruption arise.**

There have been times in Chicago's past when the criminals had a great degree of control, sometimes occupying key government positions. This made it easier for them to pass crooked laws that benefited them and their corrupt practices, and as a direct consequence, it became much harder to remove them from office.

The corruption of political figures remains an issue in 21st-century Chicago. Even though convictions for corruption are trending downward nationally, corruption continues to be a significant blight on both the city of Chicago and the state of Illinois. Even the unforeseen arrival of the COVID-19 pandemic in early 2020 did not slow matters down on this front. A report by University of Illinois at Chicago researchers Dick Simpson, Marco Rosaire Rossi, and Thomas J. Gradel found that even a constantly increasing toll of death and serious illness among its citizens could not put a dent in the level of corruption that was taking place in the city.

Most of the corruption the researchers documented was tied to public servants and business leaders, people who were in positions of power and civic authority. In July 2020, the U.S. Attorney's office announced that the state of Illinois's biggest supplier of electrical utilities, Commonwealth Edison (aka ComEd), would pay a $200 million fine to conclude a criminal bribery case it was involved in. The company offered material incentives to allies and associates of the Illinois House Speaker, Democrat Michael Madigan, such as

preferentially awarding contracts and jobs, with the ultimate goal of having him support new laws that would greatly increase ComEd's profits. Of course, there's no such thing as a free lunch, and those profits would be paid for by the citizens of Illinois.

ComEd's efforts to buy its way into Madigan's good graces spanned nine years. At first, Madigan insisted he had done nothing wrong. As a federal probe gained momentum and uncovered evidence to the contrary, he was forced to change his tune. On March 2, 2022, the politician, along with his aide Michael McClain, was indicted on 22 federal bribery and racketeering charges. The prosecution alleged that he was head of a criminal scheme that they termed "the Madigan Enterprise," a series of rackets that were designed to rake in money while gaining both power

Michael Madigan was both the long-standing speaker of the Illinois House of Representatives and chair of the Democratic Party of Illinois.

and influence for Madigan and several of his picked associates.

Facing up to 20 years behind bars if he was found guilty, Madigan entered a plea of not guilty. Barring unforeseen delays, the case was scheduled to go to trial in April of 2024.

It appears that, when it comes to rooting out corruption in the public sector, those who enforce the law in Chicago still have their work cut out for them. The city has always been a place of opportunity for a certain breed of criminal, and perhaps none more so than one of its most infamous sons: Alphonse "Al" Capone.

# The Real Scarface

For most people, the name Al Capone evokes memories of Robert DeNiro's bravura performance in the 1987 movie *The Untouchables*, directed by Brian DePalma. DeNiro gained 30 pounds to play Capone, stealing the show from Kevin Costner's straitlaced federal agent Eliot Ness. Whether smashing in the skull of a treacherous minion with a baseball bat or pulling the strings to manipulate his wide-ranging criminal enterprise, Hollywood's Capone comes across as a cold-blooded villain through and through.

The truth, of course, is somewhat more complicated. Thanks largely to several different versions of the "Untouchables" story, Alphonse Capone is irrevocably associated with the city of Chicago, yet few realize that he was actually a New Yorker by birth—he was born in Brooklyn on January 17, 1899. The Capone family were Italian immigrants who, like millions of others, had come to the United States in search of a better life six years before his birth.

Never the strongest of students, Capone lacked the potential to excel academically. He offset this with a willingness to work exceptionally hard, and he never shied away from a fight. Naturally tough, he was good with his fists and was always willing to use them

Al Capone is shown here at the Chicago Detective Bureau in 1930 following his arrest on a vagrancy charge.

when crossed. This made him a natural recruit for organized crime, and while other boys his age were finishing up their education and contemplating their future, Al Capone dropped out and joined a gang.

Every gang needs its foot soldiers, and young Capone took on the role with relish. It soon became apparent that he had a natural affinity for violence. This soon led to promotion. Capone became a trusted lieutenant, accepting a leadership position that saw his influence within the organization grow.

As a young man, Capone earned his trademark facial scars in an altercation over a woman. Enraged at an inappropriate comment Capone had made, the woman's brother slashed him across the cheek with a blade. One would think that the nickname this incident bestowed upon Capone—Scarface—would have been beneficial to a future gangster, but in reality, Capone was exceptionally self-conscious about his scars. Whenever he was photographed, he sought to angle his scarred cheek away from the camera in an attempt to hide the disfigurement.

Crime was a prosperous affair in the New York City of the 1900s and 1910s, but opportunity really came knocking when the 18th Amendment was enacted on January 16, 1920—the day before Al Capone's 21st birthday. The new law prohibited the manufacture, distribution, and selling of alcohol—though not, bizarrely, the consumption of it. One of the completely predictable consequences of Prohibition, as the amendment came to be known, was a surge in violent crime that accompanied the business of bootlegging and trafficking illegal booze.

If New York City was fertile ground for the latest wave of organized crime, then Chicago was an absolute paradise. For an ambitious man like Al Capone, the sky really was the limit. Capone worked for a mobster named Johnny Torrio, serving as his enforcer. When something needed to be done quickly, and likely with brute force, Torrio sent for Capone.

Torrio put out a hit on his boss, James "Big Jim" Colosimo. The word on the street was that Capone may have had his hand in the assassination, though there was no hard evidence and the police identified several other potential suspects—the main one being a gunman named Frankie Yale. With Colosimo dead, Torrio took over his criminal enterprise, elevating both himself and Capone to new heights of power and influence.

Torrio and Capone ruled the organized crime rackets on Chicago's South Side with an iron fist. Racketeering, bootlegging, prostitution, and even a few legitimate business ventures on the side kept the money rolling in. Their philosophy was a simple one that entailed giving competitors a choice: either join up, in which case Capone and Torrio absorbed the weaker outfits into their own organization, or else go to war with the gangsters. The latter cases exploded in episodes of violence that scarred the city, especially when innocent bystanders were caught in the crossfire.

Torrio and Capone constantly butted heads with the North Side mob, with whom they were locked in a bloody feud. On November 10, 1924, this vendetta culminated in the murder of the North Side gang's leader, Dean O'Bannion, at Torrio and Capone's order.

Retribution was swift in coming. The following January, Johnny Torrio's luck almost ran out when George Moran ("Bugs" to his friends) tried to kill him as an act of revenge. Despite sustaining multiple gunshot wounds, Torrio survived and recovered to such a degree that he was able to serve jail time. This left him plenty of time for thinking, and he came to the conclusion that the Chicago prostitution and bootlegging wars were not good for his future health prospects. Torrio's solution was to turn the whole enterprise over to Al Capone, who was only too happy to take it off his hands.

Outwardly charming, Capone was utterly without mercy when crossed, employing brutal tactics without hesitation. This cold-blooded approach was typified on the morning of February 14, 1929, when his men stormed into a garage on the city's North Side occupied by a group of his unsuspecting rivals—men affiliated with George "Bugs" Moran. As a distraction measure, they wore the uniforms of Chicago police officers.

> **Outwardly charming, Capone was utterly without mercy when crossed, employing brutal tactics without hesitation.**

Taking their targets completely by surprise, the intruders lined all seven men up against a wall then opened fire with tommy guns and a shotgun. The assassins poured gunfire into the bleeding, dying men even as they lay helpless on the garage floor, just to make sure that the job was finished. Once the shooting stopped, the gangsters fled into the street.

The event would become known as the St. Valentine's Day Massacre.

Remarkably, considering the sheer volume of ammunition that had been blasted into the victims, one of them survived the shooting. Peppered with bullet holes, he nonetheless made it to the hospital alive, where he died later that same day—without ratting his murderers out to the police. Although he was out of town at the time (which may simply have been a precautionary measure), Capone was law enforcement's number-one suspect for ordering the hit. Some historians, however, suspect that he may not have been involved at all. The truth will likely never be known.

Al Capone possessed a ruthless sense of drive and ambition, which meant that he was willing to kill anybody who could not be bought, bribed, or intimidated into doing what he wanted. He was also infected with syphilis, a sexually transmitted disease that could not be cured. He had engaged in many extramarital dalliances over the years, and Capone's wife unwittingly paid the price by also becoming infected. One side effect of the disease is that it can cause violent and aggressive mood swings, which only served to further destabilize the already vicious Capone. The illness would plague him throughout his life.

If you believe the Hollywood hype, then the architect of the gangster's demise was a dedicated prohibition agent named Eliot Ness. In reality, Ness played a somewhat less prominent role in Capone's downfall than the movies would have us believe—there was no one-on-one showdown between the two men, for example—but Ness really did contribute to finally getting Capone indicted. Although not quite the squeaky clean, square-jawed superhero of some portrayals, Eliot Ness truly was a decent lawman who could not be bought at any price—a relative rarity in the days when corruption was rife. The utter disdain he and his colleagues showed for bribery earned them the nickname "the Untouchables."

There were many who believed that Al Capone himself was untouchable. Unfortunately for him, Capone was a victim of his own success. He had grown to such prominence in the public eye that he came to the attention of none other than President Herbert Hoover. Incensed at the gangster's audacity, Hoover directed federal law enforcement to "get Capone!" Chicago was out of control, Hoover believed, and the president wanted an example to be made. As the nation's most prominent mobster, Al Capone was the perfect choice to be publicly humbled by the law.

Agent Eliot Ness of the Bureau of Prohibition recruited a team of incorruptible agents, who became known as "the Untouchables," specifically to target Al Capone and his bootlegging operations.

It is commonly said that there are only two certainties in life: death and taxes. Al Capone was responsible for many of the former, and he was brought low when he fell afoul of the latter. Considering the extensive laundry list of crimes for which he was culpable, such as murder, prostitution, illegal gambling, extortion, and racketeering, to name just a few, it seems ironic that what finally brought him down were charges of federal tax evasion.

In their efforts to get Capone, investigators from the Internal Revenue Service worked the tax angle, while prohibition agents like Ness went after him for trafficking illegal liquor. Ness and his Untouchables had experience taking down Capone's network of illegal distilleries and distribution centers; they also had a hand in drafting the bootlegging charges against him. Tax evasion turned out to be the much stronger case when the issue finally went to trial in 1931. The crime kingpin simply hadn't bothered to file tax returns on hundreds of thousands of dollars' worth of income.

Capone entered a plea of not guilty, and his legal team managed to defeat 17 of the 22 charges levied against him. After being found guilty, Capone was sentenced to 11 years in prison. He served his time in several different correctional facilities, including the infamous "Rock"—Alcatraz Island. The symptoms of his syphilis continued to worsen, inducing a prolonged degradation of Capone's mental faculties, which caused him to progressively lose cognitive function as his brain rotted away.

He was released in 1939 after seven and a half years of incarceration. Following his old boss Torrio's example, Capone went into retirement in Florida rather than going back to a life of crime. The fact that he was enfeebled, both physically and mentally, left him with little choice in the matter. He was now a mere shadow of his former self, emotionally unstable and even more prone to fits of unprovoked rage than he had been during his Chicago heyday. The authorities were justifiably confident that the former crime lord was no longer a threat to society.

As syphilis continued to enfeeble him, Capone began to suffer seizures. He began speaking to invisible people, holding entire conversations with thin air. The most powerful man in Chicago had been reduced to wandering aimlessly, sometimes completely oblivious to his surroundings, rambling incoherently like a lost soul.

Alphonse Capone died on January 25, 1947, due to a confluence of heart, lung, and brain problems. At the age of 48, he passed into the history books, not with a bang but with a whimper. All that remained was the legend.

# King of the G-Men

At the dawn of the 20th century, the United States Department of Justice—one of the most influential and powerful components of the governmental hierarchy—had an Achilles' heel. The department possessed no dedicated policing and investigative force of its own, relying instead upon agents who were on loan from the Secret Service to help support its field investigations. Sometimes, when the situation was sufficiently serious, the Justice Department loosened the purse strings and used its funds to hire private investigators to beef up its manpower.

Top officials recognized that this patchwork state could not go on indefinitely. The lack of its own investigative and enforcement arm left the DOJ something of a paper tiger. In 1908, Attorney General Charles J. Bonaparte established a group of agents devoted entirely to the needs of the Justice Department. Thus was born the Bureau of Investigation, which would later become the Federal Bureau of Investigation—the FBI.

Agents of the Bureau were commonly referred to as "G-men," short for

> **Hoover's word was law. In his mind, he *was* the law.**

government men. They garnered a reputation for dressing smartly, behaving professionally, and taking a sober, level-headed approach to law enforcement. Yet the FBI director who ruled over the agency with an iron fist for an astonishing 48 years was a colorful—and undeniably corrupt—individual.

That man was J. Edgar Hoover.

Hoover assumed directorship of the Bureau of Investigation in 1924. He was a towering, complex figure, and his influence can be seen throughout 20th-century U.S. law enforcement and politics— and not necessarily for the right reasons. During his time in office, Hoover served under eight different presidents. He thought nothing of bending or breaking the rules to get what he wanted, believing that those rules applied to others but not to him. Hoover's word was law. In his mind, he *was* the law.

J. Edgar Hoover was appointed director of the Bureau of Investigation by President Calvin Coolidge in 1924.

Empire building came instinctively to Hoover, and the Bureau grew in size and power during his tenure as director. One of the tactics he employed to expand his own sphere of influence was to make himself practically indispensable to whoever was president at the time. A bluff, hard-nosed man by nature, Hoover was nevertheless often willing to say almost anything to butter up the man in the Oval Office. This tactic met with varying degrees of success. Dwight D. Eisenhower made great use of Hoover and his clandestine services, whereas his predecessor, Harry S. Truman, had had little time for the FBI director or his agency. In public, at least, Richard M. Nixon thought so highly of Hoover that he granted him the honor of a state funeral. Privately, it was another matter. Nixon had come to see the aging Hoover as more of a liability than an asset, and his death solved more problems than it created for the administration.

In all cases, no matter what the president's personal opinion of him may have been, Hoover worked to improve their relationship and better the standing of the Bureau in the president's eyes. J. Edgar Hoover saw himself as the living, breathing personification of the

FBI. His will was the will of the Bureau, and vice versa. The two were indivisible and inseparable in Hoover's mind, and woe betide anybody who didn't fall into line.

## The Blackmail Files

Hoover maintained an expansive and detailed archive of secret reports on the professional and private lives of influential figures in each administration, going all the way up to the president. Whenever an occupant of the Oval Office was engaged in an illicit love affair (something for which John F. Kennedy was well known), word of their clandestine liaison invariably reached Hoover's ears before the president even got back to the White House. Hoover's extensive files were a Sword of Damocles hanging over the head of each and every presidency, an implied threat that the FBI director could use to get what he wanted if push ever came to shove—which it usually didn't. The threat of exposure was usually sufficient.

Hoover's infamous blackmail files weren't restricted to presidents and their cohorts. Anybody who possessed influence in American society was considered fair game. This included Hollywood actors and actresses, scientists, authors, musicians, and civil rights leaders. Martin Luther King Jr. had a file. So did Marilyn Monroe, who was suspected of consorting with communists due to her marriage to playwright Arthur Miller. The ever-present threat of communism, to Hoover, was like a red rag to a bull. The merest suspicion of harboring communist sympathies or tendencies could get somebody's phone tapped or lead to FBI agents surveilling and following them wherever they went. The blanket term used to label anybody of whom Hoover did not approve was "subversive," and Bureau agents actively monitored more than 400,000 supposedly subversive individuals—all for the good of the American people, of course.

Being both Black and a leading figure in the civil rights movement, Dr. Martin Luther King checked two boxes on Hoover's list of potential subversives. Hoover's distaste for the equality movement was rooted in that favorite bugbear of his: communism, which he believed was inextricably intertwined with it. To this end, Hoover ordered his FBI agents to do far more than monitor King and his activities. The activities they engaged in soon crossed the line into outright intimidation and harassment. The FBI director signed off on his agency sending hate mail to King and then tried to blackmail him using details of his extramarital sexual liaisons. Whenever King stayed in a hotel room, the FBI made efforts to plant bugs and wiretaps in the hope of catching him committing an embarrassing indiscretion. Hoover wanted to ruin King's reputation, smearing him as effectively as possible and destroying his credibility in the eyes of the public.

## Hoover and McCarthy

In 1958, Hoover wrote a book rebuking the evils of communism. Titled *Masters of Deceit: The Story of Communism in America and How to Fight It*, the text was intended to sound the alarm bells against the growing communist influence in the United States. There were few more outspoken and prominent anti-communists in the public arena at the time than J. Edgar Hoover, but one man who came close was Senator Joseph McCarthy of Wisconsin.

McCarthy began railing about the impingement of communist sympathizers into American life in 1950. Always a controversial figure, the senator soon launched his rhetoric to stratospheric heights, culminating in his infamous "Reds under the Bed" mantra. What he lacked in evidence (many of McCarthy's claims proved to be unfounded) he made up for in volume and sheer venom. McCarthy was nothing if not shrewd. Anybody who was paying even cursory attention to world news could see the spread of communism across the globe. American and allied servicemen were fighting and dying in an attempt to check its advance in Korea. When they were viewed in the context of world events, McCarthy's claims that "commies" were everywhere didn't seem all that far-fetched to an increasingly worried America.

Joseph McCarthy, elected to the U.S. Senate in 1946 to represent Wisconsin, began his infamous four-year campaign against Communists and other alleged subversives in 1950.

Given that both men were vehement anti-communists, it would have seemed natural for J. Edgar Hoover and Joseph McCarthy to be natural political allies. At first, that was indeed the case. However, as the senator continued to pound the pulpit loudly and aggressively, and as his search for hidden communist sympathizers took on the character of a witch hunt rather than a legitimate investigation, Hoover grew increasingly concerned. He may have hated communism, but Hoover's approach to combating that enemy was at least semi-rational and somewhat measured. Not so McCarthy, whose initial suspicions soon gave way to outright delusion.

Although they shared the same goal, Hoover finally stopped supporting and defending McCarthy from his detractors, working instead to distance himself from what he saw as the senator's growing instability. As far as the FBI director was concerned, Joseph McCarthy had turned from being an asset into a liability.

His instincts were correct. Until 1954, the senator had effectively enjoyed free rein to "investigate," prosecute, and condemn those he accused of being communists or communist sympathizers. Unfortunately for him, he tried to go a bridge too far by crossing swords with the U.S. Army. McCarthy's initial complaint involved what he claimed was inadequate security at an Army facility, but in typical McCarthy style, he began firing off accusations that members of the Army's legal team had ties with communism. If he couldn't make a case based on facts, then invoking "the Red Menace" was McCarthy's usual fallback position.

This time, however, the senator had bitten off more than he could chew. Joseph Welch, the attorney representing the Army, delivered a stinging rebuke to McCarthy's claim that would go down in the annals of history: "Have you no sense of decency?" This drama played out live on national television, and the effects on McCarthy's reputation were catastrophic. The American public, many of whom had been supportive of his anti-communist crusade up to that point, now deserted McCarthy in droves. A few months later, with his popularity in decline, McCarthy was censured by the Senate for his distasteful practices. Shredded to tatters, his reputation never recovered. Neither did his political career. McCarthy would die three years later, in 1957, his name forever synonymous with the employment of bullying and cowardly smear tactics in the pursuit of personal gain.

J. Edgar Hoover's instincts toward him had proved to be right.

## The Lavender Scare and Other "Moral Crusades"

Another group that found itself squarely within Hoover's crosshairs were homosexuals, whom the FBI director characterized as "sexual deviants." He deemed them a threat to the fabric of American society, particularly when they walked the same halls of power in Washington as he did. Hoover believed that homosexuals were extremely vulnerable to being blackmailed by foreign intelligence services into handing over secret information. This bias culminated in Executive Order 10450, signed by President Eisenhower in 1953, which barred gays and lesbians from government service on the grounds that their "sexual perversion" was a risk to national security.

In this particularly bleak moment of U.S. history, thousands of federal employees were stripped of their security clearances and ignominiously fired, often on the flimsiest of evidence. The basis for such an investigation was usually a claim of homosexuality or a similar aspect of their private lives.

This cull came to be known as the "lavender scare." Some of those who were ousted were so devastated that they took their own lives. Many of them were dedicated, lifelong public servants with unblemished track records.

Rumors swirled around the possibility of a relationship between J. Edgar Hoover (right) and his deputy, Clyde Tolson, even while Hoover was spearheading the reckless crusade against homosexuals that would become known as the Lavender Scare.

There have been many allegations over the years that the vitriol Hoover showed in this regard arose because he was a closeted gay man who allegedly like to dress in women's clothes. The debate about Hoover's private life continues to this day. Some believe that he engaged in a long-term relationship with FBI deputy director Clyde Tolson, something that, if true, would have bordered on political suicide for both men were it to be discovered. The fact that Hoover never married, instead living the life of what was then called a "career bachelor," helped fuel such rumors. Undoubtedly, Hoover and Tolson worked closely together. Were they lovers? With both men now dead, the definitive answer is lost to history.

Hoover's FBI also embarked on what could be termed a "moral crusade" against pornography and obscenity, employing very broad and loose parameters to both terms. Sexually explicit films, books, and magazines were targeted, as were theatrical performances, works of art, and even music. Other "subversives" to earn the director's ire (and the close scrutiny of his field agents) included African Americans, anybody whose political tendencies leaned toward the left, and those who protested wars, such as the Vietnam War. Such beliefs were "un-American," in his view, and those who espoused them needed to be watched carefully.

During World War II, FBI agents surveilled and apprehended enemy spies and saboteurs operating within the United States. This strong work was a credit to both Hoover and the Bureau, but the FBI's wartime service was tarnished by its involvement in the rounding up and internment of Japanese citizens following the attack on Pearl Harbor. This is more a negative reflection on the unfairness of the government's short-sighted and xenophobic policy, however, than upon the agency whose job it was to implement the law.

## The FBI and the KKK

The Bureau found itself on the right side of history by opposing the Ku Klux Klan. The Klan's home-bred form of domestic terrorism resulted in the intimidation, torture, and murder of African American citizens. Even before his appointment as director, then-assistant director Hoover responded to Louisiana governor John Parker's entreaty for help by deploying a team of field agents to assist him in countering the Klan's reign of terror.

The FBI and the KKK remained opponents for decades. In the summer of 1964, matters came to a head in Mississippi, when Klan members kidnapped and murdered three civil rights workers, whose burned-out vehicle was found abandoned. FBI agents investigating the case code-named it MIBURN, short for "Mississippi burning."

The case made national headlines, with President Lyndon B. Johnson taking a personal interest. J. Edgar Hoover provided him with regular updates on the case as it progressed. After an exhaustive search, the remains of the three dead men were finally unearthed on August 4. Over the same period of time, FBI agents worked diligently to gather evidence and assemble a case against the Mississippi arm of the Klan. The rot and corruption went deep; local law enforcement was in it up to their necks, all the way up to and including the sheriff himself.

Johnson and Hoover had demanded results, and their agents delivered. It took three years, but the perpetrators were finally brought to justice and sent to jail. The fight against militant white supremacy in the United States was far from over, however. It continues to this day.

J. Edgar Hoover remains a controversial figure, but it should be remembered that, in addition to the corrupt practices in which he was a willing participant, Hoover also did a great deal of good. In its early days, the Bureau was far from the slick, professional organization that he envisioned. Hoover set about changing that immediately, advocating for scientific advances in law enforcement such as widespread fingerprinting of suspects. On the other hand, his ham-handed refusal to allow women to serve as field operatives in the Bureau remains a black mark against his name. This rule would remain in place until after Hoover's death in 1972.

## The FBI after Hoover

With the benefit of hindsight, it cannot be denied that J. Edgar Hoover was able to accumulate an unhealthy amount of power and influence. This was partly because of his ability to hitch his wagon to the incumbent president's star. After his tenure at the FBI ended with his death in 1972, many of Hoover's abuses of power finally came to light. It became apparent to even the most biased observer that some degree of distance needed to exist between the office of the president and that of the FBI director, a "separation of church and state" that would allow the Bureau to retain its impartiality to the highest possible degree.

A case in point is that of former director James Comey. Comey had been appointed to head the FBI in 2013, under then-president Barack Obama. Arguably the most prominent Bureau investigation under the Obama administration was a probe into the actions of Secretary of State Hillary Clinton, who had stored confidential emails on a private, non-secure server (more details on this later can be found in the chapter covering the Clinton family). No case was brought against Clinton, but there were those on both sides of the political aisle who saw Comey's handling of the situation as questionable. Clinton's supporters believed that the FBI director had undermined her subsequent presidential campaign, in which she lost the election to Donald Trump; her detractors maintained that Comey had been negligent by failing to find Clinton guilty of any crime.

James Comey delivers remarks following his 2013 nomination by President Obama to the position of FBI director.

During the turbulent presidency of Donald J. Trump, the president and the FBI director clashed over what the former perceived to be a lack of Comey's personal loyalty to Trump. Comey stated publicly that the FBI was actively investigating claims that Russia had worked to undermine the U.S. presidential election in Trump's favor, a claim that enraged the president. This ultimately culminated in Comey's firing, followed by a subsequent string of acrimonious insults, retorts, and allegations against him.

Just how was it that Hoover was able to get away with his blatant abuses of power for so long? The man was a master self-promoter, never passing up an opportunity to put himself and the Bureau in the spotlight—and always in the most positive of ways. When it came to expertise in public relations, Hoover had few equals. The fact that he was able to so entrench himself in the office of FBI director that he remained there for 48 years is as remarkable as it is disturbing.

Recognizing this, the rules concerning the FBI directorship were changed following Hoover's death in 1972. Now, an FBI director can hold the post for no longer than ten years before having to make way for somebody else—unless an extension is specifically granted by Congress. This term limit is just one of many ways in which J. Edgar Hoover's complicated legacy continues to affect the political landscape many years after his death.

# An Offer You Can't Refuse

Say the phrase "organized crime," and most Americans think of the Mafia, known by some as La Cosa Nostra. This is in no small part due to the 1972 movie classic *The Godfather*, directed by Francis Ford Coppola and based on the bestselling novel by Mario Puzo.

At the dawn of the 20th century, Italian immigrants came en masse to the United States in search of new horizons and a better life than the one they had left behind. As the population boomed, Italian American communities formed. There was money to be made, and along with those opportunities came the scourge of organized crime.

The introduction of Prohibition in 1920, brought about by the 18th Amendment, drove the production, distribution, and consumption of liquor underground. It was no coincidence that the 1920s was the heyday of the American Mafia, as it rode to prominence and power on the back of the bootlegging trade. Prior to the advent of Prohibition, although there were Italian American criminal gangs, they did not represent organized crime in the current sense of the term. They were small, loosely knit groups, with no major hierarchy and little coordination between them.

Such was the demand for bootlegged liquor that an entire illegal industry arose to accommodate it. Vast sums of money were being made, and that dirty cash changed hands in countless ways. There were crooked cops and officials to be paid off, clandestine distilleries to be run, and fleets of trucks and cars to be maintained and kept on the road, transporting barrels of liquor to speakeasies and gambling joints; furthermore, it all had to be protected, which required a small army of foot soldiers. Everybody in the supply and delivery chain had to be paid regularly, which required accountants, bookkeepers, and paymasters. The only way to keep it all going was for the bootleggers to organize to take advantage of economies of scale.

Criminal organizations tended to gather in homogenous ethnic groups, in accordance with their instinct to trust those they already knew or who looked, talked, and acted like themselves. Members shared a common heritage and ancestry. There were large Italian populations in the major cities of Chicago and New York, which made them natural locations for criminal syndicates to arise.

The rise of organized crime in the United States was energized by the opportunities created when the 18th Amendment began the era of Prohibition. The quest to keep alcohol out of daily life spurred a deadly game of cat-and-mouse between law enforcement and bootleggers.

Prohibition wasn't directly responsible for creating the American Mafia, but the 18th Amendment gave it a major shot in the arm, helping it expand into a more efficient criminal organization. Prohibition was repealed in 1933, but organized crime only grew. Less than 20 years later, the Mafia was the single largest and most powerful criminal enterprise in the nation. In the latter half of the 20th century, the organization would continue to expand and diversify, getting involved in protection rackets, gambling establishments, prostitution rings, narcotic distribution, counterfeiting, and a host of other crimes.

Nor was its influence restricted to the criminal underworld. The Mafia became entangled with trade unions and legitimate businesses too. Rumors circulated that the organization had close ties to several U.S. presidents. There were even conspiracy theories suggesting that the Mafia was behind the 1963 assassination of President John F. Kennedy.

The Mafia operated with a steel fist inside a velvet glove. Sometimes it was effective for members simply to bribe corrupt officials into giving them what they wanted. When the lure of money failed, Mafia enforcers turned to intimidation and, where necessary, physical violence. Their methods of coercion ranged from broken bones to full-fledged executions.

If the Mafia had a spiritual home in the United States, it was New York City. In 1931, with bootlegging still going full force, the heads of the five largest and most powerful Italian organized crime families came together under the leadership of crime boss Salvatore Maranzano. Seeing himself as the preeminent mobster in New York, Maranzano had reached prominence only after murdering several rivals in cold blood, and he was well known for his ruthless streak.

Like many crime bosses had before him, Maranzano met a violent demise, assassinated by rival mobsters on September 10, 1931, at the age of 45. His death left the Five Families—the Bonanno, Colombo, Gambino, Genovese, and Lucchese organizations—at the top of the Mafia food chain but with a power vacuum above them that needed to be filled.

Maranzano was gone, but surprisingly, his role as "first among equals" was not to be filled by a replacement. Rather than accept the rule of another overlord, the heads of the Five Families chose instead to abolish the position and rule by collective, forming what would afterward be known as the Commission—essentially a governing council. The influence of the Five Families extended far beyond the Mafia strongholds of New York and Chicago. Their ambition was to rule all Italian organized crime throughout the United States.

## The Bonnano Family

What would one day become the Bonnano family had its roots in Sicily, and their criminal enterprise was initially named after their hometown of Castellamare del Golfo. Upon their relocation to the United States, the Castellamarese mob was run by Salvatore Maranzano. As previously mentioned, the organization was powerful enough that he had pushed to declare himself the *capo di tutti i capi*, or "boss of bosses," in New York organized crime, which is what ultimately led to his murder. The fact that he also demanded the other Mafia families make tribute payments to him had not endeared Maranzano to them one bit.

One of his protégés, Giuseppe Carlo "Joseph" Bonnano (nicknamed Joe Bananas), picked up the leadership reins in the aftermath of Maranzano's death in 1931, determined to make his own mark. One of Bonnano's first actions was to rename the crime syndicate after himself. For more than 30 years, Joe Bonnano called the shots on behalf of his family business. Failing to learn a valuable lesson from the fall of Sal Maranzano, in the 1960s Bonnano launched a hostile takeover bid aimed at making himself the boss of bosses.

What happened in the five-year period between 1964 and 1969 became known in Mafia circles as the Bonnano War, or by some, the Banana War. As Joe was preparing to launch hits on his rival crime bosses, word of his plans reached the ear of the Commission before he could put them into effect. Forced to abdicate his position, he was replaced as head of the Bonnano family enterprise by Gaspar DiGregorio.

Exiled by the Commission, Joe Bonnano went underground and waged war against DiGregorio—a war that also extended to the remainder of the Five Families. Bonnano loyalists were killed in a series of bloody shootouts. Joe ordered a hit on the head of the Genovese family, Johnny Biello, not just because he was a rival but also because he had ratted out Bonnano's plot to assassinate the other Commission members.

Joe Bonnano had relocated to Arizona, but his enemies were still able to reach him there. His home in Tucson was shot to pieces during an attack ordered by the Commission. Other assassination attempts targeted his supporters. In increasingly poor health, having barely survived a string of heart attacks, Bonnano was finally forced to see the writing on the wall. He retired from his life of crime in 1968.

The Bonnano/Banana War ended the following year.

The tides of fortune turned against the Bonnano family in 2013, when former family boss Joseph Massino flipped and became a government informant. The man who had once called the shots (sometimes literally) for the Bonnano criminal enterprise began covertly feeding information on his family members to law enforcement agents. He remains the most prominent mobster to ever turn against the Mafia, and the only member of the Five Families Commission to break ranks and give up their secrets.

Born in Sicily in 1905, Giuseppe Carlo Bonanno (aka Joe Bananas) migrated to the United States with his family, who were no strangers to organized crime.

Joseph Massino cooperated with authorities even when he was locked up in prison, having committed at least eight murders, and he secretly wore a wire to record information from unsuspecting gangsters. In 2013, a judge sentenced Massino to time served. A free man again, the 70-year-old promptly disappeared into the federal Witness Protection Program, hiding behind a fake identity at an undisclosed location. A condition of receiving his freedom was that Massino continue to cooperate with the FBI in ongoing investigations into mob activity, serving as an asset in the Bureau's efforts to control organized crime.

The inside knowledge provided by Joseph Massino as part of his cooperation deal helped federal law enforcement deliver a crushing body blow to the Bonnano family, but it was far from finished. In 2022, the Bonnano crime syndicate was still going strong.

In March of that same year, 67-year-old crime boss Michael "the Nose" Mancuso was released from jail on a $500,000 bond, having served a 15-year sentence for the 2004 murder of mafioso Randolph Pizzolo. It was strongly rumored that Mancuso, while serving his term of incarceration, was able to keep running the business affairs of the Bonnano family from the confines of his prison cell.

# The Profaci-Colombo Family

The Colombo family was originally named after its founder, Giuseppe "Joseph" Profaci, one of countless Sicilians who came to the United States in the early 1920s. At first, Profaci was a legitimate businessman, making a living by importing olive oil and tomato sauce. Some of his wealthiest clients were mobsters who craved a taste of home, which gave him more than a passing acquaintance with members of New York's criminal underworld.

By 1928, with the approval of the crime family heads, Profaci was running his own gang. Brooklyn was their turf, and the Profaci mob was more than willing to defend it from rival organizations. As the 1930s dawned, the olive oil importer was running prostitution rings, protection rackets, shady loans, and a host of other illegal scams.

With the birth of the Commission in 1931, Joseph Profaci found himself appointed as head of one of the five governing families. The organization he oversaw had expanded from being a relatively small-time gang to a full-fledged crime syndicate. The Profaci family was the last of the Five Families to be formally constituted.

A hefty chunk of the family's income came from heroin smuggling. Leveraging his roots in the import and export business, Joseph Profaci's favorite method of bringing the drug into the United States involved the use of fruit. At their home port in Sicily, Profaci associates packed heroin inside boxes full of wax oranges, which fooled cursory inspection (they weighed the same as a real orange would) but would not stand up to being handled and examined by a customs agent.

Joseph Profaci took great pleasure in evading taxes. In 1953, the Internal Revenue Service sued him for the unpaid sum of $1.5 million in back taxes. The crime boss simply shrugged and refused to cough up. Uncle Sam never got his money; Profaci would die in 1962 with the debt still unpaid.

It takes a strong degree of cold-blooded ruthlessness to run a criminal syndicate, and Joseph Profaci had this qualification. He did not tolerate disrespect, and he was more than willing to have a man killed if he felt slighted. Feared and respected as a strong leader, although never loved by his associates, Profaci remained unchallenged for almost 30 years. In 1959, however, he faced a stumbling block in the form of mobster "Crazy Joe" Gallo, so-called because he was a diagnosed schizophrenic.

Gallo and his two brothers, Albert and Larry, worked as hired muscle for the Profaci family. They were fearless and ruthless, but they could also be loose cannons when the mood took them—which was often. Profaci ordered the murder of a business associate who had stopped pay-

Giuseppe "Joseph" Profaci, born in Sicily in 1897, migrated to the United States in 1921, where he would found the Colombo crime family in 1928.

ing the regular tithe Profaci demanded from all who worked for him. That man was Frank "Frankie Shots" Abbatemarco, a high-ranking captain in the Profaci organization. The cash tributes Joe Profaci insisted upon made him unpopular with his subordinates, but Abbatemarco was one of the few who had dared to stop making payments. By the time the hit went through on him, Abbatemarco owed Profaci in excess of $50,000. The fact that he was gunned down in public made it a moot point—the debt would never be paid, but a very expensive example had been made of the murdered man.

Once Abbatemarco was out of the way, the Gallos felt entitled to a reward for their loyal services to the family, in the form of a share of the dead man's business interests. Demonstrating a remarkable lack of foresight, Profaci farmed out what had once belonged to Abbatemarco to other loyalists, pointedly ignoring the three brothers. The Gallos were outraged, and they showed it by enlisting the help of fellow mobster Carmine Persico to help them kidnap a group of Profaci's senior henchmen and hold them hostage.

Profaci agreed to pay the ransom Persico and the Gallos demanded to have his associates released. Once they were free, he welched on the deal, opting instead to put out a hit on Larry Gallo and one of his soldiers. The chosen assassin was Carmine Persico, who had switched sides and gone back over to the Profaci side of the fence. Fortunately for Larry, his attempted murder was interrupted by a police patrol. The incident left him wounded but alive.

> **The so-called Gallo Wars lasted two years and caused heavy casualties among both Profaci and Gallo supporters.**

The so-called Gallo Wars lasted two years and caused heavy casualties among both Profaci and Gallo supporters. Joseph Profaci would not live to see the end of the conflict he had brought about; he died of liver cancer in 1962 at the age of 64. After Profaci's funeral, underboss Joseph Magliocco ascended to the top spot. In what would prove to be a poor career move, he signed up to be part of Joe Bonanno's attempted coup against the Commission. When the rest of the Five Families leadership found out about his willingness to have them killed, it seemed likely that Magliocco would be whacked himself. Due to his advanced age and infirmity, however, the ailing capo was allowed to live on the condition that he pay a hefty $50,000 fine and retire from organized crime forever. This he did, and he died of a massive heart attack three days after Christmas in 1968.

Now effectively decapitated, the Profaci family had room at the top for a new boss. The Commission got the final say in who replaced Magliocco. The Five Families valued loyalty above all other virtues, and they knew that when Bonanno and Magliocco were scheming to have them assassinated, Joseph Colombo had been the hit man of choice. Rather than carry out the hit, he had instead let the Commission know about the plot to murder them. This was the kind of loyalty they were only too happy to reward and encourage in others.

So it was that the Profaci crime family came to be renamed after its new boss, Joseph Colombo. Colombo soon locked horns with the FBI in a very public feud that he sustained until his dying day. He viewed the Bureau's ongoing investigation into mob activities as a form of deliberately targeted persecution and suppression of Italian Americans. His response was to create the Italian American Civil Rights League, a political organization aimed at the betterment of Italian Americans. The league arranged public protests outside FBI field offices, the very opposite approach one would normally expect from the head of an organized criminal empire.

The line between fact and fiction became blurred when Paramount Pictures announced its intention to make a movie adaptation of *The Godfather*. Colombo opposed the idea of a film being made of Puzo's book on the grounds that it would show Italian Americans in a bad light. The use of the terms "Cosa Nostra" (roughly "Our Thing" in Italian) and "Mafia" angered him; Colombo saw them as slurs that were used to demean and belittle his people. It's also possible that the insight Puzo's novel provided into the inner workings of real Italian American organized crime family was a little too close to home for Colombo's comfort.

Born in New York City in 1923, Joseph Colombo grew up within Profaci's crime family, which he would eventually take over and give his own name.

In 1970 and 1971, as the movie went into production, the Mafia's antagonism proved to be a big problem for producer Al Ruddy. For reasons of authenticity, the movie had to be filmed in and around New York City. With just a snap of his fingers, Joe Colombo could give orders to his associates that would bring production to a grinding halt. Indeed, he had made a number of thinly veiled threats to that effect. Clearly, the crime boss had to be placated—but how?

At the end of the day, what Colombo really wanted was a little respect for himself, his family, and his people. Ruddy showed that respect by allowing him to read and approve the movie's shooting script—and by excising any mention of the word "Mafia" from within its pages. The offering worked. After going over the script, Colombo did a one-eighty and gave *The Godfather* not just his cautious approval; the production also benefited from the full-blown support of New York's crime families. This link with organized crime upset top executives at the movie studio, Paramount Pictures, who did their best to downplay reports of production on *The Godfather* having any sort of Mafia involvement. In all likelihood, however, the success of the film was boosted by the cachet conferred upon it by receiving Mafia assistance—or, as it was more publicly termed, the support of the Italian American Civil Rights League.

Unfortunately for him, Joe Colombo was about to have bigger worries than a movie production. On June 28, 1971, he was speaking at a League rally when a man with fake press credentials got close to the podium. The supposed reporter pulled a handgun and shot Colombo three times in the head. From the edge of the crowd, another man (believed to be a Colombo family bodyguard) returned fire, killing the assassin, who was later identified as one Jerome A. Johnson. Eyebrows were raised at the fact that the significant police presence at the rally that day was not sufficient to prevent either shooting. Stranger still, Johnson's killer has never been identified.

There was much speculation on who was behind the attempted assassination. Some laid the blame at the door of Crazy Joe Gallo. Others believed the attack to have been racially motivated, or that Joe Colombo's constant presence in the media had infuriated the Commission, who set out to have him silenced. Joseph Colombo's son, Anthony, had a different theory. He believed that the FBI had put out a hit on his father in retaliation for his ongoing crusade against them.

Remarkably, despite being shot repeatedly in the head at close range, Joseph Colombo did not die. He was rushed to hospital, where he underwent emergency surgery. The severe brain damage that he suffered inflicted permanent paralysis. Colombo lived for seven more years, albeit in a comatose state. He died in 1978. Even without his galvanizing presence, the Italian American Civil Rights League went on, and it still exists today.

The Gallo Wars ended less than a year later, with the assassination of Joe Gallo, who had been released from a prison stretch in 1971. On April 7, 1972, he was eating at a seafood restaurant in Manhattan to celebrate his 43rd birthday when multiple shooters appeared and opened fire. Shortly afterward, he was pronounced dead at a nearby hospital.

Although Colombo family soldiers claimed credit for the hit on Gallo, the identity of his killers remains unproven. Nobody was ever convicted of his murder.

As tended to happen following the assassination of a boss, fresh blood came forward to lead the family enterprise onward. In recent years, the Colombo family has seen its power and influence wane, but it is still extant.

## The Gambino Family

The Gambino family traces its origins back to the rackets run in the late 19th century by Salvatore "Toto" D'Aquila. Thanks to his drive and savvy leadership, during the early 1900s the D'Aquila gang became the most powerful criminal enterprise in New York City. Its founder paid the ultimate price on October 10, 1928, when assassins shot him dead in the street. The hit had been put out by the rival Masseria crime family.

The organization's fortunes continued to fluctuate until 1957, when one Carlo Gambino assumed leadership. One of his first acts was to rename the family after himself. A case can be made that Gambino was the most powerful and influential mob boss in the history of Italian American organized crime. This is bolstered by the fact that he was one of a select few bosses to die peacefully, of natural causes, rather than meeting his end by assassination. Taking into consideration the violent circles in which he moved, this was no small feat.

Born in Sicily in 1902, Carlo Gambino emigrated from his homeland to the United States in 1921 to join the family business in New York, where he assumed control of a long-standing crime family in 1957.

The heads of the Five Families had believed that Gambino's predecessor, Albert Anastasia, had become a liability. They had wanted him removed. As his trusted underling, Carlo Gambino was in a good position to take over the reins—once his boss was permanently out of the way.

Anastasia liked to get his hair cut at the barber shop inside Manhattan's Park Sheraton Hotel. On October 25, 1957, he was sitting in the barber's chair when hit men burst in and opened fire, shooting him dead. Though the assassinated mob boss hadn't lacked for enemies, the identity of his assassins has never been determined conclusively. The likelihood is that the hit was ordered by Gambino.

**Grifters, Frauds, and Crooks: True Stories of American Corruption**

With the change in leadership, the family's fortunes reached new heights. Carlo Gambino had a sharper head for business than Anastasia, and he lacked his predecessor's vicious streak. Anastasia had drawn ire when he had men murdered for questionable reasons, the deaths bringing unwelcome instability and attention to family operations. Gambino was perfectly willing to have somebody executed, but unlike Anastasia, he was never prone to doing so frivolously. For this, among other reasons, many people believe that he was a key influence for the character of Vito Corleone in *The Godfather*.

One reason for Carlo Gambino's success and longevity in a field that saw many of his rivals incarcerated or assassinated was his tendency to fly under the radar. He eschewed the constant publicity that was courted by the likes of Joe Colombo, preferring to operate behind the scenes. He was soft-spoken and was not given to emotional outbursts, preferring to keep a cool head even when provoked.

FBI agents assigned to watch him found it impossible to catch Gambino doing or saying anything that might incriminate him. He seemed to lead a charmed life—one that was finally ended not by an assassin's bullet but by a heart condition. He died at home on October 15, 1976, of a heart attack, bringing to a close his 19 years as a head of the Gambino family and more than five decades as a member of organized crime.

Other leaders would follow. Perhaps best known was the infamous John Gotti, nicknamed "the Dapper Don" because of his immaculate sense of dress. Although the family retained its name on Gotti's ascension to supreme power on January 15, 1986, he was in many ways the polar opposite of Carlo Gambino. The Bronx-born, 46-year-old Gotti had spent his entire life working for the Mob. He gravitated to the Gambino family and served as a foot soldier, during which period Gotti served time in prison without breaking the Mafia code of silence.

After his release from prison, Gotti progressed from committing lower-level crimes to carrying out murder. His first hit, ordered against a member of a rival gang, took place on May 22, 1973. Gotti and two colleagues walked into a bar on Staten Island where James "Jimmy" McBratney was drinking, and they shot him dead. Subsequently arrested and tried, Gotti was able to bargain his conviction down from murder to manslaughter, which cost him four years behind bars.

In the winter of 1985, Gotti saw a once-in-a-career opportunity to make a power grab, and he seized it. On the night of December 16, four of Gotti's soldiers ambushed the head of the Gambino family, 70-year-old Paul Castellano, outside a steak house. The unsuspecting Castellano went down on the sidewalk in a hail of bullets, along with one of his most trusted lieutenants, Thomas Bilotti.

Although he hadn't pulled the trigger himself, Gotti had not only ordered the hit but also hung around a block away from the scene of the crime, making sure that the assassination went off without a hitch.

John Gotti, born in New York City in 1940, dramatically assumed control of the Gambino crime family in 1985 after ordering the assassination of its previous boss.

The audacious move paid off. Gotti replaced the dead Castellano as head of the family. His underlings soon learned that the new boss liked to lead a flashy, ostentatious lifestyle. As head of the Gambinos, federal officials tried to indict and convict him several times, but they were never able to make charges stick. Thus was born a new nickname: "the Teflon Don."

Gotti's luck finally ran out in 1990 when he was arrested and put on trial for racketeering, extortion, and ordering the assassination of Paul Castellano and Thomas Bilotti. In the past, the Teflon Don had been able to bribe and intimidate his way to freedom. Not this time. In 1992, after being found guilty, he was sentenced to 14 years in prison. In the event, the sentence was actually life—John Gotti died in prison in 2002, of throat cancer. The fortunes of the Gotti family never quite recovered after his loss.

## The Genovese Family

The Genovese family was established in 1930 by Sicilian-born crime boss Charles "Lucky" Luciano. The origin of his nickname is lost to the mists of time, with several completely different stories vying to explain it. Whether he was lucky in the gambling halls he once frequented, lucky because he had survived several close brushes with danger, or perhaps so named simply as a derivation of the surname Luciano, we may never know for sure. Whichever is the case, the name stuck with him throughout his life.

Luciano's family emigrated from Sicily to the United States when he was still a boy, and it didn't take long for the young Lucky Luciano to gravitate toward gang life. The advent of Prohibition saw him running a moonshine supply operation in New York City. During the bloody 1930–31 Castellammarese War, Lucky worked for Giuseppe "Joe the Boss" Masseria, fighting against his bitter rival, Sal Maranzano. Luciano had risen through the ranks to become a trusted lieutenant.

The so-called war was tearing the city apart, with each side launching tit-for-tat hits on the other, leaving behind a constant trail of bodies. In a rare case of law enforcement and the Mob agreeing with one another, everybody accepted that neither boss was willing to negotiate an end to the feud. The bloodshed would only stop once either Masseria or Maranzano was dead. Luciano was ambitious, and he was more than willing to eliminate his boss if it would further his own advancement. The fact that Masseria's side was losing the Castellammarese War helped make up his mind. All Luciano asked of Maranzano was that he be given Masseria's territory once he was dead.

The hit took place on April 15, 1931, at—where else?—a Coney Island restaurant. Luciano was the architect of the assassination but let others carry out the actual killing. Shot repeatedly in the back while playing a hand of cards, Joseph Masseria had no idea what hit him.

Being promoted to Maranzano's second-in-command might have been enough for some men, but Lucky Luciano had grander ambitions. He was no fan of the way his new boss was running things, and he decided he could do better. Tipped off to his new hireling's plans, Maranzano set plans in motion to have him killed, but Luciano beat him to the punch, organizing a series of brutal hits that left Maranzano and a number of his associates dead, and Lucky Luciano as ruler of the entire criminal enterprise.

True to his instincts, Luciano was far better at expanding the Italian American crime empire than either of his predecessors had been. Rather than wasting time, resources, and lives on perpetuating old feuds, he sought to build networks with other organizations for mutual profit. A shrewd businessman, Lucky Luciano reaped huge financial rewards as a result. He lived high on the hog, but all that came to an end in 1936 when the federal authorities put his life and operations under intense scrutiny.

Prosecutors zeroed in on Luciano's massive fortune, which he could not explain away as the proceeds of legitimate business. Upon his conviction, the judge sentenced Lucky Luciano to be jailed for between 30 and 50 years. Like many heads of crime families, being incarcerated didn't keep him from pulling the strings of his criminal enterprise. Even while stuck behind bars, Luciano commanded fear and respect.

He might have been a criminal, but Lucky was nothing if not a patriot. When the United States went to war against the Axis powers in 1941, the crime boss was still imprisoned but determined to serve his country in its hour of need. By 1943, the Allies had set their sights on invading Sicily. The local knowledge and connections held by men like Lucky Luciano might prove invaluable, some believed, when Operation Husky went ahead.

Never a man to lack courage, Luciano proposed that he be released from prison and sent to Sicily, where he could organize support for the Allied landings and arrange for local guides to accompany friendly units once they were ashore. The audacity of the scheme was astounding. Was the U.S. government really willing to send one of the country's top criminal masterminds, a man it had worked so hard to take off the streets, into a foreign land and simply trust that he would work to further American national interests?

Born in Sicily in 1897, Charles "Lucky" Luciano came to the United States at the age of six and soon commenced his life of crime.

As things turned out, it was not. Luciano was still able to assist his adopted country's war effort in another way, however. He gave orders to his Sicilian associates to tell the U.S. Naval Intelligence planners anything they wanted to know about their country of birth. He also arranged for contacts still living in Sicily to cooperate with the Allied forces once the invasion was underway.

In 1946, having served just a fraction of his sentence, Lucky Luciano was suddenly granted parole. The stated reason was for his "wartime services." Freedom came at a price: deportation and permanent banishment from the United States. He could never return to the U.S. again—not while alive, at any rate. He died of a heart attack in 1962. With his debt to society deemed to have been wiped clean, the authorities allowed his body to be repatriated to New York City. He is buried in Queens.

Although Frank Costello took the top job in 1937, the man who would give the family its current name, Vito Genovese, was Lucky Luciano's underboss. Genovese took over in 1957 and ran the organization until his death of a heart attack in 1969.

Undeniably the most colorful Genovese family boss would be Vincent "Vinny the Chin" Gigante—also known as "the Oddfather." New York City born and bred, Gigante began his working life as a prize fighter, then worked his way into the employ of Vito Genovese. He proved to be a good soldier, and duly became initiated—in Mafia terms, a "made man," and one who could pretty much write his own ticket.

> **Undeniably the most colorful Genovese family boss would be Vincent "Vinny the Chin" Gigante—also known as "the Oddfather."**

On the orders of Genovese, Gigante carried out a hit on Frank Costello on May 2, 1957, shooting him in the head at close range. Incredibly, the bullet creased the skull of the crime boss, failing to kill him. Still, enough was enough for Costello. He knew his days were numbered and that he would probably not be as fortunate the next time a hit man came calling. Costello willingly retired and turned over total control of the family to Vito Genovese.

In 1959, Gigante and Genovese went to jail for the crime of trafficking narcotics. Released after five years, Vincent Gigante cooked up a scheme to avoid ever doing time again: he would pretend to be insane. The higher he climbed the Mafia career ladder, the bigger a target he became for law enforcement. He decided to put on an act to convince them that he was mentally ill, just an everyday man with mental health issues, rather than the mastermind of a vast network of criminal enterprises.

A stranger meeting him on the street would never have realized that the man dressed in a bathrobe and pajamas, stumbling along the sidewalk, muttering at birds and inanimate objects, was the head of the infamous Genovese crime family. He intentionally spread false rumors about the state of his mental health, even going so far as to get professional clinicians to give him documentation of false diagnoses, including dementia and schizophrenia.

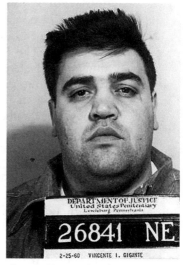

With every passing year, the organization's income grew—as did the tall stories about Gigante. He relished both aspects of his life. Behind closed doors, "the Oddfather" was his normal, rational self. In public, he thought nothing of going to the toilet in the street, right in front of shocked passers-by. The FBI agents assigned to surveil Gigante couldn't help but admire their quarry's acting chops and sheer cunning, as he frustrated every attempt they made to bring him to justice. His lawyers were able to convincingly plead that he was mentally incapable of committing the crimes of which he was being accused, and the court bought it.

Vincent Gigante, born in New York City in 1928, rose to power in 1981 as the boss of the Genovese crime family and evaded imprisonment for many years by feigning mental illness.

Playing the mental health card could only take him so far, however, and in 1996, justice caught up with Vincent Gigante. After listening to claims and counter claims about the mental state of the accused, the presiding judge ruled that he was in fact competent to stand trial. At the trial's conclusion, Gigante was sentenced to 12 years' imprisonment. Like other bosses before him, he continued to run the family from his jail cell.

In 2003, he finally confessed in a courtroom to what the FBI already had been saying for decades. The claims of mental incapacity had all been a sham. The confession wasn't altruistic in nature. It was motivated by self-interest, part of a plea deal that would help Gigante avoid a lengthier prison sentence. If all had gone well, he would have been released seven years later. Unfortunately for him, all did not go well. He died on December 19, 2005, while still a federal prisoner.

The Genovese family continues to operate to this day.

## The Lucchese Family

The last, but by no means least, of the Five Families is the Lucchese family. Its founder, Gaetano "Tommy" Reina, was born in Corleone, Sicily, in 1889. The Reina family came to the United States while Tommy was still a boy and made their home in Harlem. After learning the ins and outs of organized crime with the Morello crime family, by 1920 Tommy Reina had formed his own outfit, with Tommy Gagliano as his number-two man.

Ten years later, on February 26, 1930, Reina was shot dead outside his aunt's home. Lucky Luciano would later claim responsibility for ordering the hit. The executioner had been Vito Genovese.

With Reina dead, the leadership void was filled by Joseph Pinzolo—but not for long. Unpopular with his underlings, Pinzolo's short-lived reign ended on September 5, 1930, when he was fatally shot in Brooklyn.

Tommy Gagliano was waiting in the wings for his shot at the top job, and he would steer the Reina organization for the next 20 years. His underboss, Tommy Lucchese, took over from him in 1951 in a bloodless, nonviolent transfer of power. It was here that the family took on the name it would keep through the present day. His tenure was profitable and stable, ending with his death from a brain tumor in 1967.

The bosses that followed Lucchese worked to expand the reach of the family operation, branching out into legitimate and profitable industries. The most recent official boss, Vittorio "Vic" Amuso, gained notoriety for a series of brutal killings committed throughout the late 1980s. During his trial in 1992, Vic Amuso steadfastly insisted he was innocent of the nine murders and plethora of racketeering and corruption-related charges of which a jury declared him guilty. He was sentenced to life imprisonment and chose not to lodge an appeal.

Amuso continued to run the Lucchese family from confinement, with the help of a succession of acting bosses on the outside. It continues to operate today.

## The Mafia into the New Millennium

Beginning in the 1980s and continuing through the 1990s, a series of high-profile law enforcement operations that led to multiple convictions served to degrade Mafia operations throughout the country. The rise of the internet and online gambling also put a major dent in its revenue stream—until the Mafia adapted and turned to the internet itself to streamline its own betting operations.

Renowned author and former investigative journalist Selwyn Raab, an acknowledged expert on all things related to La Cosa Nostra, observed that the Mafia benefited greatly from the September 2001 terror attacks. In the aftermath, at the direction of the Bush administration,

> **The rise of the internet and online gambling put a major dent in its revenue stream—until the Mafia adapted and turned to the internet itself to streamline its own betting operations.**

federal law enforcement turned much of its attention away from organized crime and redirected a large portion of its resources to the war on terror. This took a lot of heat off the Five Families, which, as a consequence, would have a decade in which to regrow their operations while the FBI was busy elsewhere.

Recognizing this, in January of 2011 the FBI launched the largest roundup of Mafia personnel in the agency's history: 127 suspects were arrested, the majority of them known members of the organization. The remainder were confederates—associates who had facilitated the many criminal operations run by the Mafia. More than 800 FBI agents were involved in the massive bust, which took place across the northeastern United States. The Five Families were singled out and lost many key members in the swoop.

Despite the best efforts of the FBI, today's Mafia maintains its international reach and influence. Organized Italian American crime still has a presence in the 21st-century United States, albeit at a significantly lesser level by comparison to its heyday. The days when groups of rival mobsters went to war with one another are long gone. There is no longer blood in the streets, trussed-up bodies found in dumpsters or rivers, or other similar tropes made popular by Scorsese movies or hit television series such as *The Sopranos*.

The Five Families do still run their operations, however, and they remain a force to be reckoned with—and respected.

# The Whistleblower

S ay the word "whistleblower," and one of the first people to come to mind is Francesco (Frank) Serpico. Serpico joined the New York Police Department (NYPD) in 1959. An honest and idealistic young man who had grown up in Brooklyn, he was motivated by a desire to protect and serve his fellow New Yorkers. The beat cops he saw patrolling his neighborhood as a boy were respected and admired. Law enforcement seemed like a good career fit, and after graduating from the NYPD academy, Serpico spent the next 12 years in a variety of positions, including working the streets as a patrolman and investigating cases as a plainclothes detective.

Unfortunately, all was not as it seemed within the ranks of the NYPD. The more time he spent in uniform, the more he realized just how deep and widespread was the corruption that ran throughout the department. Many cops were on the take, either actively involved in criminal behavior or turning a blind eye to the crimes of others. Many of them benefited financially from abusing their position of trust. This did not sit well with Serpico, who believed that the last person who should get away with breaking the law ought to be a cop.

By his own admission, Frank Serpico was something of an outsider within the department. He spent his free time keeping himself to himself, rather than socializing with other cops. Serpico

The NYPD has a long history with allegations of misconduct, as evidenced by this 1887 political cartoon where a citizen begs the mayor for protection from the police.

didn't fit the mold of the "thin blue line" brotherhood, didn't hang out grilling brats and drinking beer with his fellow officers. More damning still, he refused to take dirty money when it was offered to him.

Unsurprisingly, word of Serpico's "excessive" honesty quickly spread throughout the precinct. Some began to label him as untrustworthy because he couldn't be bribed. This made some of his fellow cops very nervous. Was Frank Serpico a rat—a stool pigeon?

They got their answer when Serpico started talking openly about all the grift he saw going on. Ignoring the old adage that one should never speak truth to power, he spoke out to anybody in city administration who seemed willing to listen. Most heard him out but then turned a blind eye. Finally, in 1970, the city formed the Knapp Commission, formally known as the Commission to Investigate Alleged Police Corruption. Serpico and a fellow detective, David Durk, both stepped up to testify.

Grift was a way of life for much of the NYPD throughout the 1960s and 1970s, as it had been for years. Many cops saw skimming money off the top of criminal enterprises as simply accepting their due, something to which they were entitled. Bribes were nothing more than perks of the job. A cop who was not on the take, like Frank Serpico, was far more likely to raise eyebrows than one who was. The peer pressure for him to accept bribes to "prove himself" as one of the boys grew steadily. Still, Serpico steadfastly refused to become part of the problem. Instead, he became a threat to the status quo.

Frank Serpico's story almost ended on February 3, 1971—and so did his life. Now working for the NYPD's narcotics division, he was participating in a raid on the home of a heroin dealer. Serpico was the first officer through the door of the apartment. He was immediately faced with the gun-wielding occupant, who raised his pistol and shot Serpico in the face.

Two fellow officers had accompanied Serpico on the bust. Rather than return fire or at the very least call in for help, they fled the scene, leaving the detective to die alone. In all likelihood, Serpico would have died in the doorway of that apartment had not a well-meaning member of the public made a 911 call regarding the gunshot. When word got out that Serpico had been shot, it is said that few of his colleagues shed a tear. He was, by that time, a virtual pariah.

With hindsight, it is easy to see why some believe that the whole thing was a setup, designed to rid the department of its most vocal whistleblower. That may or may not have been the case, and the truth will probably never be known, as no formal police probe was launched into the incident.

> **With hindsight, it is easy to see why some believe that the whole thing was a setup, designed to rid the department of its most vocal whistleblower.**

The Knapp Commission was still ongoing at the time of Serpico's shooting. At its termination in 1972, the committee's report agreed that the NYPD was indeed rife with corruption, and Serpico made a number of recommendations aimed at cleaning the department up. That same year, once he had mostly recovered from his wound, Serpico decided he'd had his fill of trying to reform the NYPD, and he chose to take retirement. He saw the award for bravery—the Medal of Honor—given to him by the department as nothing more than lip service, particularly as it was not accompanied by a certificate.

Immediately after his retirement, Frank Serpico collaborated with the acclaimed journalist and author Peter Maas. The result was a book that recounted Serpico's involvement with the NYPD corruption scandal. In 1973, his story reached a much broader audience with the release of Sidney Lumet's movie, *Serpico*, based on Maas's book. Al Pacino played the title role. The film did well at the box office and garnered some positive reviews, but it did not lack for detractors. Serpico himself was not overly enamored with the result, and neither was David Durk.

Frank Serpico's name has become linked forever with calling out corruption, thanks in large part to the story's film adaptation, which starred Al Pacino (pictured) as the title NYPD officer.

Needless to say, the NYPD administration and many of the cops within its ranks hated the film. It was pointed out that although corruption was indeed rife, the movie implied that Serpico was one of just a handful of honest cops on the force. That was an exaggeration.

Both within and outside the police department, Frank Serpico had become a polarizing figure. Some saw him as a hero, one of the courageous few who were willing to speak out and oppose corruption within the ranks of law enforcement by breaking the so-called "blue wall of silence" that surrounded cops on the take. Others, including many police officers, viewed the whistleblower as a traitor, somebody who had betrayed them and everything they stood for by throwing his fellow officers under the bus.

In the aftermath of his career with the NYPD, Serpico stuck to his guns. He has received a stream of death threats over the years, ever since he testified as part of the Knapp Commission, but he remains a resolute and unabashed advocate for combating police corruption and reforming what he sees as the unhealthy culture of law enforcement. Now in his mid-eighties, a still-undaunted Serpico maintains that the problem is bigger than individual cops but arises from the way police departments perceive themselves and their relationship with the public they serve. Using his Twitter account, Serpico still calls attention to cases of injustice and corruption when they come his way.

It may have taken 50 years, but Frank Serpico's story does have a happy ending. In February of 2022, the New York Police Department awarded the 85-year-old former detective a new Medal of Honor. This time, it was accompanied by a certificate of acknowledgment. This may be the closest to a gesture of vindication that the former detective ever receives from the NYPD.

# The Sheik, the Scam, and the Feds

Operation Abscam was one of the longest-running and most complex covert investigations in the history of the FBI. Aspects of it were so colorful and bizarre that the case almost seems like it was ripped from the pages of a Hollywood screenplay—indeed, it would be filmed in 2013 as *American Hustle*, with actor Christian Bale starring in the lead role.

At the beginning, it seemed like nothing more than a run-of-the-mill corruption case. In 1977, a con artist by the name of Melvin Weinberg showed up on the Bureau's radar. As a criminal, Weinberg was relatively small time. He had a lifelong history of petty crimes and swindles, eventually graduating to scams based on offering fraudulent loans through a front company called London Investors. The scam was simple. Once the dummy loan was drawn up and signed, Weinberg would pocket the fees he charged for processing the transaction and then abscond with the money, leaving the confused customer empty-handed. His most famous victim was the Las Vegas entertainer Wayne Newton.

Busted by FBI agents, Weinberg was offered the opportunity to become a paid informant. It was an attractive deal. Rather than go to prison for three years, he would instead be placed on parole. An additional sweetener came in the form of the Feds dropping all charges against his girlfriend, Evelyn Knight. There was even a financial inducement to accompany his new position in the form of regular cash payments and bonuses for a job well done. The more criminals he helped the FBI put behind bars, the more he would be paid. Accepting the offer was a no-brainer for a man who had extensive experience in weighing up his options.

Among Melvin Weinberg's scam victims was legendary performer Wayne Newton.

Weinberg was an expert grifter, and he had the silver tongue needed to gain the confidence of unsuspecting marks. Perhaps surprisingly, he was a more accomplished undercover performer than most of the FBI agents who were assigned to work with him. Under the auspices of J. Edgar Hoover, who had died five years earlier, the idea of an FBI agent going undercover to pull off a sting operation was deeply frowned upon. Hoover felt that it was bad for public perception to have his G-men out of their smart suits and wearing disguises; in his eyes, it made them appear just a little too close to the people they were supposed to be arresting. For the five decades that Hoover dominated the Bureau, undercover operations were few and far between, and they required extensive clearance before being given the green light. As a result, Bureau agents had relatively little experience in undercover operations.

> **Weinberg was an expert grifter, and he had the silver tongue needed to gain the confidence of unsuspecting marks.**

In the 1970s, under the direction of Clarence M. Kelley and then William H. Webster, attitudes within the Bureau changed. Both Kelley, who served from 1973 to 1978, and Webster, who took the reins from 1978 to 1987, wanted to make a dent in white collar crime, and clandestine work was now an acceptable option for supervisory agents to employ, if they saw fit to do so. The field operations team that utilized the talents of Melvin Weinberg was overseen by FBI agent

John F. Good, and it was comprised of a handful of agents with varying degrees of experience.

Things started out small. Weinberg had experience in setting up and running a fake company, one that was convincing enough to fool those who were a little too eager to part with their money, and so was born Abdul Enterprises, Ltd. The con artist put the word out that the business was owned by a multimillionaire sheik who had made a fortune in the oil business. This immensely wealthy Arabian entrepreneur was amassing a collection of fine art, the story went on, and was only too happy to pay top dollar to acquire it.

The hook was baited, and it wasn't long before the crooks started coming out of the woodwork. The operation, which would not be named Abscam (short for Abdul Scam) until after its first successful operation, was up and running in the first quarter of 1978. Working out of New York, the team was able to recover two pieces of stolen artwork, and they also brought the thief responsible to justice.

Weinberg had been the point man throughout, brokering the deal and stepping forward to meet the art thief in person, giving the FBI agents the opportunity to arrest him red-handed. The capture served to validate Weinberg's standing in the eyes of the FBI. It was a sign of greater things to come.

Successful con artists tend to be detail oriented, and Melvin Weinberg was no exception. He and his FBI handlers concocted an increasingly elaborate and convincing series of ever-changing cover stories for Abdul Enterprises and the mysterious sheik behind it. To lend further credence to their drama, they brought on board outside agencies, including one major bank, to buttress their claims, just in case anybody got suspicious and did some background checks. The charade was designed to hold up to all but the closest scrutiny.

The early days of Operation Abscam were not entirely plain sailing, but they still proved to be a solid success. There were wrinkles to be ironed out as the team learned how to work together. Weinberg proved capable of thinking on his feet, no matter how unpredictable a situation turned out to be. Two of the FBI agents donned Arabic attire to portray the sheik during meetings with potential suspects. Each sting was recorded, and the tapes were kept to be used as evidence during future courtroom cases.

What had started out as an attempt to catch and indict crooked businessmen later switched its focus to encompass potentially corrupt public servants. An early target was Angelo J. Errichetti, who served two terms as the mayor of Camden, New Jersey. Elected in 1973, Errichetti worked hard to meet the needs of the people of Camden, many of whom liked and respected him immensely. At the time he first came to the attention of Operation Abscam, the mayor was also pulling double duty as a senator for the state of New Jersey. Once the FBI heard rumors that Errichetti was corrupt and taking money for his own purposes, the Abscam agents set out to put his integrity to the test. Good and his team knew they would have to tread carefully. Angelo Errichetti was a man with power and influence at the uppermost level of state politics. They couldn't afford to mess up.

In a meeting recorded for the FBI's Abscam investigation, on August 22, 1979, U.S. representative Michael Myers, second from left, holds an envelope containing $50,000 that he just received from undercover FBI agent Anthony Amoroso, left. Also shown in the photo are Angelo Errichetti, second from right, and con man Mel Weinberg.

In December of 1978, an unsuspecting Errichetti met with Melvin Weinberg. The rumors were proven to be true when the mayor accepted $25,000 at the meeting, with the agreement that he would use his influence to smooth the way for some gaming licenses to be granted. This met the definition of a bribe: a public official taking money and bestowing favors in return, which amounted to abusing the powers of his office.

Although Errichetti was caught dead to rights, the FBI agents did not bring him into custody for immediate prosecution. Instead, they kept him under surveillance and watched as he unwittingly ensnared other politicians. The web of corruption kept growing, under the direct observation of the Abscam investigators, as the targets became ever higher in profile. One such example was U.S. senator Harrison Williams of New Jersey.

As part of Abscam's ongoing efforts, Errichetti established an investment group, which he invited Williams and several others to join. The concept was simple: the group would build and operate a titanium mine, then sell the processed titanium to the U.S. military and other industrial buyers. Titanium is an essential component in warships and other key weapons systems, and the more of it that the mine could produce, the richer its owners would be. Establishing a titanium-processing operation wouldn't be cheap, so meetings were set up between Senator Williams and the "sheik" and his entourage—in actuality, FBI agents who were part of Operation Abscam.

So far, everything fell within the boundaries of legal entrepreneurship. Now came the shady part. To finance the get-rich-quick scheme, Errichetti's investment group would need to acquire some serious funding—so they asked the sheik to invest $100 million. In return, Senator Williams would agree to use his position of influence to make sure that future Defense Department contracts for titanium supplies would be awarded to the sheik's organization. This would guarantee rich profits for all concerned, but it also constituted a serious abuse of power by the senator. Although he did not take a cash bribe, Williams had already secretly accepted an ownership share in the mining operation, and he could have been expected to make a lot of money—if it hadn't all been a scam designed to test his integrity.

Once the agents believed they had enough evidence to indict Senator Williams, they turned their attention to other public figures.

Within the halls of the FBI, Operation Abscam had gone from being a relatively limited, small-scale endeavor to a high-profile case, all in less than two years. This was mainly because corrupt senators were becoming a major part of the agents' haul. Along with the increased visibility and prestige, there also came an influx of resources and better technical equipment. The bribes they were able to offer got larger. All eyes were on the small group of agents and their con man for hire as they continued to investigate and indict suspect after suspect.

In early 1980, with 26 suspects facing an array of corruption and bribery-related criminal charges, there was concern that word of the sting operation might finally leak out. The FBI decided to wind things up. There was already a backlog of cases that were overdue to go before a judge and jury. With the field investigative portion now closed down, federal grand jury trials began for those who had been indicted.

Mayor Angelo Errichetti was given a six-year prison sentence, of which he served less than half.

In December of 1983, former representative John W. Jenrette of South Carolina was sentenced to two years' imprisonment, five years of probation, and a $20,000 fine after being caught verbally accepting $50,000 as part of an Abscam sting. Congressman Jenrette had accepted the bribe as an advance payment on using his influence to allow the sheik to become a U.S. citizen. The judge and jury watched covert videotape of Jenrette agreeing to take the bribe and declaring that he "had larceny" within him.

John Jenrette served as a U.S. representative from South Carolina from 1975 to 1980. Three years later, he was convicted of accepting a bribe in an Abscam sting conducted in 1980.

Senator Harrison Williams was found guilty on multiple charges, including conspiracy to defraud the United States, conflict of interest, and bribery. Williams denied having done anything illegal. The Senate Ethics Committee disagreed, and it recommended that he be expelled from his elected position. The judge sentenced Williams to three years' imprisonment and fined him $50,000. He was released after having served 21 months.

Representative John Murphy of New York served 16 months after being caught agreeing to take the same $50,000 bribe as his peers. His lesser sentence reflected the fact that he was found guilty of accepting an unlawful gratuity, but Murphy was found not guilty of the greater charge of bribery.

Representative Michael "Ozzie" Myers of Pennsylvania also received a three-year prison sentence. Unlike his fellow politicos snared by Operation Abscam, he seemed to have learned little from the experience. Essentially unelectable once he was released in 1985, Myers set about building a career as a political consultant. Things did not go well. In the summer of 2022, decades after his involvement in the Abscam scandal should have faded into the background, Myers pleaded guilty to charges of election fraud, and in September he was sentenced to 18 months in federal prison. Myers had bribed several judges of election in an attempt to make them support candidates he backed. This was achieved by casting fake votes during the election process.

Congressmen Raymond F. Lederer of Pennsylvania and Frank Thompson of New Jersey were also convicted and imprisoned for accepting bribes as part of Operation Abscam. Florida representative Richard Kelly, a former judge, was imprisoned for 13 months.

Today, the FBI views Abscam as one of its more notable successes, and the Bureau devotes a page on its website to highlighting some of the details. Not everybody was as enamored with the operation as the Bureau, however. As quoted by journalist Al Kamen in the *Washington Post* on December 10, 1983, John Garrett Penn, the presiding judge at the John Jenrette trial, told the court that nothing less than prison time would be an appropriate sentence for the disgraced congressman's crimes, given the position of public trust he had occupied. The judge went on to express his concern at the concept of federal agents attempting to "test someone—to give him an inducement to see if he will commit a crime."

Penn's disapproval of Abscam boiled down to the fact that neither Jenrette nor any of his fellow politicians exposed by the sting operation had sought out bribes; instead, the FBI had gone to them and dangled a particularly juicy carrot in front

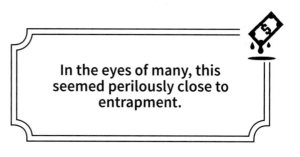

In the eyes of many, this seemed perilously close to entrapment.

of their noses to see if they would take it. In the eyes of many, this seemed perilously close to entrapment, luring somebody in and encouraging them to commit a crime, and then arresting them for it. Entrapment is seen as an unfair practice, and while inciting or pressuring a suspect to break the law is not an illegal tactic for law enforcement personnel to use, it is forbidden for them to encourage a person to do something illegal that they would not otherwise have done.

During a courtroom trial, a defense attorney may choose to use entrapment as a defense for their client. Sometimes the defense is successful; other times it is not. In the case of Abscam, the claim that the senator and congressmen were entrapped arose many times during the various trials. Every single attempt to use this defense was rejected, despite the fact that the FBI had deliberately set up its sting operation based on the word of a proven con man and known criminal—Melvin Weinberg. Some of the convictions were only upheld after the case was thrown out and went through an appeals process, but all of those indicted would ultimately be found guilty.

FBI director William Webster served from 1978 to 1987, heading the agency during the Abscam sting operations.

Although the end results involved the successful prosecution of seven corrupt senior public officials and a number of less-prominent individuals, the FBI caught plenty of flak for its methods. Allowing a con artist to hold an influential position in a Bureau investigation would never have been permitted under J. Edgar Hoover. How could somebody with such a questionable background be considered a reliable witness by the Department of Justice? Even Congress itself was unhappy with the way the operation had been conducted, and its members had to be formally reassured that the FBI had discontinued its field investigations. Senators and representatives were wary that they could become the next target of the corruption probe. Finally, the Bureau formally assured them that a number of members who had been approached by Abscam agents were innocent and that matters would be taken no further.

Today, few people remember Operation Abscam. At the time it took place, however, it was a national cause célèbre that preoccupied the American public and the media for months. One aspect worth noting is that six of the seven major indictments were levied against Democratic politicians, something that caused outrage in 1980—an election year. The current claims that the FBI has been politicized echo those that formed part of the blowback against Abscam, lending weight to the old adage that holds that history really does repeat itself.

# Tammany Hall

For any student of U.S. history, one name stands head and shoulders above all others as a byword for corruption: Tammany Hall. This was one of the names given to an 18th-century society comprised of powerful politicos; it was also known as the Sons of St. Tammany and the Society of St. Tammany, to list just two names of many.

Why "Tammany"? The name derives from that of Tamanend, an influential Native American chief who had a reputation for kindness and compassion. Tamanend, as leader of the Lenni-Lenape nation, had been instrumental in brokering peace between the English settlers and the Indigenous tribes in Philadelphia. A number of Tammany societies had sprung up across the country in the wake of the War of Independence. After Tamanend's death sometime in the early 1700s, the societies' namesake became both iconic and revered, synonymous with the concept of amity.

Formed in 1789 by one William Mooney, a veteran of the war, the Society of St. Tammany was envisioned as a necessary counterweight to the fledgling Federalist Party. The Federalists, headed by such luminaries as Alexander Hamilton, favored a strong, centralized government to oversee their new nation. Prominent figures such as Aaron Burr opposed the Federalist worldview, believing it to be too elitist, and Burr headed up the Society of St. Tammany as it grew into a force to be reckoned with in the arena of national politics. The

Why "Tammany"? The name derives from that of Tamanend, an influential Native American chief who had a reputation for kindness and compassion.

building in which meetings were held was known as Tammany Hall.

For what was ostensibly a charitable and benevolent organization, intended to help enfranchise the working man, the rolls of Tammany membership had one glaring omission: the Irish. Of the many immigrants stepping off the boats at Ellis Island, tens of thousands came from Ireland with the hope of starting a new life in the land of opportunity. Many sought relief from the horrific famine that blighted the land of their birth. What they found instead was a land filled with squalor, bigotry, and, all too often, racially motivated violence.

William "Boss" Tweed, an incredibly well-connected lifelong New Yorker, headed up the Tammany Hall political machine from 1858 to 1871.

Throughout the 19th century, it became clear that throngs of newly immigrated Irishmen were an untapped potential resource for politicians. They were ineligible to vote, and the thinking went that if Tammany could not only enfranchise them but also influence them to lean toward its own political persuasion, then the power of the Democratic Party in New York would be greatly bolstered.

Tammany Hall would offer Irish immigrants material assistance and respect. In return, the recipients of its generosity were expected to go to the polls on election day and cast their votes for the Democratic candidate. By and large, that's exactly what they did.

As Tammany Hall's power and influence over the lives of New Yorkers grew throughout the 1800s, it was inevitable that corruption would somehow creep in. If a single figure embodies that corruption above all others, it must be William Magear Tweed (1823–1878), commonly known as "Boss."

An immensely powerful Democrat, Boss Tweed was a big believer in cronyism, strategically placing his sycophants in key positions throughout the city and state government. The ever-increasing group came to be known as the Tweed Ring. It worked to further Tweed's personal interests and its own, which in most cases dovetailed neatly with the Democratic party's political agenda.

Throughout the 1800s, New York City was a powder keg. Tensions ran high between a multitude of different economic, ethnic, and religious groups, many of whom chose to settle their disputes with violence. Corruption ran rampant, not just through the government but also the police force and other municipal institutions. It was common practice for authority figures to turn a blind eye to crimes both major and minor, so long as palms were sufficiently greased in advance.

Tweed became immensely wealthy on the back of his corrupt practices, grifting for money with countless crooked schemes and investing much of the proceeds in land and property. He soon came to own vast tracts of New York City real estate. Having his hand in a host of public building projects, Tweed deliberately allowed their budgets to overrun and then skimmed money off the increasingly bloated costs, which was all coming from the city coffers.

Matters came to a head in the summer of 1871, in what later came to be known as the Orange Riot. Members of the city's Protestant community (the Orange Order) applied for permission to hold a parade. New York Catholics strenuously objected, on the basis that such a public display of support for Protestantism was an insult to their own beliefs. At first, Tammany Hall sided with the Catholics and refused to grant a parade permit. There was good reason to do so: the prior year had seen a similar march quickly devolve into a vicious street brawl.

The Protestants persisted, however, and ultimately, threats of violent reprisals if the event was not given permission to proceed led to a reversal of the decision. The Orange Parade was allowed to go forward as planned. A military escort was provided for the marchers to avert further trouble. It didn't help. Violence flared along the parade route, which became something akin to a pitched battle between Catholics and Protestants. The troops not only opened fire but also fixed bayonets and used them in an attempt to keep order. When the dust settled, more than 60 participants lay dead, and almost three times that number were wounded, some of them seriously. The public was outraged, and there were calls for heads to roll. Tammany Hall drew significant criticism, with Boss Tweed himself deservedly shouldering much of the blame.

To make matters worse for him, Tweed and his cronies were also the subject of scathing reporting from the *New York Times*, whose reporters were out to blow the lid off corruption in New York City. Satirical cartoons depicted Tweed as a fat, corrupt, twisted figure of ridicule—which wasn't far from the truth. In the aftermath of the Orange Riot, more exposés were printed, shining a light under the rocks of Tweed's many corrupt schemes. Tammany Hall was fast losing the confidence of New Yorkers, and it became apparent to everyone that Boss Tweed had to go.

Go he finally did. Tweed was arrested, tried, and imprisoned, primarily as a result of his grand-scale fraud and theft. The public had had enough of the Tweed Ring and its corruption, and they made their feelings known at the ballot box at the next election, when his cronies' seats were in jeopardy. After getting booted out of Tammany Hall, many of Tweed's appointees also joined him behind bars.

One of many contemporary political cartoons satirizing the corrupt Tweed and Tammany Hall, famed cartoonist Thomas Nast's "Tammany Ring" depicts Tweed and his cronies passing off the blame for missing public funds.

Boss Tweed had a cushy time in jail. His cell contained luxuries such as books and ostentatious furniture that other prisoners could only dream of. His wealth and influence meant that he was serving time on Easy Street, but the perpetually greedy politician just couldn't help himself. By 1875, Boss Tweed had grown sick of prison life and decided to make a break for freedom. Remarkably, he was successful, slipping away from his captors and boarding a ship for Europe, by way of Cuba. Unfortunately for him, when the ship docked in Spain, he was recognized, captured, and extradited back to the United States—where a less-comfortable cell awaited at the Ludlow Street Jail. It was here that William Tweed would die, on April 12, 1878, from complications of pneumonia.

Had he been an honest and scrupulous man, Tweed's legacy could have been a great one. Instead, his incessant greed and crooked nature meant that his name, and that of Tammany Hall, remain to this day synonymous with fraud and corruption.

# Storm in a Teapot

Although not widely known today, at the time it took place, the 1922 Teapot Dome scandal rocked the U.S. government to its core. There had never been a greater scandal in U.S. history to that point. It had all the hallmarks of a page-turning novel, and each new twist and turn dominated the newspaper headlines for weeks.

World War I had ended in 1918, and the United States placed great emphasis on being a major player on the global maritime stage. That relied upon having a strong, modern navy with which to defend international trade routes, project power, and support U.S. interests around the globe. Like other navies, the U.S. Navy was engaged in a years-long program of phasing out coal power and replacing it with oil, which would allow its warships to roam further and sail faster than their coal-fueled predecessors.

All that oil had to come from somewhere; most of it would be mined from oil wells scattered across the United States. Although the so-called War to End All Wars was now over, the possibility of another major conflict was an ever-present threat. As a preparatory measure, the government maintained a network of strategic oil reserves, set aside exclusively for the Navy's use in the event of a sudden, unexpected increase in needs. One such oil reserve was established at Teapot Dome, Wyoming; another, in Elk Hills, California.

President Warren G. Harding had already proven himself to be a friend of "Big Oil," particularly when the oil companies were willing to throw their support behind his cause. Also a big advocate of oil drilling was Harding's newly appointed secretary of the interior, Albert Fall. When Fall petitioned Harding for oversight of the strategic oil reserves to be transferred to the Department of the Interior, effectively taking control away from the Navy, Harding agreed.

It didn't take a genius to see that this was a case of the fox guarding the henhouse. Fall wasted no time assigning drilling rights to the reserve oil fields to executives at civilian oil companies. At around the same time, hundreds of thousands of dollars suddenly came Fall's way, mostly in the form of Liberty bonds and sketchy "loans" on which he made no repayments. It was blatantly obvious that the secretary of the interior had been paid off by special interests representing the oil industry.

> **Calling the backroom deal "a notable departure" was putting things much too lightly. It was a kickback deal, plain and simple.**

*Wall Street Journal* reporters first broke the story on April 14, 1922, in an article titled "Sinclair Consolidated in Big Oil Deal with U.S." In part, it read: "A contract has just been signed by the government and the Sinclair Oil interests for development of Naval Oil Reserve No. 2, Teapot Dome, Wyoming, estimated to contain between 150,000,000 and 200,000,000 barrels of high-grade oil." It went on: "The arrangement entered into marks one of the greatest petroleum undertakings of the age and signalizes a notable departure on the part of the government in seeking partnership with private capital for the working of government-owned natural resources."

Calling the backroom deal "a notable departure" was putting things much too lightly. It was a kickback deal, plain and simple. Before long, uncomfortable questions were being asked about contracts between the government and the oil companies. It soon became apparent that Albert Fall had been caught red-handed in a corrupt attempt to line his own pockets.

That an official as high ranking as the secretary of the interior should be caught defrauding the national interest was almost inconceivable. As more facts came to light and the public outcry intensified, Congress stepped in, forcing the cancellation of the contracts and returning oversight of the oil fields to the Navy. A surprised President Harding suddenly found himself beset by critics and accusers on all sides.

After the Teapot Dome scandal, President Harding embarked on a train tour of North America. Photographed here during the tour's stop in Seattle, Harding would be dead within a week from an apparent heart attack.

When it came to matters of corruption, Warren G. Harding did not have an easy presidency. Several members of his inner circle of friends and advisors had developed a reputation for dishonesty and crooked dealings. They were nicknamed the Ohio Gang, which derived from their past association with the president when he was a rising star on the Ohio political scene. The behavior of the Ohio Gang had tarnished the reputation of Harding's presidency before Teapot Dome ever reared its ugly head. Now, the oil reserve scandal took the attacks on Harding to the next level. Based on the fact that he had rubber-stamped the transfer of the oil reserves, many saw the president as being directly culpable for the scandal.

**Grifters, Frauds, and Crooks: True Stories of American Corruption**

While embarked on a nationwide tour in 1923, Harding is alleged to have confidentially asked Herbert Hoover (who would go on to become president himself): "If you knew of a great scandal in our administration, would you for the good of the country and the party expose it publicly, or would you bury it?" Hoover advocated exposure.

Known as the Tour of Understanding, Harding's epic 15,000-mile journey was scheduled to take him by train across the continental United States, Canada, and Alaska; neither of the latter two places had ever been visited by a U.S. president while still in office. There can be no doubt that the multiple scandals in which his administration was mired contributed to Harding's desire to get away from it all for a while and, hopefully, refocus the attention of the press on something positive instead.

> **It is likely that the stress brought on by the unfolding Teapot Dome scandal contributed to the president's demise.**

In theory, it was a good idea. In practice, the immense stress under which the president constantly found himself finally caught up with him on August 3. He and his entourage checked into San Francisco's luxurious Palace Hotel. Later that evening, he collapsed and died in the suite he shared with the First Lady.

To be fair, the president wasn't exactly the picture of health. He had already been diagnosed with a number of medical ailments, and he had also showed signs of heart failure. He had taken ill in the days leading up to his death, although Harding had dismissed the symptoms as insignificant. Because no autopsy was ever conducted, the cause of his death remains speculative to this day.

It is likely that the stress brought on by the unfolding Teapot Dome scandal contributed to the president's demise. He was succeeded in the White House by Calvin Coolidge, who rode out the remainder of the scandal with as much aplomb as he could muster. Coolidge had no time for the Ohio Gang, all of whom lost their influence and standing with the passing of President Harding.

Today, the words "Teapot Dome" stir up images akin to those of Watergate or Tammany Hall: they have become synonymous with corruption at the highest levels of political power and, to the casual student of history, have sadly overshadowed much of the good that was done by the Harding administration.

# Nixon's Plumbers

When the Watergate Hotel checked in its first guests in 1965, nobody could have predicted that its name would one day become synonymous with political scandal and corruption.

It was the middle of the swinging sixties, and for socialites, the Watergate was the place to be seen in Washington, D.C. The brightest lights flocked there. It wasn't unusual to find politicians from the Hill drinking and dancing with movie stars while the paparazzi waited outside for a chance to snap their picture.

The Watergate didn't *really* hit the front pages until 1972, however, when it became the stage for events that would ultimately bring down the presidency of Richard M. Nixon.

Nixon was no stranger to scandal. In 1971, a whistleblower named Daniel Ellsberg leaked a report on the causes and current progress of the Vietnam War to the *New York Times*. The 7,000-page report, titled "History of U.S. Decision Making in Vietnam, 1945–68," became known to the public as the Pentagon Papers. Its contents were damning, outlining a catalog of lies that successive U.S. administrations had fed to the American public in an effort to keep them on board with the war.

Richard Nixon is sworn in by Chief Justice Earl Warren on January 20, 1969, for his first term as president.

Ellsberg knew the intricacies of the report intimately. After all, he had been one of the authors and had read the entire thing from beginning to end. His experience studying U.S. involvement in Vietnam had turned him into a resolute opponent of what he had come to see as an unwinnable war.

Despite legal proceedings started by his administration's lawyers—proceedings that were contested all the way up to the Supreme Court—Nixon was unable to prevent major U.S. newspapers from publishing key highlights of the report. The infuriated president set Ellsberg squarely in his sights, and he determined to exact his revenge on the man who had dared to reveal abuses of power in his administration. What Nixon did not foresee was that he would instead dig his own political grave.

"Tricky Dicky," as he came to be known, operated a secret unit of spies and agents known as the Plumbers, so called because their mission was to plug leaks that threatened his administration. Each Plumber had a background in espionage and covert operations, and many had come from the CIA or the FBI. They targeted Ellsberg incessantly, trying to dig up dirt they could use to undermine his public image.

The Plumbers also had bigger fish to fry than Daniel Ellsberg. Nixon's principal opposition was the Democratic Party. Treating them as if they were an enemy army, on June 17, 1972, the Plumbers infiltrated the headquarters of the Democratic National Committee at the Watergate Hotel. Their mission was to plant bugs—electronic listening devices—with the hope of gathering intelligence about the Democrats' political strategy and day-to-day

**Making full use of what he saw as plausible deniability, the president threw his Plumbers to the wolves, stating publicly that he had no knowledge of their actions.**

operations. Unfortunately for them, they were caught red-handed, wearing gloves and carrying equipment they'd used to break in.

Despite strenuous denials that he had anything to do with the burglary, it soon became apparent that the men had close ties to the Nixon White House. Making full use of what he saw as plausible deniability, the president threw his Plumbers to the wolves, stating publicly that he had no knowledge of their actions. In a blatant attempt to whitewash the scandal, he ordered a formal investigation into the affair, which found no links between the break-in and his own administration—an outright lie.

The denials bought Richard Nixon sufficient time, and mitigated the political damage just enough, to let him win the election in November of that same year, in a landslide victory. Two tenacious *Washington Post* reporters, Bob Woodward and Carl Bernstein, dug into the matter and brought to light further proof of malfeasance within Nixon's inner circle. At his trial in March of 1973, under threat from the judge of being given the harshest prison sentence allowable, the Plumber James McCord confessed in a written statement that a cover-up had been orchestrated at the highest levels of government. McCord oversaw security for CREEP—the Campaign for Re-Election of the President, an organization that raised money to fill Nixon's so-called "war chest." His close tie with the sitting president was undeniable—and extremely damning.

In the wake of McCord's confession, the entire tissue of lies surrounding Nixon's involvement with the Watergate break-in, as part of a much broader conspiracy to destabilize his opponents, started to break apart. The senatorial committee hearings convened to get to the truth of Watergate were televised, and a stunned nation watched Richard Nixon be implicated by his own people. Testimony under oath revealed that he had known about the break-in and the subsequent cover-up all along.

Worse still, the hotel break-in was just the tip of the iceberg. With Nixon's approval, operatives violated the rights of many other private citizens, most of whom were believed to oppose the president and his reelection. The increasingly paranoid Nixon had taken to secretly recording conversations he was part of. The contents of those tapes did not show the president or members of his inner circle in a good light.

The tapes were subpoenaed by the Watergate committee. In a bid to keep their contents quiet, Nixon offered to submit "summaries" rather than the actual recordings themselves. The appointed special prosecutor, Archibald Cox, refused to accept them. He wanted the committee members to hear the unexpurgated recordings for themselves. On October 20, in a brazen move even by his standards, Nixon responded by trying to fire Cox. His attorney general and deputy attorney general both resigned in protest, refusing to carry out the culling of Cox despite the president's insistence. With the AG and the DAG both gone, Solicitor General Robert Bork stepped into the role of acting attorney general. Bork obeyed Nixon's order to get rid of Cox and shut down his office.

After resigning his presidency over the Watergate scandal, Richard Nixon boards Army One to depart the White House.

Still, Nixon clung to power with mounting desperation. The Watergate hearings dragged on into the following year. The longer the proceedings went on, the worse President Nixon looked in the eyes of the American people. By the summer of 1974, even many of his most ardent supporters had turned against him. The Watergate scandal could only end in one way: his impeachment and subsequent resignation. On August 8, 1974, bowing to insurmountable pressure, he resigned.

Richard M. Nixon was the first president in the history of the United States to resign his office. Announcing the news on national television to a stunned nation (and an audience of millions around the world), Nixon, true to his word for once, was gone the following morning.

Richard Nixon was succeeded in the White House by his vice president, Gerald Ford. "Tricky Dicky" had once proudly proclaimed to the public: "I'm not a crook!" Yet in September of that same year, despite the fact that some of those he commanded would end up going to prison, the man who was "not a crook" accepted a pardon from Ford. This brought down the curtain on one of the ugliest and most corrupt episodes in U.S. presidential history.

# "I Have No Recollection ..."

It has been said many times that the United States does not makes deals or negotiate with terrorists. While this is indeed the nation's officially stated policy, the truth is that the U.S. government *has* engaged in shady, under-the-table dealings with terrorist groups on several occasions. Arguably the most infamous example was the Iran–Contra scandal, which left the administration of President Ronald Reagan with a lot of egg on its face.

Like his predecessors in the White House, Reagan believed in opposing the ideology of communism and its spread around the globe. He had stated that clearly in the run-up to the 1980 presidential election. On the other hand, the Cold War was at its height, and the last thing Reagan wanted was to be responsible for engaging in a "hot" war directly with the Soviet Union. His counterpart in the Kremlin, Mikhail Gorbachev, felt the same way. Both men knew that such a war could easily escalate to nuclear Armageddon and that the safest way to chip away at the other's power was to engage in small-scale proxy wars.

To this end, the United States implemented what came to be called the Reagan Doctrine, a declaration of its willingness to support fringe groups who themselves opposed Soviet influence and occupation directly. The administration took care to refer to these groups as freedom fighters. Others labeled these entities terrorist organizations. U.S. support came in the form of money, equipment, weapons, and military training. In other words, the United States would do whatever it could to help give the Soviets a bloody nose, short of actually going into battle with its own troops.

OLIVER L NORTH
DOB 10 7 43

Known to much of the world at the time as the face of the Iran–Contra affair, Colonel Oliver North took the reins on the operation—and much of the heat.

One such fringe group was the Nicaraguan Contras, counterrevolutionaries whose objective was to overthrow the leftist Sandinista regime in Nicaragua. The Contras were riddled with corruption, relying on drug money for funding and committing human rights abuses such as torture and murder, but this did not dampen Reagan's willingness to deal with them. He continued to support the Contras and their anti-communist agenda.

Seeking to curb the United States' association with what some saw as being little more than a heavily armed mob, albeit one with the potential to cause significant problems for U.S. foreign policy, Democrats enacted a series of laws known as the Boland Amendment, named after Rep. Edward Boland of Massachusetts. This legislation was intended to prevent the Central Intelligence Agency (CIA) from meddling in the state affairs of Nicaragua. The first act of the Boland Amendment went into effect in December of 1984.

Because of the wording of the initial amendment, the Reagan administration was able to find workarounds that would still allow them to funnel supplies to the Contras. By 1985, another international crisis was looming for the United States, this time concerning Iran. Hezbollah terrorists, with backing from Iran, were holding seven American citizens captive in Lebanon. Reagan wanted the hostages freed and, against the advice of many of his advisors, approved a deal in which American arms would be sold to Iran in exchange for freeing the hostages.

Iran and Iraq were engaged in a bloody war. U.S. policy dictated that it would not support Iran in that conflict, a response to Iran's role as a supporter of terrorist organizations around the world. Turning a blind eye to this inconvenient fact, the Reagan administration accepted money from Iran for the weapons shipment, then immediately paid a hefty chunk of it to the Contras in Nicaragua.

In October of 1986, the Sandinista regime's military shot down a C-123 cargo plane. Two of the three-man crew were killed. The survivor was a 35-year-old American

> **The Reagan administration accepted money from Iran for the weapons shipment, then immediately paid a hefty chunk of it to the Contras in Nicaragua.**

named Eugene Hasenfus. Taken under interrogation, he admitted to being a U.S. military advisor working in support of the Contras. More damning than that were the contents of his crashed aircraft: military supplies that were destined for the Contras. In a massive propaganda coup for the Sandinistas, it soon emerged that such flights were being operated by the CIA, in direct contravention of the Boland Amendment.

At first, President Reagan denied U.S. involvement, but he subsequently reversed course and ultimately admitted the truth. The ensuing scandal was a major embarrassment for his administration, garnering negative international headlines and condemnation.

One of the more colorful characters who appeared at the 1987 Iran–Contra hearings was United States Marine Lt. Col. Oliver North, a staff member of the National Security Council. In addition to being a key player in the scandal, North also did his utmost to cover it up. The televised hearings had all the hallmarks of high theater, featuring accusations, conspiracy, intrigue, and all manner of twists and turns the likes of which thriller writers such as John le Carré and Tom Clancy would have appreciated. The American public was glued to their television sets, riveted as each new revelation unfolded in front of them.

Testifying before Congress, North soaked up a lot of the heat that was being directed at the highest levels of the government, particularly at President Reagan himself. By helping set up what was basically a secret organization outside of the much-better-known secret organization of the CIA, the Marine officer truly believed he was serving the best interests of his president and his country—although that service sometimes required him to conceal the truth or even tell outright lies.

Under oath, North testified that he "assumed" the president was aware of his activities. Reagan, for his part, steadfastly maintained that he had not known about the illicit activities that were taking place and claimed that he had no memory of specific events and facts relating to the scandal on no fewer than 88 occasions. How much the president truly did or did not know is likely to remain uncertain forever.

The trial by media garnered a lot of sympathy for Lt. Col. North, who came across as a patriot who had done what he believed was right in pursuit of a higher goal—the national interest.

In the aftermath of the Iran–Contra affair coming to light, President Ronald Reagan created a Special Review Board to investigate the matter. Known as the Tower Commission, its members would issue a report that landed responsibility firmly with the president's administration.

While the American public found it easy to overlook North allegedly shredding reams of highly sensitive official documents and blatantly lying under oath as part of the cover-up, Judge Gerhard A. Gesell was considerably less sympathetic when North was found guilty. Gesell handed down a three-year suspended prison sentence and a fine of $150,000. North was supposed to spend the subsequent two years on probation, but in one final plot twist, the sentence was overturned on appeal. Lt. Col. North got off scot-free.

At the time, many believed that Irangate, as it came to be called, had the potential to bring down the Reagan administration, just as its namesake, Watergate, had done for that of Richard M. Nixon. This turned out to be untrue, although 20 members of government would be indicted. Eleven of them were convicted, including Oliver North. Of those 11, some had their convictions thrown out upon appeal, and the remainder received presidential pardons, which allowed them all to walk away without consequence.

The Iran–Contra scandal remains a black mark on the Reagan administration, and it illustrates the dangers of bending the rules in pursuit of what one believes to be a loftier goal.

# Bill and Hillary

Politicians attract rumors of corruption like iron filings to a magnet. This is rarely truer than when the politician in question has their sights set on the highest office in the land: that of president of the United States.

In the case of William Jefferson Clinton, the 42nd president, and his wife, former Secretary of State Hillary Rodham Clinton, the Democratic candidate for 45th president in 2016, the allegations of corrupt behavior go back decades.

At the time of this writing, the Clintons have been together for more than 50 years. They met in 1971, when both were students at Yale Law School, and were married four years later, in 1975. A shared interest in politics led them to volunteer together on the campaign of George McGovern, who ran for president in 1972. (McGovern's bid for the Oval Office was unsuccessful.)

One year after their wedding, Bill was elected attorney general in his birth state of Arkansas, and he became governor two years later, in 1978, at the age of 32. That same year, the Clintons partnered with another married couple, James and Susan McDougal, on a real estate venture that saw them purchase 220 acres of riverside property in the Ozarks. That venture was named the Whitewater

Development Corporation, and its intent was to sell the land in parcels to those who wanted to build vacation properties on it, hopefully turning a hefty profit in the bargain. To complete the deal, Whitewater Development took out a loan for $203,000.

Bill Clinton and Hillary Rodham Clinton at President Clinton's second inauguration, in January 1997.

Unfortunately for them, neither the Clintons nor the McDougals had done their homework. The venture was not a success, leaving them tens of thousands of dollars in the red. There's nothing particularly suspect about that. Real estate deals lose money every day; that's simply a risk of doing business.

Yet the name "Whitewater" would come to be an albatross around the Clintons' necks, and they would later have cause to regret their association with the McDougals. During his time as governor, Bill Clinton enlisted the services of James McDougal as an economic advisor. McDougal soon left public service for the private sector, acquiring a savings and loan company named Madison Guaranty Savings and Loan.

With McDougal at the helm, Madison Guaranty traveled a rocky road. Along the way, it was claimed that Madison money was being used by James McDougal to pay off debts incurred during Bill Clinton's political campaigning.

Madison Guaranty employed the legal services of Hillary Clinton (who worked for the Rose Law Firm at the time) in an attempt to keep itself financially solvent. Madison Guaranty would finally go under in 1989,

> The name "Whitewater" would come to be an albatross around the Clintons' necks, and they would later have cause to regret their association with the McDougals.

amidst accusations of mismanagement and fraud on the part of McDougal. As he and others involved with Madison Guaranty's downfall were arrested, allegations were made that Bill and Hillary had been involved with the fraudulent behavior. Including the McDougals, 15 people were convicted of crimes associated with the ill-conceived Whitewater venture. James McDougal was convicted of fraud and conspiracy in 1997 and died of a heart attack in federal prison in 1998.

James McDougal claimed in a posthumously published 1998 memoir, *Arkansas Mischief,* that not only had the Clintons been his co-conspirators, but Bill Clinton had perjured himself on the stand while testifying at McDougal's trial.

Despite several in-depth probes into claims of their being involved with illegal activity, the Clintons were never found guilty of any wrongdoing. Like her husband, Susan McDougal also served jail time. Eyebrows were understandably raised when the outgoing President Bill Clinton, on his final day in the White House, gave her an official presidential pardon. As previously mentioned, he had testified in McDougal's defense in court, and many saw the pardon as his way of rewarding her personal loyalty to him.

Whitewater was the first major scandal to embroil Bill and Hillary Clinton. It would not be the last.

## Travelgate

In 1992, Bill Clinton beat the incumbent president, George H. W. Bush, to become the 42nd president of the United States. His tenure in the Oval Office, which spanned eight years, was far from smooth sailing. In May of 1993, the Clinton administration became the source of another scandal, this one going by the nickname of Travelgate—so called because it centered on the White House travel office.

On May 19, seven employees of the Travel Office were suddenly fired by administration aide David Watkins amidst claims of incompetence and mismanagement. The record-keeping and money management procedures within the travel office were incredibly arcane, as an independent audit would later reveal, but there was no evidence of major wrongdoing. (Travel Office director Billy Ray Dale would be tried for embezzlement, charges of which he was ultimately found innocent.)

The White House Travel Office is responsible for travel arrangements for the White House press corps. Though uninvolved in travel arrangements for the first family themselves, the office arranges travel for the press who cover presidential events, including getting them on the ground in time to photograph moments with Air Force One.

It did not reflect well on the Clintons that the frontrunner to take over the travel office had ties with them going back to Hillary's days at Rose Law Firm. The implication was that she had wanted Dale and his six colleagues out so that she could usher in a new travel agency that was more to her own liking—that is, one operated by pro-Clinton personal friends.

At first, Hillary Clinton claimed to have had nothing to do with the firings, a position that was also adopted by Watkins. In a controversial memo that gained national attention, Watkins subsequently reversed course, however, and claimed that the travel office workers had indeed been fired at the insistence of the First Lady. To compound matters further, Watkins then went on to lie to federal investigators who were looking into the firings.

Watkins's memo surfaced after he had been fired from his position for misusing White House resources (he had taken a presidential helicopter on a golfing trip). One particularly suggestive line, referring to White House deputy counsel Vince Foster, read: "Foster regularly informed me that the First Lady was concerned and desired action—the action desired was the firing of the travel office staff." This statement flew directly in the face of statements to the contrary made by the First Lady. An official investigation concluded that although there was strong evidence to support Hillary having been behind the firings, there was not enough to prove that she had lied about them.

Travelgate weighed so heavily on Deputy Counsel Foster that it is believed by some to have been a major reason (along with severe depression) for his suicide. Foster took his own life by shooting himself in a Virginia park a few weeks after the firings had taken place. (Foster's tragic suicide sadly went on to become fodder for outlandish conspiracy theories alleging that the Clintons had him murdered.) Both Bill and Hillary escaped Travelgate relatively unscathed, albeit with further blemished reputations, but far worse was to come.

> Foster's tragic suicide sadly went on to become fodder for outlandish conspiracy theories alleging that the Clintons had him murdered.

## Monica Lewinsky Scandal

Without a doubt the biggest political black eye on the Clinton administration was the scandal involving Monica Lewinsky, which came close to bringing down Bill Clinton's presidency. Lewinsky was a White House intern, one of many who flocked to the coveted position in the hopes of kick-starting a career in Washington politics. It was not long after she arrived, in May of 1995, that she caught the wandering eye of the president.

One year prior, in May of 1994, a former state of Arkansas employee named Paula Jones had launched a sexual harassment lawsuit against Bill Clinton. Jones alleged that in 1991, Clinton, who was then the governor of Arkansas, had sent her a message via a police officer on his security detail asking her to come up to his hotel suite. Thinking it slightly odd that the governor, whom she had never met, wanted to see her for no apparent reason, Jones nevertheless acceded to his request and went to Clinton's hotel room.

Jones and Clinton were alone in the suite. After a few minutes of small talk, according to Jones, the governor made several unwelcome sexual advances, placing his hand suggestively on her leg and moving in to kiss her. Despite her attempts to spurn him, Jones said that Clinton pulled down his pants, exposed his genitals, and tried to convince her to perform oral sex on him—which she refused. A magazine article subsequently appeared that stated that Governor Clinton had met multiple women for secret trysts and implied that Paula Jones had been one of them. The article led readers to believe that she had gone along with Clinton's advances willingly. Incensed by these claims, Jones understandably sued.

At the time of the lawsuit, Clinton was well into the first term of his presidency. Jones's demands weren't particularly extreme. She wanted him to admit that he had made a pass at her, state on the record that she had rebuffed him, and offer her an apology. If the sitting president of the United States had done exactly that, there would still have been some political fallout, but certainly nothing close to what eventually happened. True to form, Clinton doubled down and issued a blanket denial, by means of the White House press secretary. Paula Jones had never visited his hotel room and had definitely never been propositioned for sex, he insisted.

For Jones, those were fighting words. She and her lawyers wanted a speedy trial. Bill Clinton and his legal team wanted the opposite, hoping to shove the whole mess further back in time until he was no longer president. Clinton was not to have his way. Although the case would take years to come to trial, President Clinton was seemingly incapable of keeping a low profile. In a pattern of behavior that was almost identical to that identified by Paula Jones, he invited 22-year-old Monica Lewinsky to join him for a private tête-à-tête.

It is difficult to blame Lewinsky for falling under the president's spell. What impressionable White House intern could possibly refuse a private invitation from the president of the United States? He was not only her boss but also arguably the most powerful man in the entire world. The two began enjoying sexual liaisons whenever the opportunity presented itself. (The sex in question was restricted to fellatio and hand stimulation, which Clinton would later rely on when attempting to twist the truth.)

President Clinton and White House intern Monica Lewinsky engaged in ongoing sexual relations, sparking a scandal that nearly cost him the presidency.

If Bill Clinton was relying on Monica Lewinsky to keep their affair a secret, he underestimated her need to share it with somebody. That somebody was Linda Tripp, who was supposedly Lewinsky's friend but had contrived to secretly tape-record their confidential conversations regarding Lewinsky's affair with the president. The recordings were made in the fall of 1997, when Lewinsky had moved on from the White House and taken on a role at the Pentagon.

Tripp made those explosive recordings available to attorney Ken Starr. Starr was an independent counsel investigating the president in light of the complaint lodged by Paula Jones. At Starr's behest, Jones continued prodding Lewinsky for more details about her former affair with the president. Of particular interest to her was a blue dress Lewinsky had worn to a White House dinner event, which was stained with Clinton's semen after the two snuck off to the Oval Office bathroom for a sexual liaison. Their affair had lasted for 18 months.

In January of 1998, confronted with accusations of his impropriety during a grand jury investigation, Bill Clinton fell back on his tried-and-trusted tactic of stringent denial, both of the affair and of asking Lewinsky to lie about it. "I did not have sexual relations with that woman, Miss Lewinsky," he insisted forcefully during a press conference, staring into the news cameras that were broadcasting his denial to the entire world.

That was an outright lie. Sticking to the letter of the law rather the spirit, in a show of lawyer-like verbal judo more suited to a courtroom than the Oval Office, Clinton was hoping to get off the hook by telling the American people that he had never had "sexual relations" in the sense of penetrative intercourse. In other words, Bill Clinton's penis had never entered Monica Lewinsky's vagina (his definition of sexual relations)—but other things had.

"I never told anybody to lie," Clinton also maintained. "Not a single time. Never. These allegations are false, and I need to get back to work for the American people."

Seven months later, on August 17, 1998, he did an about-face, finally admitting: "I did have a relationship with Miss Lewinsky that was not appropriate." Describing it as "a critical lapse in judgment, and a personal failure on my part for which I am solely and completely responsible," Clinton nevertheless had the air of an aggrieved party who was sorry not for what he had done but for the fact that he was no longer able to conceal it from the voting public, whom he had blatantly and purposefully deceived.

> "I never told anybody to lie," Clinton maintained. "Not a single time. Never."

Tellingly, his non-apology (Clinton never actually used the words "sorry" or "apology") seemed to be aimed at everybody but Monica Lewinsky. For her, there was nothing but implied disdain ("that woman"). Toward Ken Starr, there was resentment and irritation that he had pried into what Clinton saw as his personal and private life. He tried to spin the situation to cast himself and his family as the injured parties, their privacy infringed upon by what he saw as an increasingly intrusive grand jury investigation into the president's misconduct.

The question was now being asked: had Bill Clinton perjured himself by claiming under oath that he had not had a sexual relationship with Monica Lewinsky? Having spent four years investigating Clinton's improprieties, Ken Starr certainly thought that he had. Despite having promised to be forthright and cooperative during his questioning, Clinton had in reality been defensive and, at some points, maddeningly vague. It had taken the threat of a subpoena to even get him on the stand, which many believed was not the behavior of a man with nothing to hide.

Why had Clinton lied under oath? After admitting that he was embarrassed by his own behavior, the disgraced president then tried to elicit sympathy by adding, "I was also very concerned about protecting my family."

On December 19, 1998, President William Jefferson Clinton was impeached by the U.S. House of Representatives. The charges: perjury before the grand jury and obstruction of justice. At the time, he was only the second president in the history of the United States to be subjected to impeachment proceedings. (The third would be Donald J. Trump—twice.)

I did not have sexual relations with that woman, Miss Lewinsky.

On January 26, 1998, President Bill Clinton looked the American public in the eye and issued his now-famous denial: "I did not have sexual relations with that woman, Miss Lewinsky."

With the president impeached by the House, proceedings moved on to the Senate in January of 1999. The impeachment trial was five weeks long. Theoretically, it could have ended with Bill Clinton's removal from office. At the end of the trial, on February 12, a majority of senators voted to dismiss the articles of impeachment.

The Clinton presidency had survived. Finally, Bill Clinton used the S-word, telling a nation that had long since grown tired of the media circus surrounding the investigation that he was "profoundly sorry."

It was still not the last scandal to be associated with Bill and Hillary Clinton.

# Benghazi

Ever since the 2001 terror attacks on New York City and Washington, D.C., September 11 has been a date not forgotten by Americans. On the eleventh anniversary of the atrocity, Hillary Clinton found herself at the center of yet another imbroglio—one that some would blame her for causing. Even now, more than ten years later, her name is irrevocably linked with the name of Benghazi.

Benghazi is the second-largest city in Libya. By 2012, it had a become a breeding ground for a multitude of disparate militia groups, many of which had formed after the dictator Muammar Gaddafi was killed in an insurrection. The militias all had different ideals and motivations, but many also had one thing in common: they were decidedly anti-Western, with an added emphasis for some on being anti-American.

Despite the risks, the Barack Obama administration felt it was politically worthwhile to keep a mission in Benghazi. The mission was lightly protected, and it didn't take much in the way of tactical foresight to see that the compound was a prime target for attack.

In the run-up to September 11, 2012, the consensus among U.S. intelligence agencies was that there would likely be an attack on U.S. interests in Libya somewhere, at some point. However, nothing concrete pointed specifically toward the Benghazi mission—at first. All throughout that day, crowds had formed outside the gates of U.S. installations across the Middle East, demonstrating against American interests and ideologies. These hostile assemblies were loud but were not particularly violent.

Later that same evening, the U.S. ambassador in Benghazi, Christopher Stevens, realized that his mission compound had acquired its own mob of protestors. The hostile assembly was armed with AK-47s, rocket-propelled grenade launchers, and a host of other weapons. By 9:30 p.m., the mob had stormed the mission and set buildings on fire.

Despite valiant efforts on the part of the mission staff, the ambassador and three other Americans died in the attack, which also included a mortar bombardment of the CIA annex.

A formal review of the tragedy revealed what almost everybody who had set eyes on the U.S. mission at Benghazi already knew: security at the compound had been woefully inadequate. Ambassador Stevens had requested extra measures to beef up security. Seen as being non-urgent, those requests were either ignored or denied. Stevens was an astute and savvy politician who knew which way the wind was blowing in the region. He had come close to being harmed in Benghazi more than once already, such as when a car bomb was detonated outside his hotel. However, the evidence suggests that he didn't see the true severity of the threat on September 11, 2012.

On the day of the attack, Hillary Clinton held the position of secretary of state. She drew a great deal of criticism in the aftermath of Benghazi for what many saw as the Obama administration's tepid policy on terrorism. It was her job to foresee the vulnerability of U.S. installations such as the Benghazi mission, one school of thought goes, and to take adequate measures to secure them from attack. This, she singularly failed to do.

Clinton hit back by insisting that there was "no actionable intelligence" to suggest that the Benghazi compound, specifically, was targeted for attack. Critics on the right-hand side of the aisle saw the disaster as a failure of leadership to be laid at her door and that of President Obama. Supporters on the left charged that the allegations against Obama and Clinton were politically motivated. It is certainly true that the events at Benghazi continued to be a millstone around Hillary Clinton's neck during her 2016 presidential run, for which she won the popular vote but lost the electoral college vote and thus the election.

## Her Emails

This was not helped by revelations that, during her tenure as secretary of state, she had made use of a private email server to conduct official State Department business—a big no-no. The reason for this ultimately boiled down to the fact that, when it came to information technology, Hillary Clinton was something of a technophobe. When questioned later by the FBI, multiple colleagues recalled being asked to help her with relatively simple computer operations. She didn't even know her way around a desktop PC or a Mac.

Government IT best practices strongly recommended that personal email accounts not be accessed from the same device as an official, government-issued account. This was for reasons of security, and it made eminent sense. Nonetheless, Clinton had her assistants set up a private email server from which she could access her own personal email via a Blackberry device—the only piece of information technology she was comfortable using. Even when the majority of her colleagues switched to Apple iPhones, Clinton clung to the trusty old Blackberry, resisting even the necessity to upgrade it to a newer model wherever possible.

Secretary of State Hillary Clinton was dressed down, mainly by GOP faithfuls and the media, for improper use of a private email server to conduct official business.

To be fair to Hillary Clinton, this was simply the way things were done at the State Department. Even her predecessor, Colin Powell, had skirted the IT security guidelines and had intimated to Clinton that she had to be careful—otherwise her emails might become a matter of public record, and therefore subject to subpoena. It was to be a prophetic statement.

She was far from the only employee to have a non-secure email setup; she was also, however, the head of the department, and she could easily have instituted a change of culture had she wanted to. Instead, she continued using an email server that was kept in the basement of her own home. Rather than going through State Department IT accounts, Hillary sent and received emails via a domain named clintonemail.com.

Compounding the problem was the fact that within the State Department, there was a tendency for employees to discuss and share classified or partially classified information in unclassified emails, both within the department and also to recipients outside it. So long as she could send and receive email, Hillary Clinton remained oblivious to how the technological aspects of it actually worked.

Cybercrime is a sad fact of everyday life in the 21st century, so the fact that hackers would discover and then launch a cyberattack on the private email server was inevitable. The Clinton server was attacked multiple times unsuccessfully until, in 2013, a hacker finally got in, compromising the account.

It wasn't until 2015, however, that Colin Powell's warning about her emails possibly being subject to a subpoena finally came true. Hillary was under investigation for her role in the Benghazi incident, and the investigators wanted to know how much classified information had passed through her personal email account.

In 2016, when the dust finally settled after not one but two investigations, the FBI concluded that, while Hillary Clinton and her staff had been "extremely careless" in their treatment of classified data, there was insufficient grounds for them to be prosecuted. Over the course of her political career, although allegations of corruption have dogged her and scandal has followed in her wake and that of her husband, Hillary Clinton has never been convicted of any crime.

## The Clinton Foundation and Uranium One

In 2013, the Clintons reassessed the status of their nonprofit William J. Clinton Presidential Foundation, which had been set up in 1997. Hillary had just left her position as secretary of state for the Obama administration, and Chelsea Clinton was a member of the board—and thus the Bill, Hillary, and Chelsea Clinton Foundation was born. Philanthropy is a laudable thing, as was the fact that neither Bill nor Hillary—nor their daughter Chelsea—accepted a salary from their association with the foundation.

Much like Bill and Hillary Clinton themselves, however, scandal has never been too far behind the foundation that bears their names. The foundation attracted the attention of the FBI, who investigated claims that some of the wealthy donors who contributed money were involved in "pay to play" politics. In other words, corporations and rich individuals get access to Bill or Hillary's time and support in exchange for large donations of cash. Some critics have claimed the donations might more accurately be described as bribes.

A number of the foundation's charities also paid Bill and Hillary large fees for public speaking, racking up profits for the Clintons that ran into the hundreds of millions of dollars. Donors have included extremely rich private individuals, companies, and even foreign governments. In return for their cash, they received "favors" from Bill and Hillary, helping to further their own private interests.

After Hillary Clinton was sworn in as secretary of state in 2009, questions arose about the propriety of Bill Clinton's paid speech engagements.

What drew the attention of the FBI were complaints that some of those who donated to the foundation had done so during Hillary's time as secretary of state (2009–13). The possibility of a U.S. secretary of state being effectively "bought" by private interests is an alarming one. These concerns came to a head in what would come to be known as the Uranium One deal.

Uranium is one of the most carefully tracked and closely guarded elements on Earth. It is a key component in the construction of nuclear warheads. Uranium also helps power the nuclear reactors that drive submarines, aircraft carriers, and civilian power stations.

During the hotly contested 2016 presidential election, then-candidate Donald J. Trump claimed that in 2010, Secretary of State Hillary Clinton had made it possible for Russia's energy ministry, Rosatom, to buy ownership in U.S. uranium supplies. The mechanism was for Rosatom to buy ownership in Uranium One, a Canadian company that extracted its uranium in the United States—specifically, in the state of Wyoming. When Rosatom purchased a significant ownership stake in Uranium One, therefore, one of America's oldest and wiliest enemies would have gotten its hooks deep into mining American uranium.

During his bid for the White House, Donald Trump made much of "crooked Hillary's" ties to the Russians over the Uranium One deal. Closer scrutiny of the evidence turned up no improper actions.

In a move that raised the hackles of Peter Schweizer, author of the book *Clinton Cash*, it transpired that wealthy shareholders and investors in Uranium One had also made donations to the Clinton Foundation. The big question was: Had this influenced Secretary of State Clinton to help push the Rosatom/Uranium One deal through to completion? It didn't help matters that the foundation was supposed to name all of its donors to offset the perception of impropriety when Clinton became secretary of state. A subsequent investigation revealed that the names of the Uranium One investors who donated cash to the Clinton Foundation had *not* been disclosed, as they should have been.

During his bid for the White House, Donald Trump made much of "crooked Hillary's" ties to the Russians over the Uranium One deal. Closer scrutiny of the evidence turned up no improper actions carried out by Secretary of State Clinton in relation to the deal, nor anything linking payments to the Clinton Foundation with it.

As with most probes into their business dealings, the most recent investigation of Hillary Clinton fizzled out without ever finding a smoking gun.

Both Bill and Hillary Clinton have received very public black eyes over their decades in public service, as scandal after scandal threatened to engulf them and destroy their careers. Remarkably, both are still active in the public eye at the time of writing.

# Governor of the People

In August of 2021, Governor Andrew M. Cuomo of New York bowed to a tidal wave of public pressure and resigned from office. His term as governor had been turbulent, encompassing as it did the COVID-19 pandemic—a situation that saw him go head-to-head with then-president Donald J. Trump on a regular basis.

Cuomo held daily press conferences with the news media as the pandemic began and continued throughout 2020, demanding that thousands of ventilators be supplied to his jurisdiction, which had suffered an unprecedented number of serious coronavirus cases. He threatened to use National Guard troops to seize ventilators from some hospitals and redistribute them to others that had a greater need for the life-saving equipment. It was a controversial move on Cuomo's part, and a divisive one, albeit a stance that was consistent with his carefully cultivated image as a hard-liner. Some saw him as a strong leader, doing what needed to be done to protect as many lives as possible during a time of crisis. Others saw him as dangerously reckless, proposing the medical equivalent of robbing Peter to pay Paul.

Donald Trump had little time for any Democrat, but he was particularly scathing toward Cuomo, describing his leadership during the pandemic as "total incompetence" in an August 18 tweet. Cuomo, for his part, regularly savaged Trump's performance, targeting the

Before the last in a series of scandals prompted his resignation, Governor Andrew Cuomo of New York maintained an active media presence.

president and his administration for frequent criticism. The two men, president and governor, were engaged in what can only be termed a feud.

In many ways, Trump and Cuomo were quite alike. Both had mercurial personalities and were prone to outbursts of anger, particularly toward those who worked for them. Each was the center of multiple accusations of sexual harassment. The allegations against Cuomo painted a picture of a man who treated male and female staffers very differently. Over a period of several months, multiple women came forward to state that they had suffered unwelcome sexual advances, which sometimes occurred in hotel rooms meant for official use. One of the victims was a state trooper assigned to the governor's personal protection detail.

Men faced aggressive and verbally abusive behavior, with the governor using emasculating language to berate them for perceived infractions. The verbal tirades and harassment were not restricted exclusively to men, however. Several female staffers came forward as well, some under condition of anonymity, and also claimed that they too had been the target of the governor's rage over the course of their careers.

For his part, Cuomo denied the allegations of impropriety, stating publicly that he had never meant to make anybody feel uncomfortable. "To be clear," Cuomo said, "I never inappropriately touched anybody, and I never propositioned anybody, and I never intended to make anyone feel uncomfortable."

> The word that former staff members frequently used in reference to working for Andrew Cuomo was "toxic."

The word that former staff members frequently used in reference to working for Andrew

Cuomo was "toxic." In the political realm, he had cultivated an image as an energetic and aggressive leader who was not afraid to shake the tree to achieve his objectives. Yet there is a big difference between the use of aggressive political tactics surrounding an issue and aggressive treatment of human beings. Cuomo's reported treatment of his employees suggests that the line was crossed repeatedly during his tenure as New York governor. His behavior was that of a bully, not a leader.

When interviewed by journalists regarding their experiences working with Cuomo, former colleagues and employees painted a picture of a man who could be charming and gracious one minute and then turn on a dime the next, his short fuse leading to sudden outbursts of anger. He was also believed to have been vindictive, leading a number of those who spoke out against him to be afraid of reprisals. These fears were not unreasonable. Cuomo had already threatened to destroy the personal lives and livelihoods of others who had crossed him in the past. Some claimed that Cuomo had threatened to harm them physically.

While this behavior coming to light certainly contributed to Andrew Cuomo's political downfall, it was not the sole factor. During the first year of the pandemic, the governor's office mandated that COVID-positive residents of nursing homes be re-admitted to those facilities if they were deemed "stable," a controversial order. To make matters worse, it would later be discovered that the Cuomo administration was publicly underreporting the number of nursing home deaths by as much as 50 percent. Governor Cuomo had been pushing the narrative that, in terms of COVID-19 deaths, his state was performing better than many others—a narrative that was subsequently shown to be false. The extra deaths, which numbered in the thousands, were intentionally concealed to prop up the Cuomo administration's public image. To add insult to injury, Cuomo earned millions of dollars from

> **Rather than accept responsibility for his behavior, Cuomo used his resignation speech to issue a puzzling non-apology.**

sales of his book *American Crisis: Leadership Lessons from the COVID-19 Pandemic*, in which the author is self-portrayed as being a hero.

Rather than accept responsibility for his behavior, Cuomo used his resignation speech to issue a puzzling non-apology, decrying the "unfair" treatment he had received at the hands of his accusers and the media. Playing the victim card to the hilt, the disgraced outgoing governor made clear his conviction that he was the target of an orchestrated smear campaign rather than somebody whose past behavior had finally caught up with them. Never mind the fact that the New York attorney general released a report supporting the claims made by 11 women that Andrew Cuomo had treated them inappropriately. He left office still denying having committed any major wrongdoing. His ouster, Cuomo maintained, was "politically motivated."

The blowback was not confined to Andrew Cuomo himself. His brother, Chris, was an anchor with Cable News Network (CNN). It would subsequently emerge that Chris Cuomo had been complicit by trying to dig up potentially discrediting information on at least one of his brother's accusers. He had taken part in crafting Andrew Cuomo's public defense against the harassment claims that mounted against him, helping to set the public relations strategy.

CNN at first placed Chris Cuomo on suspension while an independent review was conducted, and the network eventually terminated his employment with them once the final report was turned in. It would not be long before it was revealed that the former CNN anchor was himself accused of sexual harassment—claims that Chris Cuomo denied.

The Cuomo brothers retain a presence in the public eye. It is a safe bet that the American public has not yet seen the last of them.

# The House of Trump

Donald John Trump was born in 1946 in the city with which his name would be associated throughout his life: New York. He was born into a wealthy family. Trump's father, Fred, had made his fortune in the world of real estate and could afford to give his children a private education.

After graduating from the New York Military Academy, young Donald embarked upon a university education that focused on business and finance. He was clearly destined to follow in his father's footsteps. By the time he entered higher education, the United States was at war in Vietnam. Trump received multiple deferments that kept him out of military service, including one on medical grounds for the stated reason of "bone spurs." Although this would come back to haunt Trump as a form of criticism years later, the fact is that millions of young men of his generation received deferments for this or similar reasons. The vast majority came from middle-class or wealthy families.

After graduating with a bachelor's degree in economics, Trump did indeed go to work at his father's real estate company, managing properties in various parts of New York City. By 1974, he was running the company.

> **Under Donald's direction, the Trump name would become a bona fide brand. Its hallmark characteristics were grandeur and glitz.**

Under Donald's direction, the Trump name would become a bona fide brand. Its hallmark characteristics were grandeur and glitz, as evidenced by such creations as the Trump Tower. Constructed on busy Fifth Avenue, the 58-story skyscraper would add to Trump's growing fame.

One of the earliest scandals involving Trump came to light in 1973, when he and his father, Fred, were accused of racism in relation to some of the tenants who rented apartments from them. Donald was head of the Trump Management Corporation, where he was responsible for overseeing thousands of rental properties owned by the Trump family.

Donald Trump wears his signature red Make America Great Again hat during a 2016 campaign speech.

Trouble came when the Department of Justice took Fred and Donald Trump to court, alleging that they were offering less-favorable rental terms to "people of race and color" and sometimes refusing to rent apartments to African Americans at all.

Calling the charges "ridiculous," the younger Trump pushed back against the government lawyers by countersuing for $100 million. This would become a standard tactic whenever he felt threatened, which he would return to over and over as time went on.

Two years later, both parties agreed to settle the issue. Trump promised the government that he would not discriminate against potential tenants on the grounds of race. A key point was that he refused to admit to having done so in the past; the written terms of the agreement did not involve an admission of culpability on the part of Trump Management Corporation.

Trump's first marriage, to fashion model Ivana Zelnickova, produced two sons, Don Jr. and Eric, and a daughter, Ivanka. Donald and Ivana divorced in 1992, having been married for 15 years. Another marriage followed in 1993, to actress Marla Maples, producing one daughter, Tiffany. Trump's third marriage took place in 2005, and it was also to a model. His newest wife, Melania Knauss, gave birth to a son, Barron, the following year.

## *The Apprentice*

The year 2004 saw Donald Trump's media star on the rise when he became the center of the hit reality TV show *The Apprentice*. Love him or hate him, nobody could deny that the man had star power. Turning a blind eye to his string of entrepreneurial misfires, the show painted Trump as an uber-successful business mogul—a man with the Midas touch, turning everything around him into gold. Trump dominated every scene he appeared in as a gaggle of eager contestants competed for the grand prize: a position working at one of Trump's business organizations. The show's ratings soared, garnering 20 million viewers in its first season.

> **Love him or hate him, nobody could deny that the man had star power.**

Depending on one's perspective, *The Apprentice* made for either compulsive viewing or train-wreck television at its worst. Viewers tuned in regularly to watch the 21st-century equivalent of gladiatorial combat staged in the business world, with Trump delivering the final thumbs up or down, accompanied by his catch phrase: "You're fired."

Although *The Apprentice* buttressed his reputation for being a skilled negotiator and successful entrepreneur, Donald Trump has been associated with multiple failed business ventures. While that may not be particularly unusual (many entrepreneurs fail, sometimes spectacularly, before finally making it big), Trump's business failures have had a way of courting controversy—and lawsuits.

## Trump University

One such venture was the ill-fated Trump University. The pitch: for a hefty enrollment fee, students could learn the secret real estate sales techniques of Donald Trump—secrets with the potential to make them a fortune. Trump University claimed that its cadre of instructors would be "hand-picked" by the man himself, something he would later deny having done. On paper, Trump U promised to be a training ground for the best of the best, building the next generation of savvy investors and titans of industry.

In reality, it was anything but. Launched in 2005, Trump University did hire some academic luminaries to help craft and teach the curriculum. However, some of the instructors were grossly underqualified to teach anything. Some did not even possess a college degree themselves. Few had any background in training and education. One was a convicted felon.

This parody of a diploma highlights the scam that was Trump University, an unlicensed, illegal business venture that folded after only six years.

Trump U turned out to be little more than a system for bilking enthusiastic customers out of their money, returning nothing but dubious "trade secrets" in return. In hindsight, many of its customers thought it was a scam. Completing courses didn't confer a degree or any sort of academic standing for students; they got nothing concrete whatsoever to show for their time and money. It is safe to say that nobody got rich as a result of their studies at Trump's online school—with the possible exception of Donald Trump.

In advance publicity for the school, Trump had waxed lyrical about using the online format to bring education to the masses, helping more people become successful and leveling the playing field. As a concept, it had much to commend it, and had Trump kept the tuition fees affordable, Trump University might have stood a chance. Instead, he chose to set prices high, with some students ponying up tens of thousands of dollars to take classes. Few, if any, experienced the kind of wild financial success they had been promised at the outset.

By all accounts, Trump was a hands-off boss when it came to his university, preferring a "set it and forget it" approach to management. As profits began to decline, so did funding for the various programs on offer. Trump University went out of business in 2011, having survived for just six years. Inevitably, lawsuits followed.

The state of New York sued Trump University for operating an "unlicensed, illegal educational institution from their headquarters in New York City, which purported to teach students Donald Trump's real estate strategies and techniques." Due to a failure to follow the rules, Trump University was indeed an illegal business venture.

A class action lawsuit, comprised of students who claimed that they had been defrauded of tens of thousands of dollars by Trump University's false promises, was settled in 2018 for $25 million. Once again, Donald Trump refused to admit that he had done anything wrong.

## Business and Bankruptcies

There has been much debate about Trump's ability (or lack thereof) as a businessman. The fact remains that Trump businesses have gone bankrupt no fewer than six times, at the time of writing. Many see this as a sign of failure on his part. Trump's own perspective is somewhat different: he sees bankruptcy as a perfectly legal and valid tactic to be used in the acquisition of wealth. Indeed, he has said as much, and he claims to view the business world as "nothing personal"—that is, his business ventures are no reflection on him. Considering the world of real estate and entrepreneurship as something akin to a giant-sized game of Monopoly, Trump sees himself as playing with house money. When questioned about the bankruptcies in interviews, he tends to dismiss the insolvency of his hotel and casino ventures, and he likes to emphasize the fact that none of his bankruptcies were *personal* bankruptcies. In this, he is correct.

Another attempt to buff Donald Trump's image came in the form of a book, ostensibly authored by him, though the vast majority was written by coauthor Tony Schwartz. Indeed, Schwartz has stated publicly that he wrote the entire book himself. *Trump: The Art of the Deal* was published in 1987. The book reads like a distilled (and considerably cheaper) version of Trump University, outlining his thoughts and insights on the ins and outs of doing business.

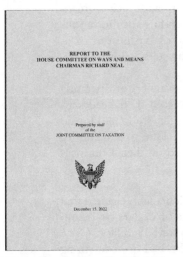

REPORT TO THE
HOUSE COMMITTEE ON WAYS AND MEANS
CHAIRMAN RICHARD NEAL

Prepared by staff
of the
JOINT COMMITTEE ON TAXATION

December 15, 2022

After a four-year legal battle rising all the way to the Supreme Court, the U.S. House Ways and Means Committee released six years of Donald Trump's tax returns alongside their report.

Schwartz opined in a May 8, 2019, tweet from his personal Twitter account: "Given the Times report on Trump's staggering losses, I'd be fine if Random House simply took the book out of print. Or recategorized it as fiction."

The report to which Schwartz refers is a May 8, 2019, article in the *New York Times* written by Russ Buettner and Susanne Craig. Its title is provocative: "Decade in the Red: Trump Tax Figures Show Over $1 Billion in Business Losses." The journalists dropped the bombshell revelation that, at the very same time Trump's face was staring at readers from the front cover of *The Art of the Deal*, espousing the entrepreneur's reputation as a legend of the business world, Trump was losing a fortune on enterprises that hadn't panned out the way he wanted them to.

This was information that Donald Trump understandably didn't want to be made public. After all, who would want to buy a book full of advice from a businessman who wasn't making any profits? But Trump's tax returns told the true story, and for the unidentified source who provided them to the *New York Times*, they made for far more compelling reading than *The Art of the Deal*. The upshot was that in the space of ten years, between 1985 and 1994, Trump's businesses had lost in excess of one *billion* dollars. The only financial benefit, so far as Trump was concerned, was that he had lost so much money that he did not have to pay any tax for eight of those ten years.

In response to the article, an attorney representing Trump countered that the contents were untrue, although no specific rebuttals were provided. Unlike other major party presidential nominees, Donald Trump fought tooth and nail to avoid releasing his tax returns. In all likelihood the picture they painted was at odds with the image of a successful entrepreneur he wanted to present to the world.

## Accusations of Assault

Among the more frequent types of scandal to dog Donald Trump are claims of sexual misconduct, harassment, and assault.

In 2005, Trump was secretly recorded speaking crudely to *Access Hollywood* host Billy Bush. The conversation happened on the set of the popular soap opera *Days of Our Lives*, on which Trump was making a cameo. It is likely the future president had no idea his mic was live when he began telling a story about seducing a married woman and the advantages that being famous conferred upon him.

"I did try and f— her," Trump can be heard saying on the tape. "She was married. I moved on her very heavily. In fact, I took her out furniture shopping. I moved on her like a bitch, but I couldn't get there, and she was married."

Worse was still to come. "I'm automatically attracted to beautiful [women]," Trump continued. "I just start kissing them. It's like a magnet. Just kiss. I don't even wait. When you're a star, they let you do it. You can do anything. Grab 'em by the pussy. You can do anything."

*You can do anything* gives a clearer insight into the way Donald Trump perceives women than anything else he had publicly said.

When the tape came to light during his 2016 presidential campaign, Trump dismissed it as being nothing more than "locker room banter," adding that Bill Clinton had said far worse to him in the past. Although many were disgusted by what he had said, it didn't seem to harm his chances of being elected.

Claims of Trump sexually assaulting women go back to at least 1980, when, according to businesswoman Jennifer Leeds, Trump forcibly kissed and groped her in the first-class section of an airliner heading to New York.

A host of other women have also come forward, many with similar reports. Some involve Trump kissing them without their consent. Others have accused him of sexual assault. Many of the alleged assaults are said to have occurred at various locations in New York City, although Trump's Florida club and resort, Mar-a-Lago, is also the scene of several reports.

For his part, Trump has categorically denied all of the assaults, going so far as to imply in some cases that the female plaintiffs were not attractive enough to even garner his attention.

Seen here in 2007 at the Adult Entertainment Expo, actor and director Stormy Daniels received hush money from the Donald Trump campaign in 2016 to keep their one-off liaison quiet.

Not all of Trump's alleged sexual malfeasances were nonconsensual. Porn actress Stormy Daniels (whose real name is Stephanie Gregory Clifford) stated that she had a brief tryst with Trump in 2006. Trump was married to his wife Melania at the time. It is claimed that Daniels met Trump in 2006 at a celebrity golf tournament, joined him for dinner, and then accepted an invitation to join him in his hotel room. Trump was a decade away from the presidency at the time, but he was well known, thanks in part to his starring role on *The Apprentice*.

There was a 33-year age gap between the two; Trump was 60, Daniels just 27. Per Daniels, this was their sole sexual encounter, although the two did keep in touch for months afterward. Trump made vague promises about getting her TV work, which ultimately never materialized.

Although there were rumors and gossip here and there, the story flew mostly under the radar until Trump garnered the Republican presidential nomination. Even considering the playboy image that he coveted so much, Trump and his team knew that if word of his supposedly having an affair with a porn actress were to emerge, the optics would be bad for a would-be president's image.

The solution Team Trump came up with was to offer Daniels $130,000 in hush money by way of an intermediary—attorney Michael Cohen. All the actress had to do in return was to sign a non-disclosure agreement (NDA) and keep quiet about her affair with Trump. She signed and took the money.

Nonetheless, in January of 2018, the story hit the press anyway. The *Wall Street Journal* revealed the details of the NDA and the amount of money that had been paid to Daniels in exchange for her silence. Both Trump and Daniels, communicating via their respective lawyers, denied the story.

Still, the story refused to die. By March, Daniels had changed her tune. She would later say that many of her denials occurred because she had been threatened and intimidated. Donald Trump was now president of the United States, and many found the fact that his lawyers were trying to slap Daniels with a $20 million claim for damages to be in poor taste. (According to the terms of the NDA, each violation of the agreement would render Daniels liable for a $1 million penalty.)

Hitting back, the actress granted a tell-all interview to CNN's Anderson Cooper. Cooper had just completed an interview with Playboy model Karen McDougal, who had confessed to having had a long-standing affair with Trump. Some of the details McDougal recounted concerning her sexual liaisons with Trump bore close parallels to those told by Daniels. By way of White House spokesperson Hope Hicks, Trump had vehemently denied the affair with McDougal.

The case dragged on through the courts for the next several years. Michael Cohen spent three years imprisoned (half of the sentence within his own home) after being convicted of campaign finance crimes and lying to Congress. He was released in November 2021.

## Raising His Royalties

In an August 24, 2016, article titled "Donald Trump Used Campaign Donations to Buy $55,000 of His Own Book," *Daily Beast* reporters Olivia Nuzzi and Ben Collins exposed another shady tactic employed by the real estate mogul. It's not unusual for a presidential candidate to release a book—often either ghostwritten or co-written with a professional author—in the run-up to an election. It serves three purposes: First, having a book published lends credibility to the candidate in question. Second, it's a reminder to potential voters every time they see the book on store shelves that this person is running for office—a form of free marketing. Lastly, income derived from the book in terms of royalties goes into the author's pocket, providing a healthy stream of revenue.

There's nothing at all wrong with this, per se, so long as everything is kept aboveboard. In the case of Trump's book *Crippled America: How to Make America Great Again* (renamed *Great Again: How to Fix Our Crippled America* for the paperback reprint), the problem came when his electoral campaign shelled out more than $55,000 to buy thousands of copies of the book from the retailer Barnes and Noble. That money came from donors to the Trump campaign, and it found its way back into Trump's personal coffers in the form of royalties—payments made to the author on each copy of a book that is sold.

The books were given away to attendees at the Republic National Convention, along with other pro-Trump swag. The fact that they were gifted to potential voters is not the problem; the concerning issue lies with Donald Trump lining his pocket with book sales that were essentially made by himself *to* himself, taking the donated money of political supporters and converting it into royalties that the publisher would pay him personally. If the middleman were cut out, those donors were basically putting their money straight into Donald Trump's wallet. Under the rules governing the electoral process, this is an illegal use of campaign funds and violates federal election standards.

## Financial Gain for the First Family

After ascending to power in the 2016 presidential election, Donald J. Trump headed one of the most controversial administrations—if not *the* most controversial—in the history of U.S. politics.

It has long been understood that presidents and their family members who choose to run personal business enterprises are not supposed to leverage their position in the White House to promote or otherwise further their own financial interests. In direct contravention to this rule, shortly after the Trumps took up residence in Washington, visitors to the official White House website (www. whitehouse.gov) were greeted with a message extolling the virtues of Melania Trump's personal sales line of jewelry products. This included what was essentially an advertisement for where they could be found—the television network QVC.

Donald Trump makes his acceptance speech at the Republican National Convention in 2016, where his campaign gave away copies of Trump's book.

A spokeswoman for the First Lady defended the website entry by claiming that the reference to QVC was not an attempt to sell whitehouse.gov visitors on Melania's jewelry but rather simply a factual point in her biography. Nevertheless, the site was swiftly amended to remove the reference to the QVC retail outlet.

Not to be outdone, Trump's daughter Ivanka had her own line of clothing on the market. Seeking to leverage the perceived popularity of the Trump brand, the First Daughter aimed her expensively priced product at professional, working women. Unfortunately, sales had not been good, leading some major retailers to drop the line from their inventory in early 2017. This led to one of Donald Trump's many infamous tweets, calling out Nordstrom for treating his daughter "unfairly."

Over the course of his presidency, Trump's Twitterstorms would become near-legendary, prompting even some members of his own party to wish somebody would take his phone away. At the time—March of 2017—eyebrows were raised at the fact that a sitting president of the United States was taking time out of his day to chastise a clothing store for dropping his daughter's product line. This was not illegal behavior for a president, but many saw it as being deeply questionable.

To compound matters, Kellyanne Conway, counselor to the president, told a national TV audience on the Fox News network to "go buy Ivanka's stuff." Because of Conway's close working relationship to the president, Trump's supporters took this message as coming directly from him—which it basically did. Because she wasn't the president herself and therefore did not enjoy the privileges and protections of the position, Conway should at the very least have been subject to corrective action of some sort. That didn't happen. Her remarks had been made in support of her immediate supervisor's daughter and her personal business affairs. The ethics of the situation were, again, deeply questionable.

## Family Favors

*Merriam-Webster's Dictionary* defines nepotism as "favoritism (as in appointment to a job) based on kinship." Nepotistic appointments usually involve placing somebody who is less-than-qualified to meet the responsibilities of a position in that role regardless, often sidelining those with vastly more experience and the appropriate qualifications.

Despite claiming to staff his administration with experts, the perceived loyalty that accompanies being a family member was more important to Donald Trump than a proven track record. This is how Trump's daughter Ivanka and her husband, Trump's son-in-law Jared Kushner, wound up with plum spots as the president's senior advisors. Neither was remotely prepared or qualified to assume the role of advising the president on matters either important or trivial. The fact that Jared and Ivanka were loyal to Trump was all he cared about.

Trump was warned by government lawyers that his appointment of Jared and Ivanka to upper-echelon White House positions was illegal, unethical, and violated Justice Department guidelines. Indeed, former presidents had been blocked from taking similar action since 1967, when Congress passed a stringent anti-nepotism law to prevent exactly what Trump so blithely did. Several presidents have run afoul of the law to some degree, but all have obeyed it—until Trump.

Although both Jared and Ivanka forfeited their pay before accepting the job, they benefited from their top government positions in a number of other ways.

Trump's daughter Ivanka and son-in-law Jared Kushner wound up with plum spots as the president's senior advisors. Here, the two are seen joining the president for a 2017 meeting at the White House with Chancellor Angela Merkel of Germany.

Nor did the nepotism stop there. The son of Trump's right-hand man, the lawyer and former New York City mayor Rudy Giuliani, was hired as "special assistant to the president and associate director of the Office of Public Liaison." The job came with a salary of $95,000 per annum.

It goes without saying that Trump is far from the first politician to appoint friends and family to plum jobs; however, with unqualified appointees filling some top-level spots, critics pointed out that 170 other essential positions remained unfilled going into the final year of his presidency.

Although the Trumps vacated the White House in January of 2021 following the election of Joe Biden to the presidency, the family remained mired in controversy. Entire books have been written about the 2020 election, with claims and counterclaims flying back and forth regarding fraud and corruption at the highest levels. Just as this manuscript was being turned in for publication, FBI agents served a warrant at Trump's Mar-a-Lago club resort (and erstwhile residence) to recover 15 boxes and hundreds of pages of classified documents that the former president had removed from the White House upon leaving office and did not voluntarily return upon request.

In March 2023, Trump affirmed his intention to remain in the 2024 presidential race even if he is under indictment in relation to his handling of the classified documents or alleged tampering in the 2020 election. No matter what one's opinion is of Donald J. Trump and his family, one thing cannot be denied: their story is far from over.

# Cash in the Freezer

The more powerful and influential a corrupt public figure becomes, the more difficult it is to bring them to justice. For example, consider the 2005 case of Louisiana congressman William J. Jefferson.

The congressman's downfall began with a tipoff to the FBI from a Virginia-based businesswoman named Lori Mody, who claimed that Jefferson had approached her with a distasteful proposition. He could ensure that a major deal with a foreign business went through with a minimum of fuss, the congressman promised. In return, all she had to do was give up a partial share in the ownership of her company.

Over the six-year period between 2000 and 2005, Jefferson took close to half a million dollars in bribes. He also accepted other forms of bribery, such as stocks in a host of different companies, all of which stood to gain from being in the congressman's good graces. In turn, he led official delegations to Africa and exerted his influence upon agencies and companies in Nigeria, the Republic of the Congo, Equatorial Guinea, and Botswana. Bribes flew back and forth. Jefferson's wheeling and dealing lined a lot of pockets—most notably his own.

The next time he met the businesswoman who had turned him in, Jefferson had no idea that she was wearing a wire. Law enforcement was listening to his every word.

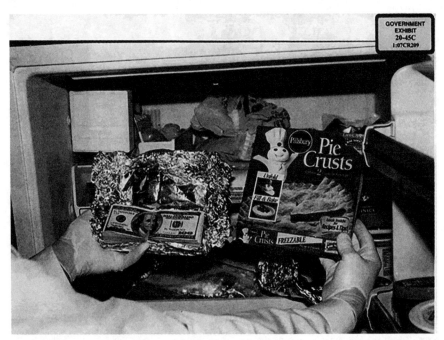

Tipped off by a constituent who was being shaken down, the FBI conducted a wire sting and raid to nab Rep. William J. Jefferson of Louisiana in a bribery and corruption investigation. Agents found the informant's bribe disguised as food in the congressperson's freezer.

Keeping Jefferson under covert surveillance, agents watched as the congressman accepted $100,000 in cash from the FBI informant, which he intended to use to bribe the vice president of Nigeria into smoothing over a trade deal. The cash handover was captured on camera, and it would prove to be strong evidence in the criminal case against the corrupt politician. He would never get the opportunity to make that bribe. The video footage provided a sufficiently strong foundation for the FBI to obtain a warrant to search Jefferson's residence.

FBI agents moved in quickly. During a search of the house, they uncovered $90,000 of the bribe money inside the congressman's freezer. It had been wrapped in aluminum foil and stuffed inside a cardboard box meant for Pillsbury piecrusts.

Whenever a public official turns rotten, it is an affront to the public he or she was elected to represent. In the case of William Jefferson, the congressman not only took money unethically from outside commercial interests, but he also used both government time and taxpayer money to line his pockets. That time should have been used to meet the needs of his constituents, not to bribe and negotiate with international officials.

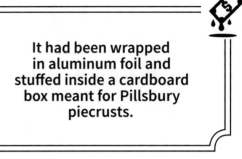

**It had been wrapped in aluminum foil and stuffed inside a cardboard box meant for Pillsbury piecrusts.**

On November 13, 2009, after being found guilty on 11 counts by a federal jury, the disgraced former congressman was sentenced to 13 years' imprisonment. The judge ordered him to forfeit $470,000 of his ill-gotten gains.

The congressman wasn't acting alone. Some of those who helped him achieve his ends overseas were unwitting accomplices, simply trying to do their jobs. As FBI agents dug further into his business dealings, however, they uncovered firm evidence against a businessman named Vernon L. Jackson and a congressional staffer named Brett Pfeffer, each of whom had willingly colluded with Jefferson and had accepted bribes themselves. Both would be found guilty and receive prison sentences—87 months for Jackson, who had paid the congressman hundreds of thousands of dollars to push the interests of his private company, and eight years for Pfeffer.

In 2017, a judge released Jefferson from prison, throwing out most of the convictions against him. He had served five and a half years.

# Quizzed

In 1950s America, television audiences were glued, day in and day out, to a new entertainment phenomenon: the TV quiz show. Many of these shows were honest brokers, but unbeknownst to their legions of avid viewers, some were rigged.

Although the technology behind television dates to the 1920s, commercial TV in its most popular and widespread form only began to take hold in the late 1940s. The TV game show, which is still with us some 70 years later, was in its infancy during the early 1950s. As with so many aspects of public life, it wasn't long before the quiz shows were mired in their own unique form of corruption.

Looking back, it is easy to see the appeal of the TV quiz. Americans love a winner, and many also love to gamble. The prospect of the guy or gal next door making a fortune by answering questions, sometimes risking it all to win big, spoke to suburban America in a way that few other things did. On TV, it really was possible to become an overnight success story—if one possessed the requisite amount of knowledge, coupled with a healthy dollop of good luck. The fact that these dramas were played out nightly right there in the living rooms of everyday Americans only helped spur the shows on to even greater success.

Charles Van Doren (right) competes within the isolation booth of the rigged quiz show *Twenty-One*, with host Jack Barry holding the quiz cards.

By 1956, one of the most popular TV quizzes was titled *Twenty-One*, so-called because two contestants were pitted against one another, each attempting to become the first to score 21 points. An element of tension was injected into the format by having each contestant sit in an isolation booth, keeping them in the dark regarding their opponent's progress. Television audiences loved the sometimes-nail-biting competition, particularly when the two competitors were neck and neck.

It was possible for a skilled or fortunate *Twenty-One* contestant to win tens of thousands of dollars in prize money—especially if they were able to cheat. Herbert Stempel was one such contestant, a reigning champion of *Twenty-One*, having worked his way up from nothing to having a pot worth a small fortune. Stempel was, by all accounts, a very smart young man, one with a passion for learning and the acquisition of knowledge, no matter how trivial. As such, he was well suited to being groomed as a quiz show champion. Trivia was Stempel's thing, and his ability to recall even the most obscure of facts showcased an almost perfect memory.

In front of the cameras, Herb Stempel was the hard-working, educated American boy making good. Behind the scenes, however, things were rotten on the set of *Twenty-One*. In October of 1956, Stempel was given his shot at fame and fortune, but only on the condition that he be willing to play the role that the producers wanted him to play—a nervous, socially awkward, yet brilliant young man. Only the last part was true to Stempel's actual personality.

He was fed answers in advance, and Stempel was also given the questions that he and his opponent would be up against on every episode. With each successive show, the amount of money in Herb Stempel's kitty continued to rise. Given thick-framed glasses and clothes that barely fit, he was set up to portray a bookish, nerdy character, contrasting with those contestants who were more conventionally attractive. The idea was that, when the time was judged to be right, Stempel would take a dive, bowing out in favor of a new champion on the rise.

Although he had all the answers, Stempel made sure to get a few wrong, just to make things look convincing. On December 5, less than two months after his first appearance on *Twenty-One*, the producers let him know that his time was up. They were bringing in a college professor named Charles Van Doren, who was Stempel's polar opposite in every way. Acting on their instructions, Herb Stempel deliberately answered a key question incorrectly, losing his title and position to the newcomer.

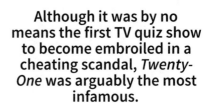

**Although it was by no means the first TV quiz show to become embroiled in a cheating scandal, *Twenty-One* was arguably the most infamous.**

Stempel's motivation for putting himself out of a job was simple. He agreed with the producer of *Twenty-One* that, in exchange for bowing out of the show, he would be given work on future TV projects that were said to be in the planning stages. None of the work that Stempel had been promised ever materialized, however. Bitter about the broken promises, he finally came forward and confessed to his part in the quiz show fraud that had bamboozled countless American viewers.

With his conventional good looks and natural charm, Charles Van Doren had won over the hearts of the public. When word got out that *Twenty-One* had been fixed, many found it difficult to believe. Nobody wanted to admit that their handsome TV hero actually had feet of clay. Van Doren had used similar tactics as Stempel, pretending to fumble in his memory for answers, intentionally missing the odd question to bolster his credibility, all while having seen the answers in advance.

Why did the producers insist on fixing the show? Because if they hadn't, it's likely that it would not have survived. *Twenty-One* debuted to relatively lackluster ratings. It had to be spiced up. Despite the veneer of reality that it portrayed, the show was in truth more fiction than fact—a carefully choreographed dance between two rivals who were operating under orders rather than a genuine battle of intellectual peers.

Although it was by no means the first TV quiz show to become embroiled in a cheating scandal, *Twenty-One* was arguably the most infamous. In 1994, Robert Redford directed a dramatized version of the events surrounding the imbroglio in the motion picture *Quiz Show*, starring Ralph Fiennes at Charles Van Doren and John Turturro as Herbie Stempel.

# "I Think I Killed Somebody"

Few producers have had as big an influence on 20th-century music culture than Harvey Phillip Spector. It is equally true that few, if any, have courted such controversy.

Raised by his mother after his father took his own life, the 19-year-old Phil Spector began his music career in a band called the Teddy Bears. He proved to be equally talented at songwriting and working behind the scenes as he was at performing in front of an audience. Spector was also deeply driven to succeed. Few in the music business manage to start their own record label at the age of 21, as he did in 1961. Spector had a cofounder named Lester Sill, and their label, Philles Records, seemed a neat amalgam of their two names.

Some of the biggest names of the 1960s music scene, such as Tina and Ike Turner, performed songs written or produced by Spector. Popular female group the Ronettes, who would become famous with such hits as "Be My Baby" and "Walking in the Rain," signed with Spector's record label in 1963. Group member Veronica "Ronnie" Bennett began a relationship with Spector, and she ultimately went on to marry him. The producer was married when their relationship began, but he didn't let that stand in the way.

Legendary music producer Phil Spector, seen here working with the Modern Folk Quartet, contributed to some of the greatest successes of the 1960s.

On the surface, Phil and Ronnie Spector might have seemed like the perfect glamorous, glitzy showbiz couple. Underneath it all, however, the music producer was abusive and domineering. His ex-wife would eventually reveal in her memoir that he had kept her under lock and key in their mansion, located in upscale Beverly Hills, refusing to let her out unless it suited him to do so. To make sure she could not leave, Spector had the property enclosed with a barbed-wire fence. Guard dogs prowled the grounds.

Their six-year marriage was a nightmare from which Ronnie felt lucky to finally escape, at the insistence of her mother. She left in 1974 and filed for divorce. In light of future events, it is possible she had a very narrow escape. Spector had already threatened to hire a hitman and have her killed if she ever left him. She revealed that Spector placed a gold coffin in the basement of the mansion, topped off with a glass lid, and told her that he would keep her dead body in there after he had her murdered.

Spector had been obsessed with violence and the threat of it since 1958. At a gig with the Teddy Bears, he was beaten up by four men, who took turns urinating on him. Humiliated at the loss of control he had suffered, Spector took to carrying a handgun with him everywhere he went. When the mood took him, the gun was used to threaten Ronnie. She was one of a string of women Spector would hold at gunpoint.

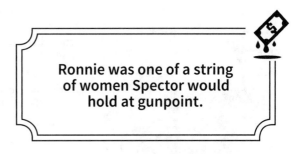

**Ronnie was one of a string of women Spector would hold at gunpoint.**

Even the many celebrity artists he worked with were not immune to having the producer pull a pistol on them, as John Lennon learned to his shock the day Spector fired off a round in the recording studio. Some see it as an eerie precursor to the way in which the Beatle would eventually be murdered by crazed fan Mark David Chapman. Lead singer Debbie Harry of Blondie and bass guitarist Dee Dee Ramone got the same treatment.

Phil Spector spent the decades between the 1970s and 2000s careening erratically between states of notoriety and obscurity. Sometimes, he could be found in the company of the world's most famous musicians and movie stars. Other times, he became a hermit, shunning the outside world as the grip of mental instability overwhelmed him. Friends and hangers-on never stuck around for long. He was too unpredictable for most people's liking. Most of those he employed, Spector ended up firing.

With the benefit of hindsight, it is easy to see that the record producer's volatile behavior was likely to end in tragedy. On February 9, 2003, 40-year-old actress Lana Clarkson was shot dead in Spector's Los Angeles home. Spector had spent the previous night drinking his way through several well-known LA night spots and watering holes. He met Clarkson at the House of Blues and invited her back to his mansion in Alhambra, which was known as the Pyrenees Castle.

Lana Clarkson had appeared in the 1982 classic *Fast Times at Ridgemont High* and had a list of television and movie credits to her name. Police officers who responded to Spector's residence found her body slumped in a chair, with blood congealing on her face and neck. At her feet was a Colt .38 revolver belonging to 67-year-old Spector, which forensic evidence would later determine had fired one bullet into the dead woman's open mouth.

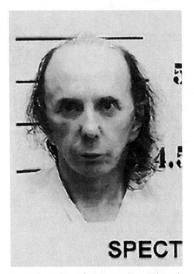

SPECT

In early 2009, after one mistrial and a subsequent guilty verdict, Phil Spector was sentenced to 14 years in prison for the murder of Lana Clarkson.

The closest thing to a witness was Spector's limo driver, Adriano De Souza, who had discreetly remained outside while his employer and guest went into the Pyrenees Castle. De Souza would later testify to hearing a single gunshot, after which Spector emerged from the mansion and told him: "I think I killed somebody."

After his arrest, Spector's story changed. At first, he said that he killed Lana Clarkson by accident. Then he switched gears and claimed that the actress had taken her own life, an unlikely thing for somebody to have done just two hours after arriving at the home of a stranger. Detectives and the district attorney weren't buying the frazzled Spector's suicide story. Spector found himself on trial for murder, not once but twice.

The first attempt to try him, in 2007, ended in a mistrial. One year later, Phil Spector was tried a second time for the murder of Lana Clarkson. This time, he was found guilty and sent to prison for life. He could theoretically have been released on parole in 2024, but Spector contracted COVID-19 while incarcerated and died on January 16, 2021, at the age of 81.

Despite his having been a groundbreaking and highly influential music producer, today he is remembered more for his erratic behavior and its tragic consequences.

# It Ain't Cool

M ovie fans can be some of the most passionate, articulate, and intelligent people one could ever wish to meet. The word "fan" derives from "fanatic," and there is indeed a vocal subculture of those whose love for and knowledge of film and its history border on the fanatical. For many years, the only way such people could find each other was by word of mouth or by attending film festivals.

Then, along came the internet.

Movie fandom exploded in the mid-1990s. Internet chat rooms permitted people of similar interests to congregate in the digital online space, ideally to exchange ideas, trade opinions, and—if they were movie fans—talk about their love of movies. Many film fans liked to argue the relative merits of their favorite pictures, while others were equally happy tearing them down. In this lay the genesis of the amateur film critic culture that pervades the internet to this day.

Until the advent of the World Wide Web, film criticism was mainly the purview of professional journalists. Movie reviews could be found in the pages of newspapers or on such TV shows as *Siskel and Ebert at the Movies*, in which the critics Gene Siskel and Roger Ebert rated the latest movies with a thumbs-up or the dreaded thumbs-down. Being a movie critic required a journalistic pedigree, at the very least—not just a ticket purchased at the box office.

Harry Knowles founded the *Ain't It Cool News* site in 1996, establishing himself as a film critic and celebrity.

All that changed with the arrival of websites such as *Ain't It Cool News*, one of the most popular in a tsunami of online forums for film fans to congregate and make their voices heard. Known informally as AICN, the site was the brainchild of Harry Knowles, a movie uber-fan based in Austin, Texas. After an accidental fall in 1994 that left him unable to get out of bed for months, Knowles found the internet to be a lifeline, a positive interest he could develop while bedbound. He had grown up immersed in movie and comic-book subculture, developed a love of film in all its forms, and acquired in-depth knowledge of movie history that he would eventually parlay into a highly successful career in the entertainment industry.

Sitting at home in his room, Knowles began putting together a simple website that was just a shadow of the behemoth it would soon become. (The name came from a line spoken by John Travolta in the 1996 John Woo–directed actioner *Broken Arrow*: when accused of being out of his mind, Travolta's character snaps back, "Yeah, ain't it cool?")

The great allure of AICN was the string of juicy rumors and gossip that was posted there on a regular basis. One of the few people to write articles for the site under his own name, Knowles recruited informants from movie sets and production crews to send him the latest news on troubled film shoots, sensitive casting news, and other movie-related scoops. Each informant was assigned a code name. Two of the most popular regular writers for AICN were Moriarty and Quint, named respectively after Sherlock Holmes's professorial nemesis and the grizzled shark hunter from Steven Spielberg's *Jaws*.

> **The great allure of AICN was the string of juicy rumors and gossip that was posted there on a regular basis.**

Much of AICN's power—and later, its notoriety—came via movie test screenings. A test screening is a secret event hosted by a movie studio in which members of the public are invited to a theater to watch a work in progress. This is usually the rough cut of a movie that is typically due to be released a few months later. Sometimes, the producers and directors attend in person. It's an opportunity for them to figure out which parts of the movie play well with audiences and which ones don't; which jokes get a laugh and which don't; whether audience members rise to their feet cheering at the rousing finale or sit in dead silence, underwhelmed and unmoved.

At the end of each test screening, those who attended are given score cards, which they use to rate various aspects of the film they just sat through. It isn't unusual for entire sequences of a movie to be reshot or removed based on the reactions of the audience. For the studio, there's a lot riding on each test screening. That's why attendees are asked not to talk about the movie they just saw; when the blockbuster finally hits movie theaters, it may well appear in a very different form to the cut they were shown.

Bad word of mouth can sink a movie before it ever has a chance to make its money back. A massive tentpole studio movie can cost hundreds of millions to make and tens of millions more to promote. If word gets out in advance that the film is a turkey, it may never recover at the box office.

Such was the case with 1997's now notorious *Batman and Robin*. The movie studio, Warner Bros., was expecting a smash hit when the film was released in hundreds of theaters that summer. The preceding Batman movie, *Batman Forever*, had performed remarkably well. *Batman and Robin* was packing some serious star power, with the likes of George Clooney and Arnold Schwarzenegger headlining the cast.

Then came the test screenings. Reports that were sent to Knowles and published on AICN savaged the film. Knowles himself described the movie as a "200-megaton bomb." It was not intended as a compliment. "The masochist in me loved it. I had attended a train wreck and sat third row center."

After a relatively strong debut, word of mouth on *Batman and Robin* led to an immediate and drastic drop in box-office business the following week. Most moviegoers agreed that the movie was indeed the ugly mess that AICN had predicted it would be, and—fairly or not—executives at Warner Bros. blamed Knowles and his spies for damaging the movie's performance. (It should be noted that although AICN took much of the flak for this, other movie

Much of AICN's power came via movie test screenings, in which members of the public are invited to a theater to watch a current work in progress.

sites also posted atrocious reviews for the film.)

Before the movie's release, a sequel was already in the works. The poor performance of *Batman and Robin* killed it stone dead. It would be eight years before Batman graced movie screens again. The amateur internet movie critic had helped drive a stake through the heart of a massive movie franchise, and the world of filmmaking would never be the same.

Harry Knowles wasn't out to savage films for the sake of it. He simply hated bad movies, and he felt he had the right to protect moviegoers from wasting their money. When he felt that a movie was being treated unfairly by the studio or by the public, Knowles used his platform to defend it. He reported on 1997's James Cameron–directed epic *Titanic* in glowing terms despite the whirlwind of negativity that plagued the film prior to its release.

Also in 1997, Knowles found himself in conflict with lawyers for Sony Pictures, which was in production on the movie adaptation of Robert A. Heinlein's science fiction classic *Starship Troopers*. AICN had posted images of the movie's monster adversaries, known as the Bugs. Sony claimed that AICN's hosting of the pictures, which had been sent to Knowles without the studio's knowledge or permission, was a case of serious copyright infringement—and they were right.

Knowles took the pictures down, though he remained defiant in the face of Sony's claims. Shortly afterward, the studio suddenly changed its tune. Attempting to court the good graces of AICN's founder (and, by extension, its many ticket-buying readers), Sony flew Harry Knowles out to attend the premiere of *Starship Troopers*. It was a complete 180 from the legal threats they had been making, and the move showed how highly sought Knowles's good opinion was.

Throughout the early days of AICN's rise to prominence, which was built largely on the back of a phalanx of unpaid writers, Knowles always insisted that his opinion was not for sale. He maintained that no movie studio could buy him for any price or inducement.

Sadly, as time went on, that didn't seem to be the case.

All success draws criticism, and the *Ain't It Cool News* phenomenon was to be no exception. The lion's share of bile was directed at Knowles himself—specifically, at the preferential treatment accorded to him by the movie studios whose products he would then go on to review. Harry Knowles was regularly flown to LA on the studio's dime to visit movie sets and attend gala premieres. His hotel room was paid for, and he was provided with spending money for the duration of the trip.

> **All success draws criticism, and the *Ain't It Cool News* phenomenon was to be no exception.**

After Knowles was vocally critical of the script for the 2000 movie *How the Grinch Stole Christmas*, its director, Ron Howard, flew him out to tour the sets in person, explaining his vision for the project to the internet movie critic. Then came a private advance screening of the movie at Universal Studios. Knowles duly wrote a glowing review and posted it to his site. Director Ridley Scott screened his sword-and-sandal epic *Gladiator* for Knowles and a cadre of his friends. More movie extravaganzas followed, many of which received strong word of mouth from Harry, even when the movie itself was weak.

The more all-expenses-paid trips he took to premieres and movie sets, the less negative Harry Knowles's reviews became—for the most part. (A notable exception is the poor review he gave the remake of *Rollerball*, despite being given the VIP treatment by its director, John McTiernan.) Over time, the reviews became every bit as much about his experiences meeting the movies' stars and directors as they were about the films themselves.

Writing about the Guillermo del Toro horror flick *Blade 2*, starring Wesley Snipes, Knowles penned what some claim to be the worst movie review ever written. The entire review employs the conceit of del Toro using his film to perform oral sex on a woman—in uncomfortably explicit detail. Even an open-minded reader might easily find the review disconcerting, to say the least.

The writing also betrayed a side of Harry Knowles that would cast him in an entirely different light some years later.

The likelihood is that Harry Knowles started out with the best of intentions: parlaying the popularity of AICN into success as an internet movie critic. Knowles's claim that he sought to protect moviegoers from wasting their money on bad films had the ring of truth about it.

Somewhere along the way, however, he lost his way. The power and influence he enjoyed were turned to a darker purpose. Knowles regularly hosted movie screenings and festivals at Austin's Alamo Drafthouse movie theater. In September of 2017, a female moviegoer came forward to say that he had groped her at the Alamo Drafthouse on multiple occasions.

The Alamo Drafthouse, a cinema-lover's cinema founded in Austin, Texas, played home to many of Knowles's events but severed ties with Knowles after assault allegations broke.

When confronted with the allegations, Knowles denied them. Days later, four more women came forward, each accusing him of similarly inappropriate behavior. One woman described him as "a predator," alleging a pattern of sexual harassment that had gone on for years. A Twitter user named Alejandra shared unsolicited, sexually suggestive messages sent to her from what appeared to be Knowles's account. "Your eyeliner makes you good enough to eat," declared one, followed by, "obviously, I'm talking cannibalism, baby. You can have my vienna sausage anytime."

"I thought it was just me getting creepy stuff from Harry," came one reply. "Thanks for speaking up. You're stronger than me."

There were claims that Knowles's alleged lewd behavior had been an "open secret" for years and that a number of the women he harassed did not speak up for fear of recrimination. Harry Knowles had a great deal of influence on the Austin film scene, and it's not unreasonable to think he would have had the power to blackball somebody from working in that community if he were so inclined.

In the aftermath of these claims, some of Knowles's most prominent writers began to jump ship from AICN, stating that they could no longer be a part of it in light of its founder's behavior. Advertisers followed. Sponsorship deals fell through. The Austin Film Critics Association expelled Knowles from the organization. Alamo Drafthouse banned him from every one of its movie theaters.

Shortly after the scandal broke, Knowles announced that he was stepping away from AICN and turning the reins over to his sister, Dannie. When asked online what his future plans were, Knowles tweeted back: "Therapy, detox, and getting to a better place." Unwilling to completely distance himself from the site he had started and grown so dramatically, he would continue to influence the site from behind the scenes—something that a few of his contributors found unacceptable.

There was also no admission of culpability and no apology. The latter would finally come more than two years later, on March 11, 2020. Posting at—where else?—*Ain't It Cool News*, Knowles apologized "to the women I hurt. I apologize to the readers I disappointed."

One hopes that the apology was sincere and was motivated by a desire to make amends. Some readers believed Knowles to have been genuinely contrite. Others saw it as a non-apology. Only Harry Knowles knows for sure. No charges were filed against him, and no criminal complaints were ever made.

In spite of the allegations against its creator, *Ain't It Cool News* still exists today. The site looks much as it always has, albeit with little in the way of contributions from "Headgeek"—aka Harry Knowles. Site traffic and readership interactivity are drastically reduced from AICN's peak.

As for Harry Knowles, although the influence he once exerted over the Hollywood moviemaking system is long gone, he remains an active presence on social media, where he continues to make his opinions known regarding movies and television.

# "Call Me Now!"

"**M**ISS CLEO HAS THE ANSWERS," declared the banner text splashed across millions of American television screens during the late 1990s and early 2000s. Beneath it was displayed a 1-800 number that would allow viewers to phone in for their "free" psychic reading.

The advice on offer covered a broad range of matters. Want to know when and where you'll meet the love of your life? Call Miss Cleo. Afraid your sweetheart is cheating on you? Miss Cleo can tell you if it is true or not. Questions about money? Business? No matter whether the affairs were of the heart or the bank account, the bombastic mystic had answers to them all.

"YOU CAN'T FOOL MISS CLEO!" a second banner insisted. After dazzling the credulous viewer with her preternatural powers, the psychic would sign off with her catch phrase, delivered with a smile and spoken in a broad Jamaican accent: "Call me now for your free tarot reading!"

Not all viewers saw the charade for what it truly was. Miss Cleo was, in fact, just a character, made up and portrayed by an actress named either Ree Perris, Youree Dell Harris, Youree Cleomili, or any one of several other names she used throughout her life. Her accent was every bit as affected as her supposed psychic powers were.

Upon calling the purported psychic's number for a "free" reading, victims would be connected to a call center filled with voice actors at rates up to $4.99 a minute.

Miss Cleo was the mouthpiece for a highly lucrative scam that was run under the auspices of the Psychic Readers Network and Access Resource Services, two Florida-based corporations overseen by Peter Stolz and Steven Feder. Callers who dialed the 1-800 number weren't connected to Miss Cleo, as the infomercials claimed, but to one of many paid "voice actors" employed by the company to give scripted answers for those seeking advice. With calls costing up to $4.99 a minute, many of the unsuspecting patrons wound up with bills that ran into the hundreds of dollars—far from the "free reading" they were promised. (Of that $4.99-per-minute rate, the voice actors themselves received less than $0.25.)

Things began to unravel after journalist Matt Bean blew the lid off the corrupt practices at the Psychic Readers network, using a phone reading of his own to confirm his suspicion that the entire thing was scripted. The Federal Trade Commission took an interest and, after an investigation, levied a host of fraud charges against both corporations. Several states, including Missouri and Florida, opened lawsuits. The phone lines rang off in 2002 for the last time.

**The actress was simply the most visible part of the corrupt money-making scheme.**

Even today, 20 years after the fraud was exposed, the whole sorry affair is still known as the Miss Cleo scandal. While the actress certainly bore her share of responsibility for bilking callers of millions of dollars, she was simply the most visible part of the corrupt money-making scheme. Harris liked to point out that she was never charged with any crime, let alone found guilty or imprisoned (as some widely circulated rumors still wrongly maintain).

However, as much as she protested her innocence, Youree Dell Harris knew full well that she was encouraging vulnerable members of society to give away their money for nothing more than a fiction. The marks targeted by this particular scam included the bereaved, the depressed, those who were desperate for a ray of hope. Instead, they got taken.

Youree Dell Harris died of cancer in Palm Beach, Florida, on July 26, 2016. She was 53 years old. Despite (or possibly because of) the notoriety that had swirled around the character of Miss Cleo, she had continued to give "psychic" phone readings long after the scandal was over.

# Hollywood Predator

The rise and fall of Miramax Films is a rags-to-riches-to-rags-again Hollywood story through which runs a horrifying vein of sexual abuse and intimidation on the part of its supremo, Harvey Weinstein. Even in an environment as infamously sleazy as Tinseltown, the extent of Weinstein's corruption and depravity is shocking and repulsive.

The Weinstein brothers, Harvey and Bob, formed the Miramax Film Corporation in 1979. Their intent was primarily to distribute movies they thought deserved more exposure. This was born from their love of independent films, particularly the work of filmmakers who were based overseas. At first, the Weinsteins weren't looking to make movies themselves. They were interested in putting obscure films in front of a wider audience and began picking up small, lesser-known movies for distribution throughout the United States.

Throughout the 1980s, Miramax slowly grew into a powerhouse of a company. The Weinsteins became increasingly involved with some of their pet projects, such as 1981 slasher movie *The Burning*, which Harvey had a hand in producing. This was early in his career, and Weinstein didn't yet wield the power of making or breaking the career of an actress if she didn't accede to his demands. Still, it was during the shooting of *The Burning* that some of Weinstein's more disturbing tendencies would surface.

In a 2017 interview with the *Buffalo News*, Paula Wachowiak recounted an ugly situation she found herself in while making the movie. Twenty-four years old at the time, Wachowiak was an intern on the movie and one day found herself taking checks to Weinstein's

room to be signed. Weinstein opened the door wearing nothing but a towel around his waist, which he dropped to accept the folder full of checks. After an awkward conversation about the checks, during which the folder was the only thing covering his genitals, Weinstein asked the horrified intern to give him a massage.

Much to her credit, Wachowiak refused, and she stood her ground when the producer tried to cajole and coerce her. She finally left the room with the signed checks, seriously upset. Based on reports from women who encountered him during his time as a music promoter, which pre-dated his involvement with movies, Paula Wachowiak was not the first woman to be sexually harassed by Harvey Weinstein. She was most definitely not the last.

The modern incarnation of a Hollywood casting-couch producer, Harvey Weinstein was in turns revered and feared as someone who could make or break careers.

Weinstein's M.O. was often to be naked or nearly naked when a female entered the room and then ask her to massage him, wash his back, or perform some other sexualized service. The assaults took place most often in hotel rooms and happened in different countries around the world as he traveled on business for Miramax. His chosen targets were invariably women who were within his control or his sphere of influence—women he judged had a high chance of giving in to his demands and then not talking about it afterward. Many were actresses, and a number felt pressured because they knew that if they rebuffed Weinstein's advances, he would make sure they would no longer get work in the motion picture industry.

According to statements made by many of Weinstein's victims, if a woman didn't take the hint, he would get more physical, trying to kiss or undress them against their will. Stories circulated among Miramax employees, particularly women, who sometimes went to meet with Weinstein in pairs, hoping to find a measure of protection.

As the 1980s faded into the 1990s, Miramax was going from strength to strength. Steven Soderbergh's relatively low budget *Sex, Lies, and Videotape* was a smash hit and helped really put the company on the map. Thanks to financing and investment opportunities, the Weinsteins were able to take a more active hand in producing movies. Miramax was a major player in putting independent or art-house movies out in both theaters and on home video, which was exploding in both sales and rentals. In 1993, the brothers sold the company to Walt Disney, with the proviso that they continue to run things their own way. They made millions of dollars on the deal. Miramax's profile was catapulted into the stratosphere when the company picked up Quentin Tarantino's seminal *Pulp Fiction*, which would be nominated for seven Academy Awards (and would win one). Over the years, Weinstein-backed movies have garnered hundreds of Oscar nominations.

As Harvey Weinstein's power and influence grew, he became bolder and more brazen with his various abuses. The moviemaking business is renowned for its cutthroat nature, yet even by those standards, Weinstein acquired an exceptional reputation for using bullying tactics to get what he wanted. Weinstein had a volatile temper and was easily provoked when things weren't going his way. Males and females alike were subjected to outbursts of rage, although men were spared his unwelcome sexual advances and assaults.

> **Rumors circulated among actors, producers, and crew about Weinstein's behavior, but for decades he seemed untouchable.**

Rumors circulated among actors, producers, and crew about Weinstein's behavior, but for decades he seemed untouchable. Harvey Weinstein was powerful, and therefore, he was understandably feared. Speaking out against him could end a career—or worse, which explains why so few people did so over the years. For his part, Weinstein came to regard himself as being beyond reproach. Time would ultimately prove him wrong about that.

Weinstein was almost outed in 2015 by a model named Ambra Battilana Gutierrez. After Weinstein grabbed her breasts and her thighs in a New York City hotel, she reported him to the police. Although the Manhattan district attorney's office did not file charges against the movie producer, time was running out for Harvey Weinstein.

In October of 2017, the deluge of accusations against Weinstein had reached critical mass. Until then, journalists had found it difficult to get his victims to go on the record. A story published in the *New York Times*, written by Jodi Kantor and Megan Twohey, finally remedied that. Here it was, laid out in black and white, for all the world to read: a piercing insight into Harvey Weinstein's sordid world. The revelations it contained were explosive and were supported by the testimony of multiple credible witnesses, most of whom had suffered indignity, abuse, and even outright assault at his hands.

Former actress Rose McGowan spoke out publicly against Weinstein and wrote about Weinstein's assault on her in a memoir titled *Brave*. McGowan recounted how Weinstein pushed her into the hot tub in his Utah hotel room, took off her clothes, and performed oral sex on her without her consent. (Weinstein denied that the assault ever happened.)

Revelations about Weinstein's behavior sparked a resurgence in the "Me Too" movement, which helped publicly unite many formerly quiet victims of abuse.

Ashley Judd stated that Weinstein used a variation of his frequent "give me a massage/let me give you a massage" routine and then tried to make her watch him while he showered. She made her excuses and left, but she never forgot Weinstein's appalling behavior toward her. Weinstein sought retribution by having Judd blacklisted from major film projects, such as Peter Jackson's *The Lord of the Rings*. Jackson was told that Judd and fellow actress (and spurner of Weinstein's advances) Mira Sorvino were both "a nightmare to work with." As a result, Jackson avoided casting them in his fantasy epic.

Although she did not go into specific detail, actress Angelina Jolie experienced a disturbing encounter with Weinstein that "was beyond a pass, it was something I had to escape." She refused to appear in future projects that Weinstein was involved with, such as Martin Scorsese's *The Aviator*.

Weinstein attempted damage control by paying off some of his accusers, requiring in return that they refrain from discussing the settlement in public. Yet there were so many accusations and allegations against him that it became impossible for him to silence them all. Weinstein's lawyers were quick to point out that in many cases, settlements are agreed to by the defendant to prevent themselves from being dragged through lengthy court proceedings—and that Weinstein's offering to settle, therefore, did not necessarily indicate his guilt. While this is true to a certain extent, the argument becomes increasingly less credible when one considers the sheer number of women accusing him of sexual predation—a figure reportedly close to or even exceeding one hundred.

October 2017 was a bad month for Harvey Weinstein. The "Me Too" movement, founded in 2009 by Tarana Burke in support of survivors of sexual violence, gained global attention when actress Alyssa Milano tweeted: "If you've been sexually harassed or assaulted write 'Me too' as a reply to this tweet." Milano replied "Me too" herself and penned a scathing indictment of Weinstein for *Rolling Stone* magazine the following January, stating that "Harvey Weinstein ripped a whole generation of actresses from society. An entire generation of talented, amazing, smart women that did not comply with his horrific demands was erased from the entertainment industry."

> "Harvey Weinstein ripped a whole generation of actresses from society."

Milano's tweet was retweeted more than 20,000 times. Tens of thousands of women used "Me too" as a response to indicate that they had been victims of sexual predation. Many male supporters stood in solidarity alongside them. One positive side effect of the Weinstein exposé was that a frank, long-overdue conversation about widespread sexual harassment and assault was finally beginning to take place.

Predictably, Harvey Weinstein apologized, saying, "The way I've behaved with colleagues in the past has caused a lot of pain, and I sincerely apologize for it." Considering the severity and enormity of the accusations against him, it is difficult to see this statement as anything other than pure public relations spin. Few people believed its sincerity, particularly those he had victimized. Weinstein's name became toxic overnight. He had become such a public liability that even his own company, the Weinstein Co., fired him from his position as CEO.

Apologizing from one side of his mouth, Weinstein denied the bulk of the accusations from the other. Still, they continued to mount, coming in from around the world, with some dating back to the 1980s. Actress Asia Argento stated that Weinstein had raped her in Cannes in 1997. She had been 21 at the time of the assault. Argento declared that the Cannes Film Festival had been "his hunting ground." Actresses Mira Sorvino and Gwyneth Paltrow added their voices to the chorus, as did many other women. Weinstein continued with his denials, speaking via his lawyer.

Georgina Chapman, Weinstein's wife, left him on October 11, taking their five children with her, saying that "my heart breaks for all the women who have suffered tremendous pain because of these unforgivable actions."

Convicted in both New York and Los Angeles, with more trials pending, in 2021 Weinstein was moved to the Twin Towers Jail, a stone's throw from Hollywood.

At the end of October, the Producer's Guild of America slapped Weinstein with a lifetime membership ban. Other professional organizations soon followed suit. Law enforcement agencies in both the United States and Europe launched criminal investigations into his activities in their respective nations. In May of 2018, police in New York charged Weinstein with rape and sexual abuse. He turned himself in and soon managed to bond himself out on a $1 million bail ticket—albeit with an electronic tag strapped to his ankle.

While he was awaiting trial in the summer of 2018, more charges were filed, and civil lawsuits were lodged against him by victims. Weinstein continued to plead not guilty. In 2019, an increasingly frail-looking Weinstein granted an interview in which he once again declared himself innocent. The gist of his reasoning was that he had done so much work promoting and enabling women in the film industry, how dare they be so ungrateful as to cast aspersions on his behavior now? He had donated hefty sums to charity and made sure that actresses were paid big bucks. If there was a victim in all this, his subtext seemed to say, then it was really Harvey Weinstein—the falsely accused, hard-done-by moviemaker.

Few people, if any, were buying his narrative. Still more accusations emerged prior to the beginning of his trial in January of 2020. The trial lasted for a month. At its conclusion, Weinstein was acquitted of some charges, but the jury found him guilty of third-degree rape and a first-degree criminal sexual act. The presiding judge sentenced him to 23 years' imprisonment. While he was serving his time, even more accusations surfaced.

At the time of writing, Weinstein is still in prison and awaiting another courtroom date, this one to decide the outcome of 11 more criminal charges that have been leveled against him. Just as he did before, the disgraced producer maintains his innocence. Whether he will be convicted remains to be seen, but given his advanced age and frail condition, it seems highly likely that Harvey Weinstein's story will end with his death behind bars.

We can only hope that Hollywood's corrupt practice of tolerating (and sometimes even celebrating) sexual predators will die along with him.

# Epstein's Island

It has long been said that the United States is the land of opportunity, a place where it is possible to go from humble origins to attaining great power, wealth, and influence. For some, that is the American Dream, and there are many famous examples throughout U.S. history. Take, for example, Abraham Lincoln, the rustic rail-splitter who educated himself and went on to hold the highest position in the land—the office of president of the United States.

Sometimes the American Dream can become corrupted, turning into something more akin to a nightmare. So it was with the financial mogul Jeffrey Epstein. Born in 1953, Epstein was raised in Brooklyn, New York. His parents worked solid, if unspectacular jobs and sent their two children to the local public schools. Their elder son was academically gifted and soon left the other children in his class behind. He had a natural aptitude for math but, as is sometimes seen with intelligent youths, could sometimes lack the discipline required to stay the course and finish a project. Epstein went to college but failed to graduate.

His lucky break came in the form of a job at the investment bank and brokerage Bear Stearns in 1976. Epstein's affinity for math soon got him noticed, and he was given a succession of increasingly pivotal roles within the firm that reflected his ability to understand and manipulate money.

Epstein spent five years at Bear Stearns, a period that essentially served as his apprenticeship in the world of financial wheeling and dealing. In 1981, he left the firm to start his own company. Lucrative contracts followed. This was the 1980s, the decade when greed and decadence became the very height of fashion, particularly on Wall Street. Toward the end of the decade, Epstein began catering his business to a very specific clientele: billionaires. He helped the uber-rich become even richer and lined his own pockets handsomely along the way.

Jeffrey Epstein's career rise seemed to epitomize the American Dream, working his way up from modest means to owning multiple properties, including his own Caribbean island with a sprawling resort complex. But for the young ladies lured into his orbit, Epstein's dreams were the stuff of nightmares.

Now immensely wealthy, Epstein had the financial means to cater to his dark side, a part of him that few people knew existed—at first. In 1998, he purchased his own private island in the U.S. Virgin Islands for just under $8 million. According to some, it was here, and to his upscale residences on the U.S. mainland, that Epstein brought underage girls, whom he would then sexually assault. Much of what happened on the island remains opaque. Epstein was a secretive man who took his privacy and security seriously, for obvious reasons. If the accounts of contractors who visited the island are to be believed, the residential areas were festooned with pictures of semi-naked women.

The island, one of two that Epstein purchased, was outfitted to the highest degree of luxury, a 72-acre paradise getaway for the financier. If some of the allegations against Epstein are true, however, then for the girls who were trafficked through there, it was a hellhole.

It is said that not just Epstein but also his friends and associates sexually assaulted girls and young women who were taken to the island and held captive there. Considering the location of the island, there is almost no way any of the perverted financier's victims could have made their escape. The only ways in or out were to fly, landing on the helipad, or to come by boat. Once the unsuspecting females were on the island, Epstein had control of their only means of leaving.

One of the many tragedies regarding the case is the fact that Jeffrey Epstein's term as a serial predator could, and most definitely should, have ended by 2008, when he was first charged with and convicted of sex crimes—prostituting a 13-year-old girl in the state of Florida. Because of an unbelievably lenient plea deal, rather than serving hard time, Epstein instead served just 13 months of a jail work-release program—time that he spent working in comfort out of his own office.

Why was he given such a privileged deal? Because of his vast wealth and influence. In all likelihood, if Jeffrey Epstein had been a blue-collar worker with only a few hundred dollars to his name, he would have been sent to a federal prison rather than a county jail.

> Why was he given such a privileged deal? Because of his vast wealth and influence.

Instead, he got off far too lightly and was thereby permitted to rape and abuse more innocent girls. Had Epstein been made to face federal charges instead of being charged at the state level, the chances are that he would have spent decades behind bars. Although he was required to register as a sex offender, the black mark on his record did absolutely nothing to curtail future abuses.

## In Custody and Denied Bail

Over the course of the next 12 years, Epstein continued to traffic vulnerable girls and women, both at his island and at his upstate private properties in the United States. On June 6, 2019, the net finally closed on him. When his private jet landed in New Jersey, he was arrested and taken into police custody. When questioned by detectives, he denied any involvement in human trafficking or sex crimes, claiming that as far as he was aware, all of the "women" who had engaged in sex with him were aged 18 or older. Considering the fact that some were as young as 11 years old, the claim was laughable.

Epstein was denied bail, with the judge understandably believing him to be a flight risk. Alarms were subsequently raised when Epstein was found in his New York prison cell with injuries to his neck, believed to be the result of a botched suicide attempt. He remained in prison and was placed on suicide watch.

For his 2008 conviction, Epstein received the kind of sweetheart plea deal only available to the very influential, but he still had to be listed in the sex offender registry.

On August 10, he was found hanging in his cell. With CPR in progress, Epstein was rushed to the hospital. Resuscitative efforts continued in the emergency department but were ultimately futile. The attending doctor pronounced Jeffrey Epstein dead. He was 66 years old.

The apparent suicide (as the coroner declared it to be) caused an uproar. Epstein had been taken off suicide watch, having convinced the authorities that he was not at risk for taking his own life. It would later emerge that the prison guards assigned to monitor Epstein had not been paying attention to their charge, choosing instead to surf the internet and take naps. For an eight-hour period overnight, the guards had not checked in on him once. To make matters worse, the pair then falsified duty logs in an attempt to cover up their inaction.

Jeffrey Epstein's in-custody death led to a slew of conspiracy theories. The phrase "Epstein didn't hang himself" went viral. One theory laid blame at the feet of former president Bill Clinton and his wife

Hillary, following the long-running conspiracy theory that the Clintons arrange to have their rivals and enemies murdered. Broken bones in Epstein's cervical spine led some to conclude that he had been forcibly strangled by somebody else instead of taking his own life.

There is no real evidence to support any of the theories, but it is not difficult to see why they became so popular. The broken bones in Epstein's neck can indeed occur in violent assaults, but they can also take place when a person hangs or strangles themselves. The fact that Epstein was taken off suicide watch is easily explainable when one considers the significant staffing shortages at the prison in which he died. While it is inexcusable that the guards did not check on him even once throughout the night, it is also true that the prison staff were pulling long hours of overtime shifts at the time. Rather than being paid off by some nefarious third party, it is far more likely that they were simply exhausted or demotivated.

## Prestigious Personalities

Jeffrey Epstein moved in highly prestigious circles. He socialized with presidents and princes, celebrities and billionaires. After his death, scrutiny turned to his associate, the socialite Ghislaine Maxwell, who was accused of procuring underage girls for Epstein to prey upon. At her trial in December 2021, several witnesses testified that Maxwell had coerced them into giving Epstein massages and having sexual intercourse with him.

In March 2022, despite pleading not guilty, Maxwell was found guilty on five out of six criminal charges, for sex trafficking and ensnaring underage female victims for Epstein to molest. Her legal team has launched an appeal. If it is unsuccessful, Maxwell is likely to spend the rest of her life behind bars.

Perhaps the best known of Epstein's associates was Prince Andrew, the younger brother of King Charles III of England. The prince was accused of having sex with a 17-year-old girl named Virginia Roberts Giuffre, which was allegedly arranged by Epstein, on three different occasions, one of them occurring on his private island. Prince Andrew denied the claims, but in the wake of these and other allegations, many were not convinced. An ill-advised interview given by the prince on BBC TV's *Newsnight* program in November 2019 backfired spectacularly, serving only to turn even more of the public's opinion against him. It emerged that Epstein, a convicted sex offender, had been the prince's guest at Windsor Castle and had attended other royal functions. Little wonder that the British people were outraged.

**Perhaps the best known of Epstein's associates was Prince Andrew, the younger brother of King Charles III of England.**

Prince Andrew categorically denied even remembering meeting his accuser, let alone having sex with her. That defense was easily refuted, in the form of a photograph showing Prince Andrew with his arm around the teenager's waist, while Ghislaine Maxwell hovers in the background. The picture, it is claimed, was taken by none other than Jeffrey Epstein himself—or, as the prince referred to him in the interview, "Mr. Epstein."

The common consensus was that Prince Andrew came across in the interview as emotionless and, crucially, completely unrepentant. Even if the accusations of unlawful sexual contact should prove to be untrue, he refused to accept any responsibility for having remained within Epstein's orbit despite knowing full well that he was a convicted sex offender. Her Majesty the Queen apparently agreed. She wasted no time in stripping her younger son of his royal title and the privileges that went along with it. He was not permitted to continue as the patron of numerous charities. Prince Andrew was no longer; all that remained was a man named Andrew Windsor.

Queen Elizabeth took this drastic action against her own son for one reason alone: to protect the British monarchy from being further tainted by the former prince's association with Jeffrey Epstein. Despite the fact that no criminal charges were leveled against the former prince, he still faced a potentially damaging and certainly deeply embarrassing civil lawsuit from Virginia Roberts Giuffre. Rather than undergo the humiliation of a potentially drawn-out legal process, Andrew, his reputation and public standing now in tatters, settled the case for an undisclosed amount of money in February of 2022.

# Spies Like Us

Corruption can take many different forms. In most of the examples explored in this book, we see instances of corruption that were carried out for material or financial gain. Others were evidenced by abuses of power, often performed by those who were in high office or privileged positions. Sometimes, the motivating factor was personal aggrandizement or satisfaction.

The case of Julius and Ethel Rosenberg is somewhat different. This married couple, who were convicted of passing on highly sensitive information to a foreign power, were not motivated by a desire for power or money. They did not commit their crime out of greed; on the contrary, Julius Rosenberg, who was the active partner of the two, acted as a matter of conscience.

Both of the Rosenbergs had familial connections with Russia. Julius's parents had both been born there prior to immigrating to the United States. The same was true of Ethel's father; her mother was Austrian by birth. After a seven-year courtship, they married in 1939, at the outbreak of World War II, and lived in New York. Both were avowed and unapologetic communists, as was David Greenglass—Ethel's younger brother, who, like Julius, was an engineer. Greenglass was not quite the true believer in communism that his sister and brother-in-law were, but that didn't stop him from becoming part of their spy ring.

Ethel and Julius Rosenberg, separated by a wire screen, leave the U.S. Court House in March 1953 after being found guilty of espionage.

Julius was an electrical engineer by training and found employment as a civilian working for the U.S. Army. During the course of the war, David Greenglass worked on the ultra-secret Manhattan Project at Los Alamos—the race to build a working atomic bomb. He leaked secret information to Julius Rosenberg, who in turn passed it on to Moscow.

After the defeat of Imperial Japan and Nazi Germany, there was a relatively brief period in which the United States and its Western allies were the only nations with the ability to construct and deploy nuclear weapons. Their leaders knew that Russia was rapidly gaining ground on this front, and the Western nations worked hard to guard their atomic secrets. This advantage lasted until August 29, 1949, when Russia detonated its own atomic bomb.

In addition to Greenglass, the Rosenbergs had also recruited other communist sympathizers to their cause, all of whom were scientific or technical specialists in their fields.

The spy ring began to unravel with the arrest of scientist Klaus Fuchs in 1950. Counterespionage agents scrutinized every aspect of Fuchs's professional and personal life, and the trail ultimately led them to David Greenglass and Julius and Ethel Rosenberg. Fuchs and Greenglass admitted to conducting espionage. The U.S. authorities had probable cause to arrest first Julius and then Ethel, immediately apprehending them for questioning. They were subsequently charged with conspiracy to commit espionage. Their spying did not constitute treason, as a state of war did not exist between the United States and Russia at the time.

The Rosenbergs did themselves few favors at trial. Although they denied the charges levied against them, they also chose to invoke the Fifth Amendment, the right to refuse answering questions to prevent incriminating themselves. Many understandably saw this as something that an innocent person would not have done. The choice to stand mute in court was as good as an admission of guilt in the eyes of much of the American public. Nor would the Rosenbergs name their co-conspirators.

The star witness was David Greenglass, whose testimony placed Julius Rosenberg squarely in the crosshairs of guilt. His story changed somewhat over the course of the trial, and there were lingering questions over Ethel's involvement in the affair. Greenglass cut a deal with authorities, and his reward for cooperating with the investigation was a 15-year prison sentence, of which he would actually serve less than ten years.

> **Although little argument can be made that Julius Rosenberg actively spied and passed on defense secrets to the Russians, some have questioned the validity of the case against Ethel.**

Although little argument can be made that Julius Rosenberg actively spied and passed on defense secrets to the Russians, some have questioned the validity of the case against Ethel. It is difficult to say with any degree of certainty just how much she knew of her husband's treasonous activities, although it cannot be denied that she was involved to some degree. Julius Rosenberg could have taken the responsibility for it all upon himself and attempted to exonerate his wife. He never did. Neither did Ethel attempt to throw her husband under the bus in an attempt to save herself. Say what you will about the Rosenbergs, but they undoubtedly had the courage of their convictions.

Their trial took place at the height of McCarthyism and the "Reds under the Bed" scare. Irving Kaufman, the presiding judge, refused to consider imprisonment for the Rosenbergs, stating his justification that their crime was "far worse than murder" and holding their actions responsible for the Korean War, which had already claimed more than 50,000 casualties. He concluded that Julius and Ethel had engaged in "a diabolical conspiracy to destroy a God-fearing nation."

Judge Irving noted that Julius was "the prime mover in this conspiracy," but he held Ethel equally accountable for her actions in assisting, rather than deterring, her husband, and described her as a "full-fledged partner in this crime."

After helping send his sister and brother-in-law to the electric chair, Greenglass later admitted to lying under oath to protect his wife, Ruth.

Espionage was a capital crime in 1953, and it remains so today. Anybody convicted under Title 18 of the United States Code section 794, "Gathering or delivering defense information to aid foreign government," can be sentenced to execution. Julius and Ethel Rosenberg were found guilty of conspiracy and were sentenced to death.

Both of the Rosenbergs would die in the electric chair on June 19, 1953, within ten minutes of one another. Julius went first. Ethel was given five high-voltage shocks before she finally died.

To this day, questions remain regarding the true extent of Ethel Rosenberg's involvement and knowledge of the scheme. History would ultimately show that her brother, David Greenglass, played up the extent of her activities, hoping to take some of the focus from the involvement of his wife, Ruth. He had testified to seeing Ethel typing out notes based upon the highly classified material, testimony that had gone a long way toward getting her convicted. It was only many years later that he recanted, admitting to having made it up. Greenglass had never seen Ethel transcribing anything. He died in 2014, unrepentant about his role in sending his sister and brother-in-law to Sing Sing's electric chair.

Attempts by the Rosenbergs' sons to gain a presidential pardon for their mother were unsuccessful, and it seems unlikely that history will soften its views of the couple any further than it already has.

# Sub Secrets

Throughout U.S. history, there have been those in positions of trust who were willing to sell out their nation's secrets to a foreign power for their own material gain. The damage done to national security can sometimes be incalculable.

## John Walker: Soviet Mole

During the late 1960s, former U.S. Navy warrant officer John Walker volunteered himself to become a Soviet mole. For the KGB, he was a godsend. Over the years that followed, Walker passed on a slew of naval technology secrets to the Russians, helping them render their submarines significantly quieter and more dangerous than ever. His motivation was simple: although he claimed to be ideologically disenchanted with the military and the American way of life in general, Walker was broke, and he realized he could make a fortune by putting the lives of his fellow sailors at risk.

Walker didn't just sell the Soviets technical data. He also revealed cutting-edge naval tactics—the specifics of how U.S. vessels would engage in battle against their enemies if war ever broke out. He revealed how to break the U.S. system of cryptography, allowing the Soviets access to encoded military and intelligence communications. Over the years he was active as a spy, along with a ring of co-conspirators, Walker was responsible for providing the enemy with a strategic and tactical edge that would have cost thousands of American lives in the event of World War III actually breaking out.

In a major blow to national security, John Walker successfully sold U.S. naval technology secrets to the Soviets for 18 years before his capture. Jonathan Toebbe, a civilian contractor working for the Navy, and his wife, Diana, were caught in attempted espionage by the FBI before they could do any actual harm.

In 1985, 18 years after he walked into the Soviet embassy in Washington, Walker was finally caught. His disgruntled ex-wife reported to the FBI that he was a turncoat. Her claim was backed up by their daughter. Their testimony made a credible case, and the Bureau placed him under surveillance. He was arrested, the spy ring he created was broken up, and Walker died in prison at the age of 77, before he was eligible for parole.

## Jonathan and Diana Toebbe: Would-Be Turncoats

Nearly four decades later, the Bureau would confront a similar case of corruption and espionage-for-profit. In October of 2021, FBI agents and U.S. Navy investigators arrested engineer Jonathan Toebbe and his wife, Diana, on suspicion of attempting to sell nuclear secrets overseas.

The Toebbes were well placed to obtain restricted data due to Jonathan's classified work with the Navy. He was a civilian contractor and possessed a security clearance that gave him access to highly sensitive material. Toebbe was an expert in the design and implementation of submarine power and propulsion systems, a field in which the United States leads the world. Diana was a humanities teacher.

Almost a year before their arrest, Jonathan and Diana Toebbe made clandestine contact, via the internet, with a person they thought was a spy from a foreign nation. Unbeknownst to them, the "spy" was in fact an FBI agent, who strung the unsuspecting couple along with promises while simultaneously building up a case against them for the crime of espionage.

According to the criminal complaint filed against them, on October 10, 2021, the Toebbes mailed off a packet of information along with a note asking the recipient to "please forward this letter to your military intelligence agency. I believe this will be of great value to your nation." Up for sale were technical specs pertaining to U.S. submarines, including classified operations manuals and various performance thresholds. For obvious reasons, the Navy does not like its enemies to know the limits and capabilities of its weapons systems and platforms, particularly those that rely on stealth and secrecy to survive—such as the new Virginia-class fast-attack sub.

With the fish now hooked, the FBI slowly began to reel the Toebbes in. The agents couldn't move too quickly lest they risk scaring the spies off before gathering enough evidence to convict them in court; at the same time, there was the possibility that the amateur spies were shopping the stolen secrets around to other nation states and might find a genuine buyer. The consequences for U.S. naval supremacy were potentially catastrophic if that information found its way into the wrong hands.

> **With the fish now hooked, the FBI slowly began to reel the Toebbes in.**

To keep the Toebbes interested, the federal agents sent the equivalent of $10,000—not in U.S. dollars but in the form of cryptocurrency, which the Toebbes believed would be harder to trace than cash. Jonathan was reluctant to deal face to face, fearing entrapment, but agreed to make an exchange in Washington, D.C., over the

Memorial Day weekend of 2021. Although the FBI has not publicly released the identity of the country to whom they were trying to sell data, the agency has acknowledged that it managed to place a prominent "sign" of some kind in a D.C. building associated with it.

Whatever that sign was, the Toebbes wrote back and confirmed that they had seen it. This reinforced the notion in their mind that they really were communicating with agents of another country and not being set up. In June, the couple delivered intelligence to a dead drop location under direct observation by the FBI. The data was contained on a SanDisk, which they had placed inside a peanut butter sandwich. Agents wired them $20,000 in return.

> **The data was contained on a SanDisk, which they had placed inside a peanut butter sandwich.**

Another information delivery took place the following month. The Toebbes worked as a team, with Jonathan making the physical drop-off and Diana standing watch, looking out for anybody trying to surveil them. Success seemed to have emboldened him, because in August, he made another dead drop, this one solo—a move that netted him another $20,000.

On the basis of the evidence gathered to that point, FBI special agent Justin Van Tromp obtained an arrest warrant and brought Jonathan and Diana in for questioning.

In February of 2022, Jonathan Toebbe's lawyers agreed to a plea deal that would see him plead guilty to conspiracy to communicate restricted data. The case against Diana Toebbe was less advanced than that against her husband, but as somebody who at a minimum aided and abetted her husband in selling sensitive material to what she believed was a foreign country, she was unlikely to receive a great deal of leniency. In fact, Diana ended up receiving the harsher sentence. In August of that year, both Jonathan and Diana pleaded guilty to the conspiracy, and their sentences came in November. Jonathan Toebbe was sentenced to 232 months, over 19 years, of incarceration. Diana Toebbe was sentenced to 262 months, more than 21 years, of incarceration.

"The Toebbes were willing to compromise the security of the nation by selling information related to naval nuclear propulsion systems; they are now being held accountable for their actions," said Special Agent in Charge Mike Nordwall of the FBI Pittsburgh Field Office, as quoted in a U.S. Department of Justice release dated November 9, 2022. "The FBI and our federal partners have an unwavering commitment to protect U.S. secrets and will continue to aggressively investigate and expose espionage activities conducted on U.S. soil."

To all appearances, the Toebbes were just an average, all-American couple. In reality, they are living proof of the dictum that no matter how much one tries to safeguard sensitive information, no matter how many passwords, firewalls, and locked doors are put in place, the greatest threat to data security will always come in the form of corrupt human beings.

# Black Sox, Green Bills

In the early 20th century, baseball was America's favorite national pastime. Going out to the ballgame was a big event for families. Parents and children bonded in the stands, rooting for their team to win. Fans obsessed over the stats of their favorite players, and youngsters idolized those who hit the most home runs, dreaming of being star athletes themselves someday.

At the professional level, the sport was big business. Because of their prominent standing within society, not only were pro ballplayers put up on a pedestal by their supporters, but they were also held to high standards for honesty, integrity, and sportsmanship. This only made the 1919 Black Sox scandal all the more devastating.

The scandal centered on the Chicago White Sox, who were competing in the 1919 World Series—a championship sequence where they would face their rivals, the Cincinnati Reds. A group of White Sox players conspired to throw games, fixing the result to the detriment of their own team but to the benefit of everybody who bet on the Reds—including themselves. Gamblers loved baseball, wagering big money on each game, particularly something as high profile as the World Series.

> **Game fixing was nothing new to baseball. In fact, it was something akin to an open secret.**

Game fixing was nothing new to baseball. In fact, it was something akin to an open secret. Corruption had been endemic in professional baseball since the Civil War. Those who stood to gain from it did everything in their power to keep the public from finding out, recognizing that they had a vested interest in preserving the perceived sanctity of the sport. Many fans believed their baseball idols to be beyond reproach, and to be fair, many were. Many, but not all. In reality, professional baseball was far more corrupt than most Americans realized.

The cabal of athletes who masterminded the game fixing planned their crime carefully and enlisted the help of powerful bookmakers. Chicago White Sox owner Charles Comiskey heard tell of the intended fraud before the first ball of the first game had even been thrown. Rather than put a stop to it, Comiskey chose instead to let the matter ride. It became obvious to him after the first game, in which the White Sox played well below their usual standard, that something was wrong. The Sox had lost that outing 9–1. Their second game saw them defeated 4–2 by the Reds.

Keen-eyed, longtime observers of the sport also began to smell a rat. By the time the 1919 World Series finally ended in a 5–3 game loss for the White Sox, Comiskey's suspicions were confirmed: they had lost on purpose. Word had also leaked into the press before the series was over.

The corrupt players and their gambling associates had made tens of thousands of dollars because of the losses. They had also gotten away with it—in the short term, at least. Rather than turn them in, Comiskey instead kept them on the team for the following season. This seemed like a shrewd business decision at the time, but it backfired spectacularly

Despite their acquittal, the eight players implicated in the Black Sox scandal were banned from the game.

when accusations of World Series game fixing were made public by the autumn of 1920.

The scandal soon became a courtroom trial. Under intense legal scrutiny, some of the conspirators began to confess to their role in rigging the games. Other members of the White Sox stood firm, insisting that they had never thrown a game. Lasting for two weeks in late July 1921, the trial was a tedious one, filled with claim and counterclaim of fixing and rigging. Finally, when the dust settled, the jury found all eight of the so-called Black Sox defendants not guilty. The newly acquitted men immediately went out on the town to celebrate. Astonishingly, they met up with members of the jury who had determined their fate and partied late into the night.

Many found the acquittal hard to swallow, particularly as some of the players had made confessions. A black mark would almost certainly have appeared by each of the eight men's names for the rest of their baseball careers—if, that is, they still had careers to go back to. In an unexpected ruling, Judge Kenesaw Mountain Landis, the country's first elected commissioner of baseball, slapped each of them with a lifetime ban. The Black Sox Eight would never be permitted to play professional baseball again. They became pariahs overnight and were forced to find employment outside the sport.

Even today, more than a century after the story broke, many of the details of the Black Sox scandal remain controversial and opaque. Baseball historians debate many aspects, particularly the legal elements and the jury acquittal of the eight accused players. Conflicting testimony and some outright falsehoods make it challenging to separate fact from fiction.

One point that cannot be argued is the impact that prosecuting the Black Sox players, and barring them from the game for life, had on professional baseball. Instances of game fixing and cheating fell dramatically, making the scandal one of the pivotal events in cleaning up a corrupt industry at the heart of the nation's greatest sporting passion.

# King of the Ring

In 1976, the United States was caught in the grip of Bicentennial fever. Two hundred years before, a loose-knit band of militiamen and rebels came together as the Continental Army. Under the leadership of General George Washington, they would go on to bloody the nose of the finest fighting force in the world—the superbly drilled, highly experienced British Redcoats under the command of Charles Cornwallis. Thus was ensured the birth of a new nation, one that was intended to be a meritocracy, free from the hidebound strictures of the monarchy from which it had forcibly cut ties.

Understandably, many Americans thought that the 200th anniversary was something well worth celebrating, and celebratory events sprang up across the nation. There were also those individuals who were motivated more by profit than patriotism and sensed an opportunity to cash in on this once-in-a-lifetime occurrence.

Such a man was boxing promoter Don King. King was one of the most colorful characters on the professional boxing scene. He liked to dress eccentrically and was instantly recognizable for his upstanding hair, which evoked comparisons to that of Albert Einstein. More memorable still was the fact that King had actually killed two men during his rise to power and influence in the sporting world.

Renowned promoter Don King (top right) stands with legendary boxer Roy Jones, who is being interviewed after winning his match with Felix Trinidad.

In 1954, the Cleveland-born King, then 23 years old, was making his money by working various illegal gambling rackets. King owned and operated underground gambling houses. Catching a man named Hillary Brown in the act of robbery one day, King had no compunction about shooting him dead. King escaped jail time, with the jury ruling the killing to be a case of justifiable homicide.

He would not get away scot-free the second time, however. On April 20, 1967, King kicked 34-year-old former employee Samuel Garrett to death. The two men had argued over money that Garrett owed King. Although King would subsequently claim that he had been attacked by Garrett and fought back in self-defense, the jury was told that the savage, fatal beating King inflicted on Garrett had continued even when the latter was helpless on the ground. Garrett was unresponsive, not moving, yet King still kicked him in the head. It took the bludgeoned man five days to die.

The jury didn't buy King's claims of self-defense and found him guilty of second-degree murder. That conviction should have carried a life sentence. Instead, the judge reduced the charge from murder to manslaughter for reasons that remain unclear to this day. Don King walked free from prison in

1971, having served less than four years behind bars for the crime of taking a human life. In 1983, he would be pardoned by Ohio governor Jim Rhodes.

Following his release on parole, King put in the hours and effort it took to become one of the leading promotors on the boxing scene. He had a flair for showmanship that

> **He had a flair for showmanship that became evident in some of the epic clashes he arranged, such as the infamous 1974 "Rumble in the Jungle" between Muhammad Ali and George Foreman.**

became evident in some of the epic clashes he arranged, such as the infamous 1974 "Rumble in the Jungle," which saw Muhammad Ali square off against George Foreman. The fight took place in Zaire and was watched by a crowd of 60,000. Foreman was the odds-on favorite to win, which made it all the more stunning when Ali knocked him out in the eighth round. Afterward, King's bank account bulged with profits.

One year later, King promoted the "Thrilla in Manila," in which Ali fought Smokin' Joe Frazier. Even today, it is considered one of the greatest fights of all time, a brutal slugfest that pushed both athletes to their physical limits. Ali won in a technical knockout.

Don King had a well-earned reputation for being less than forthright with his business dealings. The FBI investigated him for allegedly doctoring the physical records of fighters he represented. In 1976, the promoter teamed up with ABC Sports to create and promote the fledgling United States Boxing Championships, a televised tournament intended to capitalize on the tidal wave of patriotism sweeping the country. The American public fervently loved boxing, not just because of the good fighters the United States produced but also because of the strong showing from Team USA in the 1976 Olympic Games that summer, with seven medals for boxing (five of them gold), and the Sylvester Stallone movie *Rocky*, which was both a box office smash and a critical hit when it was released in November of that year.

The United States Boxing Championships would feature boxers from each of the different weight classes going head-to-head to find the "best in the nation." Many of the fighters were repped by King, which made the event a massive payday for him no matter who won the bouts. There was just one catch: not all of the fighters were signed with King before they entered the tournament. The wily promoter made entry into the U.S. Boxing Championships conditional on their committing to a contract with him. In other words, if the fighters wanted a shot at the title, they had to go through Don King to get there.

> **Some of the candidates were, to put it mildly, not great fighters. King couldn't care less.**

Some of the candidates were, to put it mildly, not great fighters. King couldn't care less. To lend his selections some credibility, King engaged the services of *Ring Magazine*, U.S. boxing's most-read periodical. *Ring Magazine* had long maintained a ranking system for American fighters, which the promoter now intended to manipulate. After a few words from King, some of the weaker, relatively inexperienced boxers who had signed contracts with him suddenly shot up in *Ring*'s rankings without having earned the boost by fighting anybody. Some had fights turn up on their records that were entirely bogus, giving them credit for boxing matches that had never taken place.

For its part, *Ring Magazine* not only got paid for the privilege of the U.S. Boxing Championships using its ranking system as a baseline for contestant ratings, but it also benefited from a healthy publicity boost for being a crucial part of the tournament. King arranged a series of increasingly esoteric venues for the championship fights, including the prison where he had served time for killing Samuel Garrett. The whole fiasco began to unravel at the U.S. Naval Academy in Annapolis, Maryland, when a final decision declared boxer Scott LeDoux to be the loser of his heavyweight bout. LeDoux was justifiably enraged. He had not signed with King but had somehow made it into the tournament anyway, only to lose in a decision he believed King had fixed.

As commentator Howard Cosell interviewed the winning fighter, Johnny Boudreaux, a furious LeDoux launched an attack on him. Standing on the ropes at the edge of the ring, LeDoux bellowed: "You tell it like it is, Howard! You tell the truth!"

In what must have been one of televised professional boxing's most surreal moments up to that point, one of the flurries of hits and kicks knocked Cosell's toupee off his head—live on ABC network television.

"It was so frustrating," LeDoux explained later in a televised interview. "Prior to that, I was training in Montreal, and they were asking about the fight with Boudreaux. I said that I'm gonna knock him down, kick his butt, beat him up … and they said: 'You won't get the decision. We heard on the street it's already done.'"

They were right. The fight had already been decided in favor of the boxer who was signed to Don King. King wanted to monopolize ownership of as many titled American fighters as possible, and this was his attempt to make that happen. A federal grand jury was convened to investigate allegations of fight fixing. The scandal was enough to shut down the championship tournament before it could be completed. ABC sought to distance itself from the scandal and, by extension, King. The network learned that it had been chumped by King and the falsified rankings system in *Ring Magazine*.

Controversies notwithstanding, Don King has continued to work as a boxing promoter into his nineties.

Incredibly, although a number of those involved with the scandal lost their jobs and were sanctioned for their part in it, Don King escaped without a blemish. No charges were ever filed against him. As the 1970s gave way to the 1980s, his power and influence within the field of professional boxing continued to grow. So did the dislike many of his own fighters held for him. In a number of the big-money fights he promoted, both boxers were King signees, meaning that he got paid no matter which of them was victorious. Although up-and-coming fighters were not forced to become part of King's stable, the savvy boxer knew that it was much more difficult to set foot on the ladder without a nod from the man himself.

Don King liked to make the rules and penalized those who would not bend the knee to him by freezing them out of professional boxing as much as his influence would allow. He remains a controversial and polarizing individual to this day. On the one hand, he was inducted into the Boxing Hall of Fame, an honor reserved for those who have made a significant impact upon the sport. While it cannot be denied that Don King most certainly made his mark, many would debate whether that was a good thing.

As of March 2023, Don King is 91 years old and continues to work as a boxing promoter, as he has done for more than half a century. Nobody can deny that he has left his indelible mark on the sport of pro boxing.

# Winter Wonderland

History tells us that the first Olympic Games on record were held in ancient Greece in the year 776 BCE. In all likelihood, the games pre-dated that event by hundreds of years. Held once every four years, the purpose of the games was twofold: to honor Zeus, the supreme god in the Greek pantheon, and to celebrate and encourage excellence—a trait that the Greeks considered to be one of the most important virtues.

Inevitably, as time went on, corruption seeped into the Olympic Games, as it did into all other aspects of life. In violation of the spirit of the games, the Roman emperor Nero Claudius Caesar Augustus Germanicus changed the date of the games from 66 to 67 CE, just so he could personally take part. Having all of the resources of the world's most powerful empire at his disposal should have made him a lock to win, but Nero wasn't willing to take any chances.

Nero had his sights set on witting glory in the chariot races. To that end, he spared no expense in obtaining the finest team of horses and chariot that money could buy. On the day of the race, the gods did not smile on Nero. He was thrown from his chariot mid-race and was unable to finish the race, let alone win it. It didn't matter. Although the Olympic ethos dictated that the winning charioteer be proclaimed champion, Nero had bribed the judges with vast

**In 1998, word got out of a scandal surrounding Salt Lake City's bid to be the 2002 Winter Olympic venue.**

sums of money to ensure that he was accorded the laurels and declared victor at the end.

Fast forward almost two millennia, and Olympic Games corruption would taint the United States. In 1998, word got out of a scandal surrounding Salt Lake City's bid to be the 2002 Winter Olympic venue.

The city that will be granted the honor of hosting the Summer or Winter Olympic Games is selected by the International Olympics Committee, or IOC. The committee is supposed to make its decision based on a fair and competitive bidding process that takes into account multiple factors, all of which speak to the bidding city's ability to host such a major event. To be considered eligible, candidates must demonstrate that they have sufficient financial standing, adequate infrastructure, and a track record of hosting major events.

Each member of the IOC casts their vote by means of a secret ballot. Whichever city gets the most votes is awarded the privilege of hosting the next Olympiad. In an attempt to maintain some degree of impartiality, the rules forbid any member of the committee from voting for a city in the same country of which they are a citizen.

Of equal importance is the oath taken by each IOC member that they will accept nothing of monetary value in exchange for influencing the casting of their vote.

The group charged with compiling and delivering a competitive bid for Utah's capital city to host the 2002 Winter Olympic Games was the Salt Lake Organizing Committee, or SLOC. Launching an all-out effort to win over the IOC, the committee spent in the approximate value of one million dollars on kickbacks aimed at those who, they hoped, would reward their gifts by granting their city the Games.

Allegations would later surface that, in addition to cash payments, some of the money was used to purchase expensive watches or to send IOC members and their families on vacations. Others got parts of their houses remodeled or were given prime seating for big sporting events. Salt Lake Organizing Committee money was even used to pay for the college tuition of the children of IOC voters.

Salt Lake City, seen here in its cheerful overdressings for the 2002 Winter Olympics, was selected to host the Games after successfully lobbying the IOC with lavish gifts.

In the summer of 1995, the official announcement was made by the IOC. Salt Lake City had been chosen to host the 2002 Winter Olympic Games. The SLOC's campaign had been a resounding success. Four years later, a Utah TV news reporter would break word of the scandal publicly.

In 1999, for the first time in more than a century, the IOC expelled six of its members for their role in the 2002 Winter Olympics scandal. The disgraced individuals came from Samoa, Chile, Sudan, Ecuador, Mali, and Republic of the Congo. All had been found guilty of taking bribes in exchange for awarding the 2002 Games to Salt Lake City.

In a parallel with the way in which host cities are chosen, the IOC voted on each of their expulsions by casting secret ballots. Four other committee members went on to resign their posts. When the dust settled, none of those accused were charged with criminal offenses.

Although there would be future instances of corruption unveiled within the IOC, the Salt Lake City scandal triggered a series of attempts to reform the bidding and selection process within the IOC.

In the United States, the scandal would be settled in federal court. Thomas Welch, president of the SLOC, was charged with bribery, mail fraud, wire fraud, and other corruption-related offenses, alongside the committee's vice president, David Johnson. The Justice Department declined to prosecute any other members of the SLOC.

> **The Salt Lake City scandal triggered a series of attempts to reform the bidding and selection process within the IOC.**

After hearing the evidence put forward by the prosecution, Judge David Sam declared the entire case to be so devoid of value that it "offends my sense of justice." In other words, Welch and Johnson were guilty of no crime in his eyes. Judge Sam acquitted both men of all charges.

Welch and Johnson were the only Salt Lake Organizing Committee members to be charged with a crime and were so convinced that they had done nothing wrong that they turned down a plea deal that would have gotten them off with a mere misdemeanor. Both men steadfastly maintained their right to a trial by jury. When it was over, although neither man was vindicated, they did at least leave the courtroom with clean legal records.

Many felt that what the SLOC had done was ethically questionable but by no means criminal, pointing out that the U.S. taxpayer footed the bill for an extensive investigation and courtroom trial that ultimately went nowhere. Was this a case of corruption or simply one of local officials trying to do their best on behalf of their home city?

At the time of writing, Salt Lake City is a potential candidate to host either the 2030 or 2034 Winter Olympic Games.

# Tour de Lance

Americans, it is fair to say, love a winner. This is especially true in the world of professional sports. As a nation, we don't just look up to our top-performing athletes; we idolize them, lionizing their achievements and placing them up on a pedestal. Sadly, this means that when corruption and scandal strikes, the fall is further and the damage much greater than it might otherwise have been.

A prime example comes in the form of professional cyclist Lance Armstrong, whose meteoric rise to fame was followed by an equally precipitous fall from grace.

Armstrong was born in Plano, Texas, in 1971. As a junior athlete, he was both motivated and highly competitive. His stepfather later expressed regret at how brutally hard he drove his stepson, but Armstrong's own recollection put a more concerning slant on it, claiming that his stepfather beat him mercilessly for even the most minor infractions, such as leaving a drawer open or failing to keep his room tidy.

As a teenager, Armstrong's grueling training regimen prepared him to compete in the triathlon, an event at which he would repeatedly excel. At 15, he was too young to enter his first races, but he thought nothing of doctoring a birth certificate to make himself seem eligible to enter. Perhaps foreshadowing his propensity for deceit, the trick worked.

Triathlon requires the athlete to bike, swim, and run, but Armstrong was particularly gifted when it came to cycling. His continual success caught the eye of the U.S. Cycling Federation, and soon he began racing at the professional level, earning a spot on the Motorola team. The year 1992 saw him representing the United States in the Olympic Games. The following year, he began competing in the Tour de France, winning stages twice but finding it a challenge to finish the entire race. That same year also saw him become world champion, a truly remarkable feat.

Lance Armstrong's career has seen him become triathlete, Tour de France winner, motivational speaker, disgraced athlete, and venture capitalist.

Although Armstrong was a superb athlete, in excellent physical condition, it became clear to him that something was wrong. That something was, unfortunately, an aggressive form of testicular cancer. A comprehensive and time-consuming treatment program meant that he was no longer able to race, needing to focus instead on beating the cancer, which had metastasized as far as his brain. Surgeons cut out as much as they could, and oncologists supplemented their efforts with chemotherapy. Despite the fact that testicular cancer has a relatively good prognosis if treated effectively—around 80 percent of men survive it, particularly if it is caught early (which Armstrong's was not)—it was by no means an easy road to recovery for him.

Lance Armstrong was no stranger to overcoming adversity. He attacked the cancer with all the grit and determination he had employed to win races. To call the journey back to wellness difficult would be an understatement. Some men, if put in his position, would have given up on their dreams of sporting success. That would have been completely understandable, but Armstrong was not willing to quit. Once the cancer was under control, he began to train again, slowly at first but gradually building back up to his former levels of fitness. By 1998, he was a member of the Postal Service Pro Cycling Team and back on the road to glory.

Not only do Americans love a winner, but they also love a good comeback story. An athlete returning to compete after defeating cancer checked all the right boxes. It was something everybody could get behind. Unfortunately, there was

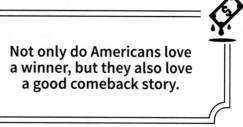

**Not only do Americans love a winner, but they also love a good comeback story.**

also a darker side, which didn't come to light until several years after Armstrong went back to professional cycling. To enhance his performance, Armstrong had engaged in a forbidden practice known as "doping," taking drugs or other substances to boost performance—in his case, the hormone erythropoietin, or EPO for short.

To be fair, he was far from the only pro cyclist doing this. The practice of doping was rife throughout the cycling world during the 1990s and 2000s. Armstrong himself would later claim that the practice was so prevalent that engaging in doping was the only way to win; without the boost it provided, it was almost impossible to remain competitive.

No matter what their chosen sport is, professional athletes are, by nature, extremely competitive. The majority abide by honest, ethical standards, but there will always be those who are willing to do whatever it takes to gain an edge over their competitors.

EPO is something that we all have in our bodies. The hormone stimulates the production of red blood cells, which are the main transport mechanism for oxygen. The more red blood cells an athlete has, the bigger the oxygen-carrying capacity, which means they tire less easily and are able to sustain intense physical activity for longer. This is particularly beneficial for performance at high altitudes, where the air is thinner and contains less oxygen. (To put this in perspective, the highest points of the Tour de France can peak at around 9,000 feet above sea level—that's almost two miles high.)

Professional athletes are regularly tested for illegal drugs and enhancers, but by its very nature, EPO can be tricky to screen for. Neither is its prohibited use confined to the arena of cycling. Any sport in which success requires aerobic endurance (which is most of them) could potentially see abuse of EPO. Championship boxing, for example, has also seen its own doping scandals.

## Too Good to Be True?

As comebacks go, Armstrong's was stratospheric. Between the years 1999 and 2005, he won the Tour de France no fewer than seven times, blowing his previous track record out of the water. As it happens, Armstrong had been producing his own blood and clandestinely storing it for use during races. This form of cheating is exceptionally difficult to detect.

Because his level of success looked too good to be true—which it was—it soon attracted the attention of the United States Anti-Doping Agency, or USADA. The agency assembled a strong case against him, but Armstrong flatly denied being involved in doping. So did his co-conspirators, including the Postal Service Team physician and trainer who not only knew about the outlawed practice but actively abetted it. The denials stood for a decade, even as the volume of evidence continued to mount.

> As comebacks go, Armstrong's was stratospheric. Between the years 1999 and 2005, he won the Tour de France no fewer than seven times.

Along the way, he used strong-arm tactics in an attempt to beat down his detractors, blatantly lying to destroy their credibility. The victims included former teammates, their families, and reporters who had written articles about Armstrong allegedly doping. In 2004, Armstrong cast serious aspersions on the work of an investigative journalist working for Britain's *Sunday Times*, David Walsh, who was among the very first to raise the possibility of doping being a factor in the cyclist's success. Armstrong tried to sue Walsh and the paper into retracting what turned out to be the actual truth. The newspaper settled, for the sum of one million pounds, and had to make a public apology.

One can only imagine how Walsh felt. Following good journalistic practices, he had spoken to multiple sources for confirmation before submitting his article for publication. These had included several insiders, such as fellow members of Armstrong's own team. Once the truth finally came to light, the *Sunday Times* sued Armstrong and got its money back in a settlement payment from the disgraced cyclist. These events were later dramatized in the 2015 movie *The*

*Program*, directed by Stephen Frears and starring actors Chris O'Dowd as Walsh and Ben Foster as Armstrong.

In 2012, Armstrong received a lifetime ban from professional cycling races. The following January, in a move that shocked many, he agreed to be interviewed by popular TV host Oprah Winfrey. In front of an audience of millions, he finally confessed to having regularly taken EPO. While he did admit to doping, the ever-confident Armstrong appeared far from contrite. He accepted responsibility but cited various reasons as to why he had broken the rules, which many viewers and critics perceived as mere excuses. The interview polarized the sporting world, with most siding against Armstrong, and opened up a huge can of legal worms.

Lance Armstrong's third place in 2009's Tour de France was reassigned in 2012 after the doping scandal broke wide open.

His various championship titles were retroactively stripped away by governing bodies. Armstrong went from making millions of dollars in sponsorship fees to being a virtual pariah almost overnight. Then came the lawsuits, which cost millions more to settle. In a landmark case, the U.S. federal government came at him with a $100 million legal action filed by the Justice Department on behalf of the Postal Service. He ultimately accepted an offer to settle for $6.65 million, a Pyrrhic victory if ever there was one.

> **The doping scandal was undoubtedly a tragedy for American sports, not least because of the revelation that a significant number of America's top-rated cyclists had only achieved success by cheating.**

The doping scandal was undoubtedly a tragedy for American sports, not least because of the revelation that a significant number of America's top-rated cyclists had only achieved success by cheating. The USADA's CEO, Travis Tygart, declared that not just

Armstrong, but also his entire team, engaged in "the most sophisticated, professionalized and successful doping program that sport has ever seen." The illusions of many American cycling fans were shattered, and their faith in the sport plummeted as a result. The impact upon the foundation that bore his name was devastating. The Lance Armstrong (now Livestrong) Foundation had made great strides in the battle against cancer, and while it continues to do so, Armstrong's tarnished reputation meant that he had to sever ties with the organization, which subsequently rebranded itself in an effort to distance itself from the negative connotations.

One positive change that came from the Lance Armstrong doping scandal was that the field of professional sports cracked down upon EPO abuse, requiring athletes to submit multiple blood samples throughout the course of a year so that a more accurate baseline could be established and monitored. This is by no means a perfect measure, but regular testing has at least made it harder for dopers to cheat their way to success.

Despite the best efforts of the USADA and the thousands of honest men and women who make up the world of professional cycling, doping remains a problem in 2023. Historically, this has always been the case. A hundred years ago, contestants in the Tour de France took cocaine to enhance their performance. Coke gave way to amphetamines, another stimulant that gave some riders "a little extra kick." Both cocaine and amphetamines are dangerous, even potentially lethal, and while EPO is not completely safe either, it is a much less risky proposition for the user.

The war against doping is far from won, and although strides have been made toward stamping it out, constant vigilance is still required to prevent the practice from spreading.

# The Art of the Ponzi Scheme

There's an old saying in life: if it looks too good to be true, then it probably is. Con artists and scammers routinely exploit the all-too-human desire to grab what looks like a great deal. The people they prey on, in turn, tend to forget another valid saying: there's no such thing as a free lunch.

One example is the Ponzi scheme, a fraudulent method of investing that lures in the unwary mark by promising high returns on the money they invest, and little to no risk. In reality, of course, there's no such thing as a high-yield, low-risk investment. If you want to win big in the short term, you have to gamble big—and be extremely lucky.

The scheme takes its name from one Charles Ponzi, a fraudster who operated in Boston during the 1920s. Like many con artists, Ponzi affected a polished and charming image. Wearing tailored suits, immaculately buffed shoes, and without a perfectly manicured hair out of place, he looked every inch the sort of savvy entrepreneur with whom investors would be comfortable placing their money.

Ponzi was literate and well spoken, possessing the so-called gift of gab. It was easy to strike it rich, Ponzi claimed: all you had to do was entrust your money to him, sit back, and let the profits roll in. He promised potential investors outrageous returns, claiming

Charles Ponzi may not have originated the type of swindle that now bears his name, but he certainly earned the associated infamy.

that they could easily double their stake—or more. The idea was a simple and convincing one, as many good lies are: Ponzi was the owner of a commercial enterprise that bought postage coupons in countries abroad where they were cheap and sold them in the United States at a significant markup. On the face of it, his sales pitch seemed plausible, and it was compelling enough to entice investors in droves.

The catch was, of course, that Charles Ponzi wasn't investing their hard-earned money in anything. The Securities Exchange Company that he touted as the basis for his get-rich-quick investments was nothing more than smoke and mirrors. Although the company did exist, it was far from the international powerhouse that Ponzi made it out to be. In reality, it was little more than a front.

There is only so much that one man, no matter how industrious he might be, can do in a day. To make serious money, Ponzi had to rope others into grifting on his behalf. He recruited a corps of salesmen who pitched his scheme to the masses. To keep them motivated, Ponzi paid them a stipend, in the form of a percentage from each new investor they brought onboard. This was lucrative enough that the first wave of Ponzi's recruits soon began to pay recruiters of their own, offering them a smaller chunk of their own profits to bring still more investors into the fold. This is the nature of a Ponzi scheme: to pay off those who jump on board at the beginning, you use funds from those who pay in afterward.

> **There is only so much that one man can do in a day. To make serious money, Ponzi had to rope others into grifting on his behalf.**

Cash continued to flow in, and within months, Charles Ponzi was living the life of Riley. He had more money than he knew what to do with and spent money like water. His new finery only made

Ponzi's carefully crafted image of the successful entrepreneur seem even more believable. Even the press started paying attention, and once word of his apparent success hit the newspapers, a tsunami of wannabe investors came running, all of them wanting a piece of the pie.

This was great publicity for Ponzi, but not all of the attention he garnered was good for him. Success brought scrutiny from the government, whose representatives soon figured out that all was not as it seemed. He stalled their investigation as best he could, refusing to cooperate or give up any of his secrets. Seeing the writing on the wall, he nonetheless attempted to brazen it out. There really were few other options. The resultant media circus captivated the nation.

Inevitably, Ponzi's luck finally ran out when auditors got their hands on his books. After some forensic accounting was completed, there was no hiding the truth: rather than being an incredible financial success, Ponzi was in fact millions of dollars in debt. The people he had bilked, some of whom had contributed their life savings, were left without a dime.

Before the people he scammed could get at him, he was taken into custody, tried for mail fraud, and sentenced to prison. The federal charges took precedence, and Ponzi spent three and a half years contemplating life behind the bars of a prison cell. After his release, the states whose citizens he had defrauded got their turn to try him in court.

The state of Massachusetts found Ponzi guilty and sentenced him to more jail time. Still the slippery customer despite his earlier stint in the clink, Ponzi decided that he had been inconvenienced enough by jailers. Chancing his luck once again, he went on the run, leading the authorities on a merry chase across the country before he was finally caught in New Orleans. His plan was to enlist as a sailor on a vessel bound for his native Italy, and he came surprisingly close to making it.

Charles Ponzi was released from prison in 1934. As he was not an American citizen, the authorities promptly put him on a boat and sent him back to Italy, never to return. His legacy was to irrevocably link the name of Ponzi with the concept of defrauding the overly credulous not just by making false promises but also by enlisting others to do the dirty work on one's behalf. Although Ponzi was almost certainly not the originator of this particular brand of larceny, he became so associated with the method that more than one hundred years later, the scheme still bears his name.

## Bernie Madoff: 21st-Century Schemer

Almost a century later, Bernard "Bernie" Madoff proved that history really does repeat itself when he resurrected the Ponzi scheme for the 21st century. Just like Ponzi, Madoff used smoke and mirrors instead of genuine investment skills to attract the attention of those who were seeking to get rich quickly and with minimal risk.

Unlike Ponzi, Madoff spent decades working on Wall Street, beginning his career in the early 1960s. He and his wife formed their own investment firm and focused their attention on trading primarily low-cost stocks. Much like Charles Ponzi, Madoff was erudite, educated, and put up a great front. He knew how to press the flesh on Wall Street, and before long, he was moving in the same circles as the rich and powerful. As time went on, Madoff became both of those things himself.

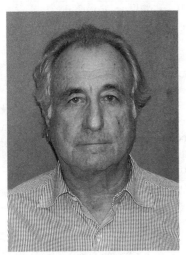

Bernie Madoff ran the largest known Ponzi scheme in history. Investigators estimated his fraud was worth tens of billions.

Bernie Madoff knew how to market himself and his brand as few others did. A key reason for his financial success was that he was picky about who he would allow to invest their money with him. When word of this got out, it attracted more wealthy individuals, all of whom wanted to be a part of the select group invited to buy into Madoff's hedge fund. Just like Ponzi before him, he promised high returns and minimal risk, no matter how volatile the stock market proved to be. Although some were doubtful of his claims (including journalists and financial analysts, some of whom smelled a rat when they started digging into Madoff's story), many others were taken in by the scam. At the end of the day, how could one distrust a man who had at one point been the chairman of the NASDAQ stock exchange?

It is unclear precisely when Madoff's Ponzi scheme began. He personally claimed that it dated back to the early 1990s, though there is evidence that it may have begun during the 1980s. What *is* known is that Bernie Madoff was able to grow his scam to such a scale that it remains, at the time of writing, the largest Ponzi scheme in history, netting somewhere in the region of $20 billion.

Madoff was able to keep the scam going until 2008, when it finally came apart at the seams. There had already been warning signs, and the Securities and Exchange Commission had even been informed, but he continued to fly mostly under the radar, defrauding his customers and racking up profits until he could no longer hide the scheme. In December of 2008, Madoff was arrested and charged with fraud, having bilked his clients (some of which were charities) of tens of billions of dollars.

Upon pleading guilty in 2009, the judge threw the book at him, sentencing Madoff to 150 years in prison. Bernie Madoff died on April 14, 2021, at the age of 82.

> **Madoff was able to keep the scam going until 2008, when it finally came apart at the seams.**

# Crash of the Titan

In the offices and on the trading floors of Wall Street, much credence and respect are given to a firm's pedigree. Certain banks and investment companies are massive, measuring their net worth in the hundreds of billions of dollars. Others are old, having been a constant presence in the financial realm since its earliest days. The true giants can claim to be both. They possess the power and influence that derive from being long established and having enormous amounts of assets and funds.

Just like the *Titanic*, they are believed to be unsinkable. To take this parallel one step further, sometimes danger, like an iceberg, lurks in the dark or beneath the surface.

One such case involved Lehman Brothers, named after the three German immigrants who founded it, Henry, Emanuel, and Mayer Lehman, who started their business in Alabama during the 1850s. The Lehmans started out with a single dry-goods store, but through sheer hard work and their industrious nature, they managed to parlay their small business into a larger enterprise that traded cotton. This meant relocating to New York, which was (and remains) the heart of the United States' financial sector.

The Civil War brought upheaval, particularly in the cotton industry, which was heavily focused in the Southern states.

Nonetheless, by 1887 Lehman Brothers was doing well enough that it joined the New York Stock Exchange. What had started out as a humble trading post had morphed into an investment bank.

Thursday, October 24, 1929, brought financial catastrophe on an unprecedented scale. The collapse of the stock market heralded the onset of a global depression that wiped out entire businesses, dynasties, and in some cases, lives. Although stories of suicidal bankers and businessmen leaping to their deaths from the upper stories of skyscrapers proved to be nothing more than urban legend, the economic crisis would lead to an increase in violent crime and starvation.

The Great Crash of 1929 kicked off a deep economic depression, which tanked many traditionally stable moneymaking opportunities across the United States and beyond. Even the formerly wealthy might find themselves accepting a helping hand, as at this Chicago soup kitchen run by mobster Al Capone.

Although many seemingly robust financial institutions went to the wall, Lehman Brothers rode out the turbulence of the Great Depression and ultimately emerged the stronger for it. Throughout the 20th century, the company expanded, strengthening its position through diversification.

As the 1990s gave way to the 2000s, Lehman Brothers found itself heavily enmeshed in the field of mortgage investments. It had been snapping up mortgage lending companies and adding them to its own portfolio of holdings. Concentrating so much of the firm's capital and focus on one specific aspect of the market seemed like a great idea at the time, but in the long run, it would prove to be a fatal mistake. Although the mortgage-heavy focus was bringing in billions of dollars in profit, a new financial crisis was brewing. While it would not quite rival the Great Depression in scale or intensity, the devastation it would wreak on financial markets would be global in scope.

By 2007, the leadership team at Lehman Brothers felt that they had every reason to be confident. With hundreds of billions in assets and credit to its name, the bank had few equals in the investment world. Low interest rates had led to a U.S. house buying boom. Even Americans with terrible credit and shaky employment history found themselves eligible for a mortgage, something they took advantage of in droves. The number of new homeowners skyrocketed. Lenders rarely stopped to ask whether all of these people truly should have qualified for a mortgage or if they represented a reasonable risk of defaulting.

The mortgage lending industry in the United States was not nearly as well regulated as it ought to have been. The housing boom led to a cash grab, and everybody wanted a piece of the lending pie. The type of mortgage given to most of these high-risk borrowers was known as a subprime mortgage. This was a term that few Americans had heard of prior to 2007, but it would be on everybody's lips once the inevitable financial meltdown started.

As with so many things in life, if it looks too good to be true, then it usually is. The catch to taking out a subprime mortgage was that the interest rates were usually variable. They tended to start out low, but they could easily increase rapidly, catching the buyer unaware—and unable to afford the higher rate. When the housing bubble inevitably burst, the cost of a monthly mortgage payment drastically shot up, leaving homeowners unable to make their payments. Their only choice was to default on their loans. The bottom fell out of the mortgage industry seemingly overnight.

Lehman Brothers was invested up to the hilt in mortgage-backed securities, the value of which had been booming up until the beginning of 2007. Suddenly, their value began to plummet as a tidal wave of mortgage foreclosures, coupled with U.S. companies laying off employees, contributed to the economy shrinking. At first, the firm's management tried to downplay the severity of the growing crisis, but as Lehman's share price continued to drop and investors saw billions of dollars wiped off its balance sheet, it became apparent that the company had entered into a tailspin from which there might be no recovery.

> It became apparent that the company had entered into a tailspin from which there might be no recovery.

Struggling to stem the financial bleeding, Lehman Brothers initiated layoffs of its own and trimmed the fat in-house wherever it seemed feasible, such as closing down some of the worst-affected parts of the business. These were temporizing measures at best, however, merely buying a little time to prop the company up. It would later come to light that executives at the bank had worked to conceal just how dire the financial situation was, hoping to maintain the confidence of creditors and investors alike. They failed, but that didn't stop the leadership team at Lehman from collecting hundreds of millions of dollars' worth of compensation even as they knew that the ship was sinking.

By mid-2008, with billions more lost from its perceived value, the writing was on the wall for Lehman Brothers, despite a series of increasingly desperate (and futile) attempts to secure more funding from investors. Even the U.S. government refused to bail the bank out, which seemed odd considering that Uncle Sam intervened to prevent the failure of other banks and private financial institutions, ultimately sinking $700 billion into shoring up the banking sector.

Lehman Brothers went bankrupt in September of 2008, its collapse sending shockwaves throughout the financial world. If an enterprise as prestigious as this could fail, the reasoning went, then was any organization truly safe?

At the time it took place, the implosion of Lehman Brothers was the largest bankruptcy in the history of the United States. As the country slowly recovered from the subsequent recession, a review of the whole sorry state of affairs showed that the financial sector was in dire need of reform, not just in the United States but throughout the entire industry. The executives at Lehman Brothers clearly over-reached by making high-yield, high-risk investments with very little oversight. In this, they were far from alone. Greed led many banks to throw caution to the wind, and the cost burden was ultimately born by the taxpayer, who ended up footing the bill for bailing them out.

Between the market crash and the collapse of the housing bubble, many mortgage holders found themselves unable to make payments and defaulted on their loans.

Although some reforms did result from the financial crash, many analysts agree that more are still needed to prevent something similar from happening in the future. If the history of global money markets teaches us anything, it is not a question of *if* there will be another global crisis—it's a matter of when.

# Up in Smoke

In January of 1954, tens of millions of American citizens opened their morning newspaper and read an advertisement titled "A Frank Statement to Cigarette Smokers."

The results of medical research studies conducted on mice had recently been released and concluded that tobacco smoking could potentially be linked with cancer. If true, then the consequences were horrifying: lighting up a cigarette, the favorite pastime of more than 40 percent of American adults, was sending them to an early grave.

*IF* it was true.

Seeing their very existence under threat, the cigarette manufacturing companies—now collectively known as Big Tobacco—struck back. Their open letter, which they had spent big money placing in hundreds of newspapers, was one of the most heinous untruths ever foisted on the American public.

The advertisement, titled "A Frank Statement to Cigarette Smokers," immediately set about attacking the legitimacy of the medical research, stating:

- Distinguished authorities point out:
- 1. That medical research of recent years indicates many possible causes of lung cancer.
- 2. That there is no agreement among the authorities regarding what the cause is.
- 3. That there is no proof that cigarette smoking is one of the causes.
- 4. That statistics purporting to link cigarette smoking with the disease could apply with equal force to any one of many other aspects of modern life. Indeed, the validity of the statistics themselves is questioned by numerous scientists.

After stating that the most important priority they had was the health of their customers, the tobacco companies who authored the statement immediately changed gears and rather snobbishly noted: "For more than 300 years, tobacco has given solace, relaxation, and enjoyment to mankind. At one time or another during those years critics have held it responsible for practically every disease of the human body. One by one, those charges have been abandoned for lack of evidence."

The tobacco companies' advertisement went on to express "deep concern" for the potential that their product might be causing cancer in smokers and pledged support for further research efforts to determine whether this was true. This would be achieved by establishing the Tobacco Industry Research Committee, or TIRC, to be comprised of scientists who were "disinterested in the tobacco industry."

Long before cigarette packs carried today's familiar mandatory health warnings, tobacco advertisements touted all sorts of benefits to smoking.

So far, so good—or so it seemed. In reality, Big Tobacco was putting up a smokescreen, more interested in profitability than it was in protecting public health. Their customers had gotten skittish in December of 1952, when the widely read *Reader's Digest* magazine published an article by Roy Norr titled "Cancer by the Carton." Norr's article pointed out that it was commonly accepted that cigarette smoke caused heart disease, ulcers, bronchitis, and a host of other ailments. Where it caused alarm was the revelation that the increase in U.S. cancer deaths seemed to keep pace with the increase in the number of cigarette smokers.

The condensed *Reader's Digest* version of "Cancer by the Carton" was just two pages long, but it had an outsize influence on Americans, coming down firmly on the side of smoking being a leading cause of cancer. *Reader's Digest* was a trusted source of information. It was no coincidence that the popularity of smoking took a major hit following the article's publication.

In the aftermath of "A Frank Statement" appearing in the newspapers just over a year after the *Reader's Digest* article, the public didn't know what to think. Was smoking safe, or was it deadly? Now that there was reasonable doubt, some people were sufficiently reassured to take up the habit again. The newspaper ad had been a success.

Even Uncle Sam was conflicted. Despite the mounting evidence that smoking caused cancer, the U.S. military issued cigarettes to its soldiers in ration packs right up until 1975. The supposedly objective research funded by Big Tobacco was little more than a whitewash. For more than 50 years after their statement, the tobacco industry stuck to the same tired old line that there was no evidence to *conclusively* link their product with the development of cancer. Meanwhile, research study after research study came to the opposite conclusion.

As the decades passed, societal norms related to smoking slowly changed. In 1971, the Federal Communications Commission (FCC) banned the advertisement of tobacco products on radio and television. In 1990, smoking was prohibited on aircraft. The mid-2000s saw an increasing number of states banning smoking in restaurants and other public places.

Since the inception of tobacco use in the United States, uncounted millions have died of cancers related to cigarettes, cigars, and similar products. Big Tobacco

> **What finally brought Big Tobacco to admit its wrongdoing was not an attack of conscience but a series of high-dollar lawsuits.**

found itself at a crucial fork in the road in 1954. Had the cigarette companies been honest about the risks of using their products, smokers could have made an informed choice. Instead, the senior management of those corporations chose to lie and obfuscate. They unquestionably have blood on their hands.

What finally brought Big Tobacco to admit its wrongdoing was not an attack of conscience but a series of high-dollar lawsuits. Shockingly, it would come to light that the cigarette manufacturers not only knew all along how addictive their product was, but they actually engineered it to be as addictive as possible—firmly hooking their customers, making it harder for them to quit, and simultaneously predisposing them to a fatal disease—all in the name of money. It would take the pronouncements of a federal court, convicting them of racketeering charges, to make Big Tobacco finally come clean.

As of 2023, smoking remained the number-one cause of preventable deaths in the United States and the world, beating out alcohol and obesity in lethality. According to the Centers for Disease Control and Prevention (CDC), about 12.5 percent of U.S. adults (some 30.8 million people) smoke tobacco despite warnings clearly printed on each pack and carton.

# Wolf on the Prowl

The late 1980s were a strange time for the stock market. Late in the decade known for materialism and greed, 1987 saw a devastating market crash that is still talked about today. Stocks rebounded in its wake, as they tend to do, and there was plenty of money to be made once more by aggressive traders and brokers.

Enter Jordan Belfort, who sensed opportunity. To capitalize on it, he set up a brokerage company named Stratton Oakmont. Belfort had minimal experience in the field of investment and finance—in fact, he already had a bankruptcy under his belt by the time he started the firm. Like many con artists, however, he was charismatic and a quick thinker. He knew how to exploit the desire almost everybody has to make money with minimal risk and employed a host of manipulative tactics to defraud those who trusted him.

Along with business partner Danny Porush, Belfort set up a so-called boiler room operation, staffed by a sales team who made cold calls to unsuspecting marks. As with today's myriad of tele-marketing scammers, the majority of those who were called didn't bite. It was the equivalent of panning for gold, sifting out the *nos* to find the rare, precious *yeses*—investors who had money to spare and allowed themselves to be talked into giving their money to Stratton Oakmont. The brokerage promised them strong returns on their initial investments, and before long the checks were being mailed in.

Investment broker and fraudster Jordan Belfort was portrayed by Leonardo DiCaprio in the loosely biographical film *Wolf of Wall Street*.

The name Stratton Oakmont sounds prestigious. It conjures up images of Ivy League schools, meeting rooms with leather furniture, and wood-paneled walls—the sort of organization with a trustworthy pedigree dating back decades. In reality, the firm's culture was anything but trustworthy. The company wasn't even *on* Wall Street, or anywhere near New York's financial district, as the cold callers liked to claim; their operation was run out of premises on Long Island.

Rather than having the feel of a Wall Street brokerage, life at Stratton Oakmont was more akin to working in a frat house gone mad—albeit a very well-funded frat house. The tales of excess associated with Belfort's company go far beyond colorful. Belfort brought in prostitutes and exotic dancers for lavish parties where alcohol flowed freely and cocaine was consumed in small mountains. If even half the escapades detailed in Jordan Belfort's autobiographical book *The Wolf of Wall Street* really did happen as described, then it is easy to see how the stories regarding Stratton Oakmont's infamous drink- and drug-fueled staff parties became the stuff of legend.

> They worked hard to push the stocks to anybody who would listen, pumping up the price to inflated levels before selling it. This is known in financial circles as a pump-and-dump scheme.

The type of investments into which Belfort's staff were putting their clients' money were penny stocks. They worked hard to push the stocks to anybody who would listen, pumping up the price to inflated levels before it and making a vast profit as a consequence. This is known in financial circles as a pump-and-dump scheme. As his income soared, Belfort purchased mansions, private jets, yachts, high-end sports cars, and even a helicopter—which he crashed into the ground while piloting it under the influence of quaaludes. Belfort had a knack for wrecking his expensive purchases, such as a top-of-the-line Mercedes that he wrote of in an intoxicated stupor.

Stratton Oakmont went out of business in 1996, a casualty of Belfort's shady practices. The firm was making too much money to be ignored and attracted too much publicity of the wrong sort.

It goes without saying that Belfort's method of profiting by bilking investors is not just unethical; it is also highly illegal. He came under the scrutiny of the authorities, who charged him with money laundering and securities fraud—both of which are federal crimes.

In 1998, following Belfort's arrest, he agreed to become an informant for law enforcement and helped FBI investigators set up and convict fellow criminals. Belfort also went to prison, but his cooperation bought him some leniency with the court. Sentenced to four years, he was out in less than two, albeit with $110 million in fines levied against his name. While behind bars, he shared a cell with actor Tommy Chong (one half of the comedy duo Cheech and Chong). Belfort claims to have regaled Chong with stories of his bizarre behavior while drunk or taking drugs, and Chong reportedly told him to write the stories down for publication.

> **His rise-and-fall book *The Wolf of Wall Street*—a nickname Belfort gave himself—became a bestseller and was turned into a blockbuster 2013 movie.**

Published in 2007, his rise-and-fall book *The Wolf of Wall Street*—a nickname Belfort gave himself—became a best-seller and was turned into a blockbuster 2013 movie directed by Martin Scorsese. Belfort was played by superstar Leonard DiCaprio in a performance that is by turns comic, dark, and viscerally compelling.

The movie made Jordan Belfort a household name. In the decade since its release, he has leveraged that fame into a career in motivational speaking, podcasting, and writing. Ever the entrepreneur, he continues to hustle his way through multiple different side gigs, but he now appears to have become the honest broker he liked to portray himself as during the Stratton Oakmont years.

Yet it is important to remember that the people Belfort conned into investing in his pump-and-dump scheme lost a grand total of around $200 million. Many had invested their life savings. Some lost their retirement to fuel his insatiable desire to live the high life.

We like to ask whether a leopard can truly change its spots. In the case of Jordan Belfort, the question becomes: Can a wolf?

# Corrupt to the Max

On October 29, 2018, a Boeing 737 Max 8 took off from Jakarta on an early morning flight. Once the undercarriage was retracted, the pilot of Lion Air Flight 610 turned the aircraft out over the Java Sea and began the climb to cruising altitude.

No sooner had the plane cleared the runway than the trouble began. An alarm sounded, telling the captain that the aircraft was about to stall. Then came obviously false readings from the altimeter and air speed indicators.

Speaking with air traffic control in Jakarta, the first officer reported "flight control problems." At that stage, neither the senior pilot nor the copilot had any inkling of just how bad things were about to get.

It soon became apparent to the flight crew that something was dreadfully wrong with their brand-new, supposedly state-of-the-art passenger jet. The cockpit instruments that pilots rely on for accurate data were painting a confusing picture, divorced from reality. There was uncertainty as to whether Flight 610 was climbing or descending. In fact, it was descending. The first confirmation the flight crew had of this was when an automated warning system began calling out the word "terrain"—an indication that a collision with the ground was imminent.

Seen here six weeks before its fatal crash, Lion Air's relatively new Boeing 737 MAX 8 crashed into the Java Sea on October 29, 2018, killing all aboard.

Lion Air 610 had been airborne for just 13 minutes when the flight crew lost all control. The plane crashed into the ocean at high speed, killing everyone aboard on impact.

The death toll came to 189 men, women, and children.

Months later, on March 10, 2019, tragedy struck again when Ethiopia Airlines Flight 302 crashed into the ground near the town of Bishoftu, Ethiopia, just six minutes after taking off. All 157 lives on board were lost.

The parallels with Flight 610 were apparent for all to see. Once again, the pilots were fed confusing and erroneous data regarding the aircraft's pitch, altitude, and speed. Despite their best efforts, the nose kept forcing itself downward. The flight crew lost their fight to keep control of the plane.

Every 737 Max in the world was immediately grounded. People wanted answers. Two crashes—with eerily similar characteristics—made it disturbingly clear that something about Boeing's premier jet airliner was horrifically flawed.

In 2011, the aircraft manufacturer Boeing began working on an upgraded, more fuel-efficient variant of its popular 737 airliner.

Designing a modern passenger aircraft is a lengthy and complex affair, requiring multiple iterations, large engineering teams, and a lengthy testing and certification process. There are always trade-offs. Designers and engineers strive to get as much bang for their buck as possible, trying out thousands of different permutations before settling on the design that will become a prototype. A multitude of changes and tweaks are made before reaching that point.

> **Two crashes—with eerily similar characteristics—made it disturbingly clear that something about Boeing's premier jet airliner was horrifically flawed.**

In the case of the 737 Max, the specification listed newer, more powerful engines than those on the original Boeing 737. The specific place on the wing at which each engine was mounted played a role in maximizing fuel efficiency; putting the engines in the wrong spot would increase drag, degrade performance, and alter the aircraft's handling characteristics. There was an optimum sweet spot, which the designers found, but the upgraded engines came with a price: their presence would put the Max slightly off balance compared to the standard 737, causing the nose to naturally want to pitch upward at an angle.

The Max wouldn't immediately replace the 737 across the board; 737s and 737 Max models would be flying the friendly skies at the same time, and the same pilots would be in charge of both different types. To certify those pilots with the minimum amount of inconvenience, Boeing needed to find a way to make them both handle in very similar ways in all circumstances. A 737 and a Max had to behave the same way whether they were pitched nose up at 30 degrees or in a slow-speed right banking turn at 15 degrees, for example. Otherwise, pilots would need to be rated on the two aircraft types separately, which would create additional overhead, incur extra expense, and make the Max harder to sell to customers who were keeping a close eye on the bottom line.

Those new engines and the pressure they exerted on the airframe to pitch upward made the Max behave differently from its predecessor. How could they make them fly in a similar manner? The solution implemented by Boeing's engineers was the MCAS—short for Maneuvering Characteristics Augmentation System. When a plane pitches upward too steeply, in what is known as the angle of attack, it runs the risk of stalling. The airflow around each wing is diminished to the point that the aircraft loses lift. An unrecovered stall results in the plane literally falling out of the sky. For this reason, an early phase of basic pilot training involves stall recovery.

> **Tragically, the sensors could sometimes be fooled into thinking that the aircraft's upward pitch was steeper than it actually was. In that instance, the MCAS would begin pushing the plane's nose toward the ground.**

The purpose of the MCAS was twofold. Its primary reason for existing was to give the newer airframe type, the Max, similar flight handling characteristics as the original 737 had, despite the fact that it was structurally different.

The secondary reason was to act as a safeguard against the 737 Max stalling. This piece of software was programmed to automatically kick in whenever the nose attained an angle of attack that the onboard computer considered to be excessive. Once specific flight parameters were achieved, MCAS would send commands to the aircraft's stabilizer, pitching the nose downward and—so it was hoped—thereby prevent a stall.

Tragically, the angle of attack sensors on the 737 Max could sometimes be fooled into thinking that the aircraft's upward pitch was steeper than it actually was. In that instance, the MCAS would automatically be activated and begin pushing the plane's nose toward the ground in an attempt to counteract a problem that didn't exist.

Airline pilots are highly educated and detail-oriented individuals. Most of them like to know the functions and operational characteristics of the aircraft they fly in minute detail. Yet the 737 Max flight crews didn't even know about the existence of the MCAS. Not only were they never taught about the system during their model familiarization, MCAS wasn't even referred to in the reference documentation each pilot received from the company in the form of training manuals.

In March 2019, the FAA grounded all 737 MAX planes pending investigation, trailing 51 other regulators in taking the safety measure. These newly constructed planes, parked at Boeing Field in Seattle, would not be released to fly for eight months.

The crew of Lion Air 610 had no way of knowing it at the time, but from the moment their plane's wheels left the runway at Jakarta, they and their flight system were being fed false information by a faulty angle of attack sensor. The 737 Max's computer was fooled into thinking it was pitched upward much more severely than it actually was. Trying to compensate (and also completely unknown to the pilots), the MCAS was invoked, automatically pushing their plane back down toward the sea—and destruction.

The angle of attack sensor had been installed in Flight 610 on October 28, 2018, one day before the crash. It was not brand new; the component was refurbished and returned by a private contractor and was found to have been improperly calibrated. It was responsible for sending out the false data on the basis of which the MCAS was automatically invoked.

The plane had been flown later that same day. The flight crew experienced similar problems but were able to maintain control of the 737 Max and land it safely at their destination. Damningly, the pilot of the October 28 flight did not report the severity of the systems malfunction the plane had experienced, as he should have done. If he had done so, airline protocol would have grounded the aircraft until a detailed safety inspection could be performed—and 189 human beings would not have died.

There were also opportunities to save those lives on October 29. The Maneuvering Characteristics Augmentation System only worked when the autopilot was switched off. If the flight crew had engaged the autopilot, the plane would have flown itself up to cruising altitude without intervention from MCAS.

Except nobody had ever told them.

One of the two angle of attack sensors installed on Ethiopian Flight 302 malfunctioned shortly after takeoff. Although the cause for this isn't known for sure, it is possible that a bird strike or piece of debris damaged the component as the plane took to the skies.

In a case of shutting the stable door after the horse had bolted, Boeing made changes to the MCAS system in the wake of both tragedies. The system was reprogrammed so that it would only engage if *both* of the onboard angle of attack sensors agreed that the plane's pitch was too high. In this way, a single faulty sensor should not be capable of invoking MCAS and causing the aircraft to crash.

> **Why didn't Boeing inform 737 Max pilots of the existence of MCAS and its potential implications? Why didn't the company train them on how to handle a malfunction with the system?**

Why didn't Boeing inform 737 Max pilots of the existence of MCAS and its potential implications? Why didn't the company train them on how to handle a malfunction with the system, which could be disengaged simply by switching the plane from manual control into autopilot? Boeing CEO Dennis Muilenberg claimed that MCAS was so deeply integrated into the Max flight control systems that it wasn't a separate entity that needed to receive its own specific training; it was, he insisted, simply a part of the greater whole, a core characteristic.

"It's fundamentally embedded in the handling qualities of the airplane," the CEO clarified. "So when you train on the airplane, you are being trained on MCAS."

This is somewhat analogous to claiming that because the heart is fundamentally embedded in the human body rather than being a "separate system," physicians shouldn't receive specialist training in cardiology. What cannot be argued is that, if Boeing had trained flight crews explicitly on the behavior of MCAS, hundreds of people might still be alive today.

Back in 2013, Boeing had made a conscious decision to not label MCAS as an additional function or system. "If we emphasize MCAS is a new function, there may be a greater certification and training impact." In other words, if they referred to MCAS as being nothing more than a part of the preexisting trim system on the Max, it would cause less hassle and expense for all concerned.

Boeing also downplayed the need for Max crews to receive additional training on the new model; under no circumstances did the company want pilots to have to undergo training in a Max flight simulator to qualify. There was a financial inducement for this. Boeing had sold the 737 Max to Southwest Airlines and, as part of the deal, had guaranteed that Southwest pilots would not need to undergo costly simulator training before they were allowed to fly the Max. The legalese agreed upon by both parties stipulated that Boeing would pay Southwest a fee of $1 million *per aircraft* if this training condition was not met. Had their pilots needed simulator time, Boeing would have found itself on the hook for hundreds of millions of dollars.

It was far more convenient—not to mention significantly cheaper—for Boeing to keep things as simple as possible and not rock the boat where the new system was concerned.

Boeing had downplayed the need for Max crews to receive additional simulator training on the new model.

News would emerge that Boeing knew about the potential for problems with the angle of attack indicator on the 737 Max prior to either of the two crashes. A warning could be sounded in the cockpit if the angle of attack values being reported by the two sensors disagreed with one another; however, that warning would only work if the customer purchased an optional feature package at additional cost. Neither the Lion Air nor the Ethiopian Airlines flight had the extra safety measure installed.

A year before either of the 737 crashes, the issue was studied by an engineering review committee and was deemed to constitute a low safety risk. Did Boeing deliberately downplay the potential hazards of MCAS, or did its top engineers simply fail to understand the prospective risks?

In March of 2021, reporter Dominic Gates of the *Seattle Times* spoke with former Boeing employee and current Federal Aviation Administration (FAA) safety engineer Joe Jacobsen. Jacobsen was highly experienced in the arena of aviation safety and would have been a key part of assessing the impact of the MCAS system—*if* Boeing had told the FAA about its existence as an addition to the Max, which it did not.

The first time he heard anything about MCAS was in the aftermath of the Lion Air 610 disaster. With the benefit of hindsight, Jacobsen told the *Times* that he and his fellow FAA engineers would have deemed MCAS a potential safety risk, requiring that additional measures be taken by Boeing to ensure that it was rendered safe.

In March of 2019, a global ban was placed on the Max. Public confidence in the aircraft was so low that practically nobody was willing to purchase a ticket to fly on one. Many governments decreed that until Boeing definitively fixed the safety concerns, they would not certify the plane to fly through their national airspace.

**In March of 2019, a global ban was placed on the Max. Public confidence in the aircraft was so low that practically nobody was willing to fly on one.**

Boeing fired CEO Dennis Muilenberg, a direct consequence of the 737 Max scandal. Muilenberg received no severance pay but, in what seems like a far cry from justice for those who had lost their lives, did retain over $60 million worth of Boeing stock and pension benefits.

More than 400 pilots assigned to fly the 737 Max banded together to launch a class action lawsuit against Boeing, alleging that the company had deliberately covered up critical safety flaws in the aircraft's design, knowingly putting their safety at risk.

In January of 2021, the Justice Department cut a deal with Boeing in which the aerospace giant would pay more than $2.5 billion in reparations for the criminal charge of conspiracy to defraud the United States. The subject of that fraud was, of course, the 737 Max. While much of the money went to the U.S. government and to Boeing's cus-

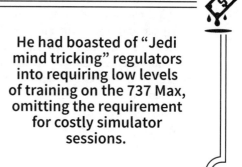

He had boasted of "Jedi mind tricking" regulators into requiring low levels of training on the 737 Max, omitting the requirement for costly simulator sessions.

tomers, $500 million was earmarked for the next of kin of the 346 passengers who died in the two plane crashes.

Acting Assistant Attorney General David Burns, speaking for the Justice Department's Criminal Division, was scathing in his critique of Boeing: "The tragic crashes of Lion Air Flight 610 and Ethiopian Airlines Flight 302 exposed fraudulent and deceptive conduct by employees of one of the world's leading aircraft manufacturers."

Burns added: "Boeing's employees chose the path of profit over candor, by concealing material information from the FAA concerning the operation of its 737 Max airplane and engaging in an effort to cover up their deception."

One Boeing employee had been charged with deceiving the FAA about the safety risks of the 737 Max: former chief test pilot Mark Forkner. The prosecution alleged that Forkner was fully aware of the problems with MCAS and deliberately kept the information from the FAA in 2016. He had boasted of "Jedi mind tricking" regulators into requiring low levels of training on the 737 Max, omitting the requirement for costly simulator sessions.

In March of 2022, Forkner was found not guilty at the conclusion of his trial. His lawyers claimed that he had been scapegoated by his employer. For its part, Boeing made no comment, and while a slew of lawsuits are currently in progress against the company, no other employees have been charged with a crime.

By the summer of 2022, the 737 Max was back in service around the world. Most of the countries that had banned the troubled aircraft had lifted them and allowed Maxes to transit their airspace and land at their airports. A notable holdout was China, whose airlines had been early and major adopters of the Max. In June of that year, Air China performed several test flights in its efforts to verify the model's safety. Although everything went according to plan, as of late summer 2022, the 737 Max was not yet making flights across China.

# The Enron Effect

Everything is bigger in Texas, as the old saying goes. Unfortunately, that can also include the extent of corruption.

Before its implosion and collapse in the winter of 2001, the energy company Enron was known for its innovation, aggressiveness, and willingness to take chances in the business market. In return, Enron had been showered with profits, making its upper echelons extremely rich. Yet in reality, Enron was a house of cards, and by December of that year, the entire thing came tumbling down.

The foundations of that house were laid in 1986, when two Texan energy companies joined to form a new entity named Enron. It specialized in the supply of natural gas but later diversified into the business of brokering contracts between gas suppliers and the customers who bought it. Enron was founded by Kenneth Lay, who would become the company's CEO.

Throughout the late 1980s and the early 1990s, the company grew steadily and prospered. Huge profits flowed Enron's way, and the future looked nothing but bright.

There was a lot of money to be made in the energy and commodities markets of the mid-1990s. By 1997, these markets were a hunting ground that gave Enron, under the direction of its newly

Kenneth Lay, founder of Enron, was found guilty in 2006 of fraud, but he died of a heart attack before he could be sentenced.

appointed chief operating officer and president, Jeffrey Skilling, plenty of scope for wheeling and dealing, cutting deals to its best advantage. Skilling took the helm in early 2001 and wasted no time in kicking the Enron engine into overdrive.

The late 1990s were a boom time for Enron, and the company grew to dominate the market. To maintain a competitive edge, Skilling and the rest of the senior leadership created a cutthroat culture in which only the most ambitious and aggressive would rise to the top of the promotional ladder. Cunning, boldness, and Machiavellian scheming were lauded and encouraged. At the top of the corporate pyramid, executives pocketed tens of millions of dollars, much of it in the form of stock options and bonuses.

While the rewards and incentives were big, the working conditions at Enron were brutal. Employees were expected to put in long hours, and whenever one sales goal was achieved, another was put in its place—one that was even more difficult to reach. This kept the rank and file on their toes, constantly striving to outdo one another in their attempt to grab the brass ring. To be perceived as weak or indecisive was career suicide. Strength, or at least the perception of it, was everything. There was no unity among the ranks. Instead, there

**Instability was baked into the Enron recipe.**

were cliques, and for any employee who didn't fit in with one, their days were numbered. Enron was a hard company to get into and an easy one to be fired from, and many of its staff lived in fear of losing their jobs on a daily basis.

At Enron, results were everything. You either performed, and performed highly, or you were gone. There was no middle ground.

On the stock market, the company's value was soaring, but this wasn't healthy growth, the kind of expansion enjoyed by stable and healthy enterprises. Enron's leadership was doing everything they could to artificially inflate the stock price, driving it ever higher and then selling off stock to cash in before everything fell to pieces.

Instability was baked into the Enron recipe. The emphasis on risk taking that permeated the whole organization eventually led to its downfall. Desperate to keep up the pace, senior executives made a series of increasingly risky investments. A few paid off, but others backfired spectacularly. Enron's balance sheet began to nosedive out of the black and into the red as the company's revenue was outstripped by rapidly accumulating debt. Bold, aggressive ventures now began to look like folly—which most of them were.

## Red Flags: Aggressive Investment and "Creative Accounting"

The outside world was beginning to take notice. Enron had profited handsomely from the soaring stock market throughout the 1990s; after all, a rising tide lifts all boats. Aggressive expansion put the company at the front of the pack. As the 21st century dawned, however, experienced investors and financial analysts took a closer look at the Texas-based company. They began to notice an increasing number of red flags and grew hesitant to put their money into Enron.

In the financial world, as in the rest of life, diversification can be a good thing—up to a point. In their never-ending quest for new realms to conquer, Enron executives started looking beyond the energy sector in which the company had built its foundation and started throwing money at an ever-increasing range of projects and industries. For those who signed the checks, it was all about demonstrating their business smarts and willingness to invest aggressively. What they were really doing was inflating a bubble—a bubble that would inevitably have to burst.

Just how much of the company's decline was attributable to incompetence, and how much to willful neglect on the part of Skilling and his cohort? One key indicator is the fact that Enron's bookkeepers were directed to engage in a series of shady accounting practices (referred to by some as "creative accounting") to hide the vast sums of money that were being lost each day. As 2001 went on, the company was no longer making serious efforts to stop the cash flow hemorrhage that was killing it. The best they could do was try to obscure the losses—to prop things up for as long as possible to extract maximum profits before the ship finally sank.

> Enron's bookkeepers were directed to engage in a series of shady accounting practices (referred to by some as "creative accounting") to hide the vast sums of money that were being lost each day.

CEO Skilling unexpectedly resigned in August, fully aware of the train wreck that was fast approaching. He was replaced by company founder Kenneth Lay.

By the fall of 2001, much of Wall Street could see that the writing was on the wall for the former powerhouse company. There is a thin line between aggressive, innovative investing and recklessness. Under Skilling's direction, Enron had stepped right over that line and kept on going. While its management team were lining their pockets, they were running the company into the ground. They had transitioned from building and growing a successful corporate enterprise to sucking out as much profit as they possibly could before the Enron gravy train pulled into the station for the very last time.

By early October, Enron's sketchy dealings had brought the company to the attention of the U.S. government, specifically, the Securities and Exchange Commission (SEC), a watchdog whose remit was to prevent market fraud. Being on the SEC's radar was a major nail in Enron's coffin. Auditors found and revealed a slew of financial improprieties hidden within the company's books. As word got out, the remaining investors deserted Enron in droves, causing the company's stock price to plummet. It was a death spiral from which Enron would never recover, one that ended in bankruptcy on December 2.

The early days of 2002 brought with them a criminal investigation into activities at Enron. Former vice president J. Clifford Baxter died in his car on January 25 of what authorities said was a single self-inflicted gunshot wound to the head. A suicide note was left inside his wife's car at the home they shared. It did not mention Enron, from which Baxter had resigned in April of the preceding year. Prior to leaving, he had expressed concern with the shady way in which the company was then doing business.

The criminal investigation found that numerous internal documents had been shredded in an attempt to cover up those practices. This discovery led to convictions for the internal auditors who were responsible. As indictments continued to mount, the lion's share were levied against executives Kenneth Lay, Jeffrey Skilling, and Chief Financial Officer Andrew Fastow.

Jeffrey Skilling, Enron's CEO during its era of shady dealings, was convicted on 19 various counts and sentenced to 24 years in prison.

Fastow went to prison for six years. He had originally been sentenced to ten but gave up information on the corrupt practices of his colleagues as part of a deal to cut his time almost in half. His wife, Lea, was also sentenced to five months for filing a false tax form.

After their conviction on fraud and conspiracy charges. the bulk of the prison time in the Enron case was issued to Skilling and Lay. In May of 2006, the 52-year-old Skilling was sentenced to 24 years behind bars. A reduction in sentence led to him being released in 2019, after serving 13 years.

Kenneth Lay, aged 64, was convicted and could have been sentenced to up to 45 years behind bars. This proved to be a moot point. In July of that same year, while still awaiting his sentence, Lay suffered a massive, fatal heart attack while vacationing in Aspen, Colorado. One can only speculate as to how much the stress of the Enron debacle might have contributed to his death.

When the dust finally settled, the rise and fall of Enron left a permanent scar on the United States business landscape. The scandal played out each night on the evening news and caused millions of small investors to lose faith in investing in big corporations. Enron had successfully hidden behind a false front, padding its profits and concealing its losses. How many other large companies might be doing the same? people wondered. Confidence in the stock market took a hit once news of the scandal broke, and while it eventually recovered, the lingering suspicion evoked by the name Enron has never quite gone away.

The chances are good that it never will.

# Anti-Social Media

Love it or loathe it, there's no ignoring it. Facebook, the social media juggernaut, is here to stay. The brainchild of four Harvard students in 2004, in 2023 the platform had almost 3 billion users worldwide—and that number continues to grow.

Facebook can be a wonderful thing, allowing users to connect with friends, family, and likeminded individuals from near and far. Yet it also has a dark side, which became apparent during one of the greatest scandals to blight the company's history: the Cambridge Analytica affair.

As part of its day-to-day operations, Facebook collects data on the activities of each and every user. Using a feature called Facebook Login, users can log in to various other websites and apps using only their Facebook credentials—an easier way to join a new site than typing out their email address, making up a new password, and performing other verification rituals. This ease of use is paid for, however, with information—specifically, with the data Facebook has collected on the user, shared with the new site.

For years, Facebook's leadership team insisted that user demographics and personal information were secure and represented no risk to those who signed up for the platform. In reality, things couldn't have been further from the truth.

In 2015, hundreds of thousands of Facebook users were presented with an app named *thisisyourdigitallife*. This was a relatively simple quiz in which users answered questions about their personal preferences in exchange for money, ostensibly for academic research. It was the brainchild of Cambridge University psychology researcher named Aleksandr Kogan.

Beginning in 2015, Cambridge Analytica used Facebook to harvest data from up to 87 million users—under the guise of a harmless quiz—most of whom did not actually take the quiz themselves. The resulting user profiles were used for targeted political advertising, fed right back through Facebook.

Paying 270,000 Facebook users to take a quiz was one thing. It can be argued that they knew exactly what they were signing up for and were given financial compensation for sharing their data. The real problem was that the app not only collected data from them, but it also had access to *everybody* on their Facebook friends list. Initial estimates placed this number at 50 million people, but because Facebook wasn't keeping accurate logs at the time the scandal took place, the true figure may have been closer to 87 million users whose data was taken without their permission. In other words, tens of millions of individuals unknowingly had their private information stolen and passed on. The app was able to gather this data because the users signed in using the Facebook Login tool, thereby agreeing to share it.

One key point is that Aleksandr Kogan was only permitted to collect data via *thisisyourdigitallife* for the purpose of legitimate academic research—not for making profits. Nor was he allowed to pass the data on to anybody else.

The data was passed on, however. So where did it go? To a British organization named Cambridge Analytica, which sells data analysis services to third-party customers. The company specialized in the political arena. Cambridge Analytica provided its services to Donald Trump's presidential campaign in 2016, which saw him narrowly beating Hillary Clinton in the contest for the White House, winning the electoral college vote even though he lost the popular vote. There are conflicting stories as to how much of Cambridge Analytica's data, if any, was actually used during the run-up to the election. According to the Trump campaign, none of it was used. Cambridge Analytica's CEO, on the other hand, claimed that the company's efforts were a key ingredient in Trump's victory.

The idea was to combine the results gleaned from Facebook users by *thisisyourdigitallife* with the vast trove of Facebook user data to target political advertisements to specific individuals. By applying proven psychological principles, Cambridge Analytica claimed, it was able to increase the likelihood of those potential voters it targeted actually casting their votes in favor of whichever candidate paid for its services.

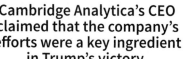

**Cambridge Analytica's CEO claimed that the company's efforts were a key ingredient in Trump's victory.**

None of this would ever have come to light were it not for a British reporter named Harry Davies and a whistleblower named Christopher Wylie, who worked for Cambridge Analytica. Davies wrote a story about the data harvesting in 2015, and Wylie came forward three years later, in 2018.

The scandal made Facebook the leading news story, particularly when it emerged that the social media giant had known about Cambridge Analytica's activities since shortly after the 2015 data transfer. At the time, Facebook had demanded that Cambridge

Analytica delete all of the user information it had taken. It then did absolutely nothing to ensure that the analysis firm obeyed that edict. No audit was launched to ensure compliance.

A public backlash was inevitable and led to the rise of the #DeleteFacebook movement. Droves of Facebook users deactivated their accounts. It's impossible to say how many, because Facebook refuses to reveal the number of users who leave the platform. A survey by research organizations Techpinions and Creative Strategies revealed that 9 percent of U.S. Facebook users deleted their accounts in the aftermath of the scandal—though with a relatively small sample size of 1,000, it's a number that should be treated with caution.

As a general rule, the first thing a corporation does when a scandal breaks is to apologize. Sometimes, those apologies are genuine. Often, they are not. Facebook creator and CEO Mark Zuckerberg said nothing for several days after the news hit the media but finally made a statement about the importance of privacy and data protection for Facebook users. Yet there were still attempts to evade responsibility. Facebook argued that because there hadn't been an actual hack or unauthorized penetration of their systems, the loss of user data wasn't truly a security breach. This argument may have been aligned with the letter of the law, but it definitely did not reflect the spirit. (Zuckerberg and company were humiliated a few months later when a genuine cyber intrusion snatched the access credentials of more than 50 million Facebook users.)

When the dust settled, Facebook suspended thousands of apps that it suspected or proved had obtained or shared data in unethical ways.

Whistleblower Christopher Wylie (right) divulged Cambridge Analytica's methods to a journalist, sparking a widespread outcry and a minor privacy movement.

In the United Kingdom, Facebook was hit with fines totaling half a million pounds (about $650,000) for failing to protect the privacy of its user data. The company paid up but refused to accept liability for its actions. On the other side of the Atlantic, the U.S. Federal Trade Commission (FTC) launched an extensive investigation into the way Facebook mismanaged the data of its users. In 2019, the two parties reached a settlement, which included a $5 billion fine and a number of internal reforms.

Facebook—which changed its name to Meta in 2021—has deep pockets, having an annual revenue of $117 billion in 2021. Things hit a little closer to home for Mark Zuckerberg in May of that year when Attorney General Karl Racine of the District of Columbia launched a lawsuit against the Meta CEO.

"We're suing Mark Zuckerberg for his role in Facebook's misleading privacy practices," Racine tweeted on May 23, 2022. "Our investigation shows extensive evidence that Zuckerberg was personally involved in failures that led to the Cambridge Analytica incident."

Attorney General Racine had sued Facebook four years prior but was not successful. This latest lawsuit was aimed not at the company per se but at its CEO personally, and at the time of writing it remained to be seen how much responsibility (if any) Zuckerberg would accept.

# Off the Rails

Of the many inventions throughout history that changed the way in which Americans lived their lives, few had more impact than the railroad. The first transcontinental railroad sought to join the eastern and western United States, allowing passengers and cargo to travel across the country in a fraction of the time it would have taken to make the journey by wagon or ship.

In 1862, while the Civil War was in its second of five bloody years, two different railroad companies, the Union Pacific and the Central Pacific, received a governmental charter to build the largest railroad in the world, under the legal endorsement of President Abraham Lincoln. The two railroads would start on opposite sides of the country and work their way toward the center, where they would—if all went well—meet up somewhere in the middle, linking up into one grand railroad.

Despite its name, the railroad would not stretch all the way from the Pacific Ocean to the Atlantic. Work on its western arm, constructed by the Central Pacific Railroad Company, was begun in Sacramento, California, in 1863, and laid track toward the east.

Its competitor-turned-ally, Union Pacific, was mandated to start out from Omaha, Nebraska, as the easternmost point of the railroad and work its way westward in the general direction of its Central Pacific counterparts. Due to a variety of logistical factors, the first rail was not laid down until 1865, giving Central Pacific a significant head start.

> **To say that as a potential investment opportunity, the railroad was a hard sell would be an understatement.**

Such a mammoth undertaking was always going to cost a fortune, even without taking into account the corrupt practices that dogged its financing and construction. For Union Pacific's portion of the railroad alone, the federal government forked out $100 million in funding. On top of that came $60 million in loans and government-backed bonds from the Treasury, along with grants of vast tracts of land on which the railroad was to be built.

It wasn't enough. Even with Uncle Sam's cash taps turned on to full flow, more money was needed to finance the vast engineering project. The only solution was to secure the extra funds from nongovernmental investors in the private sector.

To say that as a potential investment opportunity, the railroad was a hard sell would be an understatement. For one thing, the likelihood of it being brought in on time and on budget was low. Indigenous nations who understandably opposed the encroachment on their lands controlled a number of areas along the projected route, and critics pointed out that as construction went on, there would inevitably be armed clashes and bloodshed along the way. (The critics were right. Native Americans fought the railroad's progress at every turn until, ultimately, U.S. Army troops were deployed to safeguard the construction workers.)

Even without armed resistance, the construction process would be messy, expensive, and slow going. To cap it all off, once the railroad finally *was* finished, it wouldn't necessarily find a large pool of customers lining up to use its services. There was no guarantee that the massive costs incurred in building the railway would ever be recouped and turned into profit—and even if they were, it might take years.

The completion of the transcontinental railroad finally connecting at Promontory, Utah, was famously commemorated by the driving of a golden spike. History prefers this end of the story over the financial trickery of the bankers and politicians responsible for getting there.

Seeing a whole lot of risk and a relatively small amount of benefit, most investors avoided the railroad project like the plague. There was much easier money to be made elsewhere, and in a much shorter amount of time.

Enter a man named Thomas C. Durant. Having initially chosen to train as a physician, obtaining his degree at Albany Medical College as a young man, the ambitious Durant switched fields and entered the murky waters of entrepreneurship. Gravitating toward the railroad industry, Durant quickly realized that even if a railroad was unlikely to be a profitable concern once completed, there was a lot of money to be made in the building of one.

At the onset of the first transcontinental railroad project, Durant held the position of vice president of Union Pacific. He soon realized that if he wanted to make himself an absolute fortune, it would first be necessary to solve the problem of lacking private investment capital. His solution was as novel as it was dishonest.

Along with his colleague, the aptly named George Francis Train, Durant purchased a railroad financing company, the Pennsylvania Fiscal Agency, and renamed it. The name he chose was that of an established French financing company: Credit Mobilier of America.

The *real* Credit Mobilier had a solid track record of attracting private investors, most of them of moderate to wealthy means, for the purpose of pooling their money and using it to finance railroads or purchase real estate in several countries.

> **Thomas Durant's Credit Mobilier of America was a total and utter sham. It was nothing more than a shell company.**

Seeking to lure in American investors, Durant chose this established name with the goal of evoking an air of trustworthiness and dependability. His Credit Mobilier, however, bore no relation to its French namesake beyond the title of the company. Thomas Durant's Credit Mobilier of America was a total and utter sham. It was nothing more than a shell company, designed to manipulate investment capital, shares, and bonds in the most advantageous way possible for those who ran it.

Unsurprisingly, with the vast sums of money flowing from the government's coffers into the pockets of the railroad companies, Durant and a few other unscrupulous individuals saw an opportunity to siphon off a fortune for themselves—and they seized it.

The gist behind creating Credit Mobilier was that the company would build the eastern section of the transcontinental railroad on behalf of Union Pacific. Once Credit Mobilier got the contract to build the railroad, Durant and his cronies set about billing the U.S. government for its construction services at vastly inflated prices. The construction work was indeed getting done, but at almost double the actual cost it took to lay down the track. This was achieved by bond sales between the Union Pacific Railroad Company and Credit Mobilier. The profits made on the back of this crooked scheme ran to approximately $30 million, the vast majority of which went into the pockets of Thomas Durant and his fellow conspirators.

A key member was a businessman named Oakes Ames. Already wealthy, Ames was also highly influential: he was the congressional representative for the state of Massachusetts. Along with his brother, Oliver, Ames had the prestige and influence needed to attract more investment money to Credit Mobilier and Union Pacific. The Ames brothers also had a vested interest in keeping federal oversight as far away from Union Pacific and Credit Mobilier as possible. After all, Credit Mobilier existed purely to drain the railroad company of its funds, and those funds came mostly from the U.S. Treasury. If government watchdogs were to delve too deeply into the affairs of the scheme, not only would the supply of federal money stop, but Durant and Ames could be in a great deal of trouble.

To protect the scam, Oakes Ames set about bribing as many members of Congress as he could. The type of bribe he favored was not cash but stocks and bonds in the railroad enterprise itself. The congressman reasoned that the further in bed his fellow politicians were with Credit Mobilier, the less likely they were to allow an investigation into its methods of operation. After seeing the vast profits there were to be made, a number of Ames's fellow congressmen jumped on board. To sweeten the pot, if any of his intended marks hesitated, Ames gave them the stock with no money down, just an agreement that he would be repaid for it once the first dividend payments were made. It was a win-win proposition. The congressmen and senators would make a fat pile of cash, while Oakes and his ilk would gain protection on Capitol Hill.

For some of his colleagues, it did not sit well that Oakes Ames was clearly using his position of public authority to feather his own nest. There were murmurs of discontent among those who chose not to participate in the Credit Mobilier stock plan, perhaps sensing that the affair was

Thomas C. Durant, vice president of Union Pacific Railroad, was the architect of the massive railroad-building fraud scheme that would become known as the Credit Mobilier scandal.

questionable enough that it might come back to bite those involved. The railroad itself was finished in 1869. The day of reckoning for some of those who had used it for their own corrupt ends would not come for several more years.

As progress on the railroad continued, Thomas Durant and the Ames brothers had assumed a bitter rivalry. At stake was nothing less than overall control of Credit Mobilier. Durant came off worst. After a long and vitriolic struggle, Oakes and Oliver Ames finally succeeded in ousting Durant from the railroad shortly after its completion. Although it must have been a bitter pill to swallow, Durant left with a massively inflated bank balance and managed to avoid the inevitable explosion that was about to cone. Much of that fortune was lost in the great financial panic of 1873, leaving Thomas Durant little choice but to enter retirement on relatively meager means.

On September 4, 1872, the New York *Sun* newspaper finally broke word of the scandal. History tends to remember Thomas Durant as the principal architect of the scheme, not least because George Train had reaped vast profits and disappeared from the scene by the time word got out. A colorful character, Train tried no fewer than three times to become president on the Democratic ticket and would come to be viewed by some as a real-life equivalent of the globe-trotting character Phileas Fogg, the protagonist of Jules Verne's classic novel *Around the World in 80 Days*.

The issue of railroad companies exerting an undue influence upon Washington politics was something of a hot button for the American people in the aftermath of the Civil War. Popular opinion held that corrupt practices were the norm, not the exception, and word of the Credit Mobilier scandal provided fuel for the flames.

> **Popular opinion held that corrupt practices were the norm, not the exception, and word of the Credit Mobilier scandal provided fuel for the flames.**

The House convened an investigation into the affair, which originally met behind closed doors but was soon forced out into the open once the public cried foul. There was an appetite to see some of the nation's most prominent politicians humbled and even humiliated in the public eye. The list of those called upon to testify included Schuyler Colfax, who had been speaker of the House at the time he had purchased stock in Credit Mobilier but was the vice president of the United States when the investigation was underway. President

Ulysses S. Grant's administration had already struggled with allegations of corruption, and the revelations concerning the Union Pacific Railroad did not help matters in the slightest.

On February 27, 1873, Oakes Ames and New York representative James Brooks were both censured by the House. The investigation concluded that they had used their public service positions as congressmen to buttress their personal financial interests as major stakeholders of the Union Pacific Railroad. Censure is little more than a formal slap on the wrist, an acknowledgment that the representative in question has done something wrong. The investigative committee's chairman, Luke Poland of Vermont, unsuccessfully pushed to have the two men expelled from the house. Other than blotting their record with a black mark, censure had no real effect on the lives and careers of Ames and Brooks.

Every other member of the House who had bought (or in some cases, been gifted) stock was exonerated of wrongdoing. The resultant uproar in the press and public circles expressed the common view that the investigation had been a whitewash.

# The Organizer

Born into an Indiana family of moderate means, James "Jimmy" Hoffa leveraged a strong work ethic, natural tenacity, and a talent for negotiation to become the head of the powerful Teamsters Union. Hoffa's father died when his son was seven years old, killed by lung disease that he had acquired during his time as a coal miner. Conditions in the mines were poor, and young Jimmy was deeply affected by the knowledge that his father's choice of workplace had directly resulted in his death.

As a young man working in a grocery store warehouse, the 19-year-old Hoffa had his first experience with organizing a labor strike. He was the driving force behind his fellow workers walking off the job. The following year, in 1933, Hoffa joined the International Brotherhood of Teamsters (commonly known as the Teamsters Union), where his talents were quickly recognized. He began a steady climb up the union leadership ladder that would take him to the very top in a little over 20 years.

The Teamsters were (and still are) a highly influential labor organization, comprised of members from a wide range of blue-collar professions, such as truck drivers, warehouse workers, and construction workers, to name just a few. Hoffa gained the presidency of the entire Teamsters labor organization in 1957. This immediately made him one of the most powerful men in the country.

Jimmy Hoffa, president of the Teamsters Union for many years and connected to the Mob, famously disappeared in 1975.

Jimmy Hoffa was well suited to helm the Teamsters. He had a reputation for being hard but fair, a tough negotiator who always had the best interest of the workers he represented at heart. The number of enrolled union members skyrocketed on Hoffa's watch, a fact in which he took great pride. He was also famously approachable, having an open-door policy long before it became common for leaders to adopt one. He was charismatic and caring, a brilliant public orator and masterful politician. Despite whatever faults he may have had, it cannot be denied that he was a true champion for the American worker. Little wonder that so many employers hated him.

If you're thinking that it all sounds a little too good to be true, you'd be right.

It was well known that the Teamsters president had connections with organized crime, including the Mafia, which put him on the radar at the highest levels in Washington. Investigating his links with the Mob, Attorney General Robert F. Kennedy had Jimmy Hoffa squarely in his sights. In 1964, Hoffa was convicted on charges of conspiracy and fraud, and he was sentenced to 13 years' imprisonment by a federal jury. The charges alleged that, along with a handful of colleagues, Hoffa had set up fake loans out of the union pension fund and skimmed around $1.7 million to line his own pockets.

> **It was well known that the Teamsters president had connections with organized crime, including the Mafia.**

After three years of drawn-out appeals, he was sent to jail to begin his sentence. Hoffa remained president of the Teamsters while behind bars. In 1971, President Richard M. Nixon pardoned Hoffa on the condition that he stay away from the Teamsters Union until at the very earliest 1980—the year his sentence would have been fully served. As things turned out, this was a moot point, because on July 30, 1975, Jimmy Hoffa dropped off the face of the earth.

It was an open secret that Hoffa had plans to regain his position of absolute power as head of the Teamsters Union—and that he wanted to do so sooner rather than later. The Mafia had long been associated with Hoffa during his tenure as president, but as time went on, the organization came to see him as more of a liability than an asset. He was unpredictable and difficult, if not impossible, to control, something that was not true of his successor. The Mafia was deeply ingrained within the union at the very highest levels, and its leaders suspected that Hoffa was going to make their relationship public in an attempt to discredit the current union president and pave the way for his own triumphant return. This was not something that the Mafia was willing to allow.

On the day of his disappearance, Hoffa went to a restaurant in Michigan. He never returned home that night and was officially reported missing the following day. The fact that Hoffa was at the restaurant for a meeting with senior members of the Mafia sparked rumors that they had put out a hit on him, arranging for the former organized labor leader to be abducted, driven to an unknown location, and executed. This may well have been the case, although numerous theories swirl around Hoffa's mysterious disappearance to this day.

Mob hitman Richard "the Iceman" Kulinski claimed to have been paid $40,000 to murder Hoffa, snatching him from the restaurant parking lot and subsequently stabbing him to death in the back of a car. The car, Kulinski said, was then taken to a scrapyard and run through a crusher, compressing Hoffa's remains into metal. While possible, many doubt Kulinski's story, pointing out his penchant for embellishing stories and even fabricating them entirely.

**Over the decades since his disappearance, there have been numerous attempts to locate Jimmy Hoffa's body, none of them successful.**

Jimmy Hoffa was declared legally dead in 1982, and no evidence has come to light to dispute that declaration. Over the decades since his disappearance, there have been numerous attempts to locate Jimmy Hoffa's body, none of them successful. Locations as diverse as private residences, factories, landfills, gardens and farms, and even highway overpasses have all been considered as potential burial sites by the FBI. Some claims are more credible than others, but each time agents visited a location to investigate further, they ultimately turned up nothing of value. One theory even insisted that Hoffa's remains were interred beneath Giants Stadium in New Jersey, which was demolished in 2010. No evidence of Hoffa was found.

At the time of writing, despite the fact that the trail has long since gone cold, the search for Hoffa is still ongoing, spearheaded for over 45 years by the FBI's Detroit field office. In the fall of 2021, after a worker's deathbed confession claimed that he had helped bury Hoffa's remains in a Jersey City landfill, FBI agents searched the site and its surrounding area. The search turned up nothing, and some of those who have studied Hoffa's disappearance have expressed doubt that he will ever be found.

Only time will tell.

# The Root of All Evil

"For the love of money is the root of all evil," the Bible tells us. Studying the long history of organized religion in the United States provides countless examples to prove this point.

Although she was by no means the first religious figure to garner controversy and scandal, Aimee Semple McPherson was certainly one of the most colorful. Born in Canada in 1890, she moved to the United States in 1910, where she married and began to raise a family. She was not destined for a life of domesticity, however, and after experiencing her very own Road to Damascus moment, she decided instead to travel across the country, spreading the word of God and proclaiming the imminent return of Jesus. She took her family along for the ride.

McPherson was a gifted speaker and packed churches and other places of worship wherever she stopped to preach her own unique brand of Pentecostalism, known as Foursquare. Whether it came naturally or by design, she also had a flair for showmanship, particularly when it came to speaking in tongues. The crowds, often numbering in the thousands, lapped it up, especially when it came to the high point of her show: faith healing. McPherson would walk among the rows of worshippers and lay hands on those who were afflicted with ailments such as deafness or lameness. Their state of

Aimee Semple McPherson opened the Angelus Temple in 1923 as a center for her brand of Christian evangelism.

health would be miraculously transformed for the better. Those who, just moments before, could barely stand strode confidently away to rapturous applause.

The McPhersons divorced in 1921. As word of mouth grew, and McPherson's profile along with it, the next step was obvious: building a church of her very own. Aptly, McPherson chose the City of Angels as her home base, and in 1923 she realized her vision in the form of the Angelus Temple, located in Echo Park. The temple, which could hold a congregation of up to 10,000, is still in use today.

In modern terms, McPherson's organization would be deemed a megachurch, with thousands of attendees tithing hundreds of thousands of dollars. Its founder became a superstar, internationally renowned. Public radio was just coming into its own, and "Sister Aimee" embraced it as a means of reaching a much wider audience than she could ever meet in person.

## The Evangelist Vanishes

Things took a turn for the strange on May 18, 1926, when she vanished without a trace while at the beach for a swim. When she failed to return, her disappearance was reported to the authorities, and it was believed that she had drown. The Coast Guard mounted a search for her body, sending divers into the waters near Venice Beach. No matter how hard they looked, she was never found.

In the weeks afterward, the rumors began. It is a sad truth that whenever a successful woman is touched by scandal, claims of love affairs and sexual dalliances often make the rounds. These claims are often unfounded, but sometimes they hold more than a grain of truth. One theory was sparked when a woman who looked uncannily like McPherson was seen in public at a resort town along with a married radio engineer named Ken Ormiston. He worked at the radio station that McPherson owned, and reports of his being in the company of an Aimee lookalike at the time of her disappearance would come back to haunt then both in short order.

Other reports alleged she had been kidnapped, and at least one ransom note turned up, demanding the payment of $500,000 "in big bills" for her safe return. It was not the only such letter.

As the days turned into weeks, Aimee was finally believed to be dead. Her family and heartbroken followers held several memorial services. On June 23, five weeks after she went missing, McPherson turned up alive and well in Arizona. She claimed to have been drugged and kidnapped, then transported to Mexico, where she was held captive in a dilapidated shack for weeks. After her escape, the evangelist detailed a harrowing trek through the desert back to civilization, with the kidnappers dogging her trail.

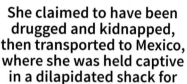

> **She claimed to have been drugged and kidnapped, then transported to Mexico, where she was held captive in a dilapidated shack for weeks.**

Although tens of thousands of her followers were delighted at her safe return, it wasn't long before some were poking holes in the kidnapping story. The press began to cry foul. Accusations of fraud began to circulate, and prosecutors began to scrutinize the testimony of not just Aimee Semple McPherson but also Ken Ormiston and Lorraine Wiseman-Sielaff, who claimed to have been the woman spotted with Ormiston and mistaken for Aimee. Wiseman-Sielaff, who bore a close resemblance to McPherson, initially claimed that the whole thing was a mix-up, but then she recanted her story and admitted that she had in fact been used by the evangelist to serve as an alibi.

It soon became apparent that Wiseman-Sielaff had a problem telling the truth. She changed her story several times. Charges were filed against Ormiston and both women by the Los Angeles District Attorney, alleging that they had conspired to commit fraud. After a protracted investigation, the outcome of which was inconclusive, and a plethora of negative publicity for all concerned, the charges were ignominiously dropped the following year. Wiseman-Sielaff cashed in on her reputation by going into show business, appearing on stage before live audiences who paid to see the woman who had been embroiled in the McPherson farrago.

Once the dust had finally settled, Aimee Semple McPherson went back to preaching. Along with the organization she founded, the evangelist was responsible for countless good deeds and acts of philanthropy. She kept little in the way of money for herself and died with an estate worth around $10,000—a mere fraction of what she had given to charitable causes or used to fund her faith-based outreach programs.

Still, questions about her mysterious disappearance remain to this day, and it is likely that the truth of the matter will never be known.

Aimee Semple McPherson was one of the first evangelists to leverage radio broadcasts to reach a wider audience. As technology advanced, giving birth to the new medium of television, an entire multibillion-dollar industry would emerge: the era of televangelism.

## Jim and Tammy Faye Bakker: The PTL Prosperity Gospel

Throughout the late 1970s and on into the 1980s, two pioneers of televangelism were Jim and Tammy Faye Bakker. Through their PTL ("Praise the Lord") organization, the Bakkers made millions of dollars preaching the gospel to vast television audiences across the United States. Both were colorful, larger-than-life characters. Their brand of Christianity would come to be known as the "prosperity gospel" and preached the message that wealth, riches, and all good things would come to those who put their faith in the Lord.

As their business empire really took off, the Bakkers developed lavish tastes and indulged in the opulent trappings of a high-end lifestyle. Jim drove expensive cars and had a private jet. Tammy Faye shopped for high-end jewelry. Profits from their burgeoning TV empire allowed the Bakkers to own multiple vacation homes, make real estate investments, and build a hotel complex, complete with its own water park—"Disneyland for Christians," as Jim liked to describe it.

Jim and Tammy Faye Bakker, televangelists preaching the "prosperity gospel" through their PTL broadcasts, were ridiculed in popular media for their conspicuous consumption even before their name was further muddied by a string of scandals.

Unfortunately, their fortune also brought challenges and tribulations. On TV, the Bakkers seemed like the perfect, all-American, god-fearing Christian couple. Behind the scenes, there were serious issues. The marriage was marred by infidelity. Tammy Faye, a highly recognizable public figure thanks to her signature fake eyelashes and heavy makeup, had secretly become addicted to prescription tranquilizers such as Valium. As her health worsened, she began to suffer hallucinations, believing herself to be attacked by demons, and matters ultimately came to a head in the form of a severe breakdown.

> **Jim had diverted more than $150 million in funds from church finances to fund his personal lifestyle.**

A 21-year-old secretary named Jessica Hahn, who worked for their organization, accused Jim of sexually assaulting her. He denied the charge, claiming that they had been involved a single sexual encounter in December of 1980, to which he said Jessica had consented. Whichever was the case, Jim paid hush money in an attempt to conceal the scandal—to no avail.

When Hahn came forward to tell her story, one consequence was that Jim Bakker resigned from his position as head of the church organization. His troubles, however, were only just beginning. With the spotlight now on his business affairs, it soon became apparent that there was a trail of shady financial dealings waiting to be discovered. Jim had diverted more than $150 million in funds from church finances to fund his personal lifestyle.

In 1989, Jim Bakker was charged with multiple counts of fraud and was sentenced to 45 years in prison. He would serve only five years of that hefty sentence. Tammy Faye was not charged with any crime.

The Bakkers divorced in 1992, while Jim was still in prison, and each subsequently married a new partner. Tammy Faye Bakker died of cancer in 2007. Jim was released in 1994. At the time of writing, he lives in Missouri and still makes a living selling faith-based trinkets and products. He remains no stranger to controversy. In 2020 he was hit with a lawsuit alleging that, in the early weeks of the COVID-19 pandemic, Bakker was marketing a product named Silver Solution that was falsely claimed to be a cure for the coronavirus. He settled the lawsuit in 2021 for $156,000 without admitting any wrongdoing.

## Jimmy Swaggart: "I Have Sinned"

Despite his high-profile prostitution scandals, Jimmy Swaggart continues his televangelism to this day.

Jim Bakker was hardly the first religious figure to indulge in the sins of the flesh, and he was certainly not the last. In 1998, one of his former associates, televangelist Jimmy Swaggart, appeared in front of a live crowd of thousands, plus tens of thousands more watching on television, and declared tearfully: "I have sinned."

Indeed, he had. Swaggart, who had made a fortune preaching the gospel and espousing the Christian virtues, was secretly visiting a sex worker whom he paid for the privilege of watching her undress. Swaggart had worked for the Bakkers during the late 1980s and had been an outspoken critic of Jim's extramarital liaisons. He, in turn, was busted by a rival preacher named Martin Gorman, against whom Swaggart had leveled similar allegations. This was payback, pure and simple. The scandal cost the errant preacher his position, and he was defrocked by the church.

Three years later, he was caught with a prostitute once again, during a traffic stop in California. Swaggart had been driving on the wrong side of the road. This time, he was far less repentant. There were no tears. Swaggart's response to the new scandal was to say: "The Lord told me it's flat none of your business."

## The Evangelical Empire of Robert Tilton

Speaking of business, there are few bigger industries in 21st-century America than televangelism. In addition to the tried and tested format of television, modern-day preachers have embraced the power of the internet to reach an even larger flock, whose members are exhorted to donate money to the church via the World Wide Web. Faith has been monetized, to the tune of billions of dollars—most of which is not taxed.

Financial corruption ultimately brought down the evangelical empire of Texan preacher Robert Tilton, perhaps best known for speaking in tongues during his TV shows and making incredible claims of faith healing. Throughout the 1990s, Tilton spent the lion's share of his airtime trying to wring money out of his congregation. His show was carried by hundreds of stations and raked in payments from the faithful all across the United States.

**The corruption scandal sent the televangelist, whose company had reportedly been making $80 million a year at the height of its success, into a public relations tailspin.**

Along with checks and money orders, viewers mailed in prayer requests to Tilton's church, having been solicited by a marketing company working on the evangelist's behalf. The company mailed each potential donor a cheap religious trinket, which psychologically primed many of them to respond by sending back money.

In 1991, scandal erupted during an undercover TV investigation by ABC News's *Primetime Live* newsmagazine when sacks filled with such requests were found in the trash. They had never even been opened. (Tilton declared that they had been planted in an attempt to smear him.)

Many of Tilton's flock were people of limited means but devout faith, who believed that their money would be used by the church to do good deeds—not to pay for the luxurious lifestyle of its pastor. Publicly humiliated and with his livelihood threatened, Tilton went to court in an attempt to block the *Primetime* segment from being repeated—and lost. Doubling down, he then sued ABC News, *Primetime Live*'s producer, and even the show's anchor, Diane Sawyer, for libel.

He lost again.

Then the lawsuits began flowing in the opposite direction: against Tilton. The corruption scandal sent the televangelist, whose company had reportedly been making $80 million a year at the height of its success, into a public relations tailspin, which knocked him down but not out.

At the time of writing, Robert Tilton is still actively preaching the prosperity gospel. His organization emphasizes the practice of donating financially to the church—tithing—and terms such payments "faith promises to God." The website offers pledges ranging from the "Patriot Founder Dream Builder," for which any amount of money qualifies, all the way up to the "Millionaire Founder Dream Builder." The cost—one million dollars.

## Peter Popoff's Faith-Healing Scam

Since the birth of organized religion, faith and money have been inextricably linked. There have always been those who are willing to exploit faith and devotion for their own personal gain. It is a sad truth that hope can make one vulnerable, and this has never been truer than in the case of so-called faith healers.

The idea of curing ailments with divine power is not new. History is littered with examples of supposedly miraculous healings. Arguably the most prominent would be those of Jesus Christ, and many Christians today believe that God has the power to heal the sick when invoked through prayer. Whether this is true is beyond the scope of this book, but there has been no shortage of men and women who have tried to cash in on this belief—with varying degrees of success.

Take the case of Peter Popoff, a televangelist who achieved national prominence in the 1980s on a popular TV show. Popoff was charismatic and knew how to work a crowd, homing in on those with injuries and chronic ailments. He knew the names of his targets in advance, and more impressively, he could also name their specific affliction. His accuracy bordered on the uncanny, and with good reason—Popoff was cheating.

The scam was simple but effective. Prior to the show, planted members of the audience would engage other attendees in conversation, with the intent of gleaning information on their medical history. Attendees were also encouraged to fill out prayer request cards, which involved detailing personal information on their state of health. This data was then collated by Popoff's wife, Elizabeth, who in turn transmitted it directly to her husband's radio receiver earpiece. Popoff would proceed to "heal" the unsuspecting mark in a theatrical display of mummery that often culminated in an apparently miraculous "get up and walk" climax.

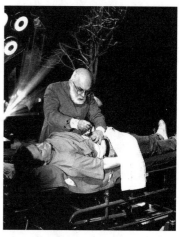

In 1986, the magician and debunker of fraud James "the Amazing" Randi, aided by several colleagues, caught the Popoffs red-handed. All it took was a radio receiver tuned to the same frequency being used by Elizabeth to communicate with her husband. She offered a running commentary on various individuals in the audience, which Peter capitalized on to great effect. The Popoffs built a multimillion-dollar enterprise on the back of Peter's supposedly supernatural abilities to

Longtime skeptic and debunker James Randi, known for deconstructing and convincingly reenacting tricks employed by purported psychics, exposed the ruse used by Peter and Elizabeth Popoff.

sense and heal illness. It took James Randi just minutes to destroy any credibility Popoff had by playing those recordings on *The Tonight Show*, hosted by Johnny Carson. The result was predictable: public embarrassment and bankruptcy.

Popoff's story doesn't end there, however. After being outed by Randi, the discredited televangelist set to work rebuilding his brand, changing its focus by veering away from faith healing and setting his sights instead on faith-based debt erasure. His next sales pitch contended that God's will was for you to be free from debt, and that Peter Popoff was the divine instrument that could help you get there—assuming you had some money to donate to him, that is. One of his more recent ventures involved "miraculous" spring water, blessed by the evangelist himself, capable of helping to erase debt, especially if the recipient is able to respond with an "optional donation."

There is no evidence whatsoever to suggest that Popoff's unique brand of "supernatural debt reduction" works, yet that is no deterrence to his legion of optimistic and faithful followers, who continue to send his ministry both money and prayers in equal measure.

It is unclear whether the majority of evangelists act out of a sincere belief or a cynical desire to make money. It is a question of prophet versus profit. Yet, in spite of the vast fortunes there are to be made and the numerous instances of corruption that plague it, evangelism does have an upside. Many televangelists, including those included in this chapter, have donated significant sums of money to charity. Some have even set up charities themselves, and while all of them benefited handsomely from taking advantage of their fellow human beings, it is only fair to point out that they also gave something back to others. For those men of faith who proved to be corrupt, this may provide at least a sliver of redemption.

# Sins of the Church

Ostensibly, the purpose of organized religion is a noble one: to care for the spiritual nourishment of those who follow its teachings. No matter what the faith or creed, there lies an underpinning moral code that insists upon doing no harm to others and caring for one's fellow human beings.

Yet the inescapable truth remains that religion has been the root cause of more wars throughout human history than almost any other cause (with the exception of greed), and of tragedy on an immeasurable scale.

Take, for example, the Catholic Church. While there are undeniably many priests whose behavior is impeccable, sexual abuse of children and vulnerable individuals runs rampant throughout the organization worldwide.

Celibacy is an integral part of the Roman Catholic priesthood and has been for the past thousand years. It has been hypothesized by some that imposed celibacy leads a percentage of male priests to sexually molest victims, usually young boys or teenage males (although sexual assaults on adult males and females also take place). It must also be borne in mind that the church has proven to be a safe harbor and a hunting ground for pedophiles; not only does it allow them to spend time unsupervised around children in a legitimate setting, but the Catholic Church also has a proven track record of covering up the awful abuses visited upon them by those priests who do turn out to be sexual predators.

Long the seat of the Catholic Church and home to its head, the pope, the Vatican's Holy See is the center of spiritual and moral leadership for the church's hierarchy and over 1.3 billion followers worldwide. Behind its sacred architecture and saintly statuary lies a long history of unholy behavior and hypocrisy.

Many experts consider it likely that the revocation of celibacy would prevent at least some priests from abusing children. Indeed, evidence suggests that the majority do not even practice celibacy, despite the rules. Richard Sipe was a Benedictine monk and Catholic priest who left the church, qualified as a psychotherapist, and went on to study the systemic abuse being conducted by priests within the organization. Sipe was often called upon as a witness in legal cases pertaining to such abuse and was considered an expert in the field until his death in 2018.

Richard Sipe's research suggested that there was a significant number of priests who only pretended to be celibate. Not all were abusing children—some were presumably in consensual, if clandestine, relationships—but in a 2017 interview with *Baltimore Sun* reporter Dan Rodricks, Sipe claimed that "6 to 9 percent of priests are involved with minors sexually." Assuming that Sipe was correct and bearing in mind the fact that a minor *cannot* consent to sexual intercourse, then the scale of sexual abuse being inflicted on them by priests is staggering.

In May of 2011, the New York–based John Jay College of Criminal Justice issued a much-anticipated report titled "The Causes and Context of Sexual Abuse of Minors by Catholic Priests in the United States, 1950–2010," commonly known as the John Jay Report. The study, which ran for 60 years, concluded that neither celibacy nor homosexuality were causal factors for priests to molest children. Those who were looking for a single reason that priests sexually assaulted children within the confines of the Catholic Church would not find it in the John Jay Report.

> **The likelihood is that the majority of victims were boys because priests were around unaccompanied boys much more often than they were around girls.**

Eighty-one percent of the abuse victims identified by the study were either boys or young men. Critics of the John Jay Report latched onto this as being proof that the offending priests were driven to molest them because the priests themselves were gay, but the likelihood is that the majority of victims were boys because priests were around unaccompanied boys much more often than they were around girls. Targeting vulnerable males as victims was not a matter of sexual preference, necessarily, but rather one of convenience and availability.

For years, priests who were accused of abusing children were not turned in to the police. Instead, their superiors swept the allegations under the rug. Rather than becoming the subject of a thorough investigation, the offending priest would instead usually be shuffled off to a different part of the country, where nobody was aware of what they had done. This was the church leadership's idea of "kindness," although it showed nothing of the sort to the tormented victims left in the abusive priests' wake.

Has the situation improved in the 21st century? Because of increased media coverage, there has been a significant rise in public awareness of sexual abuse carried out by priests. It has become harder for the church to cover up such behavior. In 2019, the senior figure of the Catholic Church, Pope Francis, spoke out against sexual abuse within the ranks of the organization, stating that "no abuse should ever be covered up, as was often the case in the past, or not taken sufficiently seriously, since the covering up of abuses favors the spread of evil and adds a further level of scandal."

The pope went on to say that "the church will never seek to hush up or not take seriously any case." Few would disagree with the sentiment. Such words lack meaning unless backed up by concrete action, however.

Rumors had long circulated concerning Cardinal Theodore McCarrick. Seminarians—theological students who made the church their calling—were targeted by McCarrick during their time studying at a seminary close to New York. By 2000, he had gained a reputation for using his position of authority to compel these young men into having sex with him at his beach house. Some reluctantly acceded. Others reported his behavior to seminary authorities, who in turn informed the Vatican, which did nothing to halt his predatory behavior. In fact, Pope John Paul II promoted McCarrick—with full knowledge of the complaints against him and despite express warnings that he was not suitable.

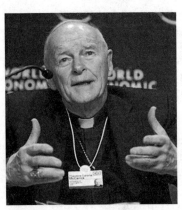

Theodore McCarrick, whose decades of abuse the church had helped cover up, resigned his cardinalship in 2018 and was defrocked in 2019.

In July of 2018, McCarrick resigned as a cardinal. The church had finally gotten around to investigating the claims against him and uncovered evidence suggesting that he may have sexually molested an altar boy 40 years before. The investigation was damning, not just of McCarrick's behavior but also because it uncovered proof that a host of church leaders had both known of his behavior and chosen to ignore it. In 2019, the 90-year-old McCarrick was defrocked by express order of Pope Francis.

Following his expulsion, McCarrick was subsequently indicted, which was a historic moment in U.S. history; never before had such a highly placed member of the church been brought up on charges of sexually assaulting a minor.

At the time of writing, Theodore McCarrick is the subject of both civil and criminal lawsuits pertaining to multiple claims of repeated sexual abuse. It is alleged that McCarrick abused his position of authority and trust at practically every level of his career within the Catholic Church to target vulnerable youngsters. If true—the claims have yet to be tried in a court of law—then his behavior was nothing less than predatory, the very antithesis of the way in which a holy leader ought to behave.

In the past, the church has proven to be a safe haven for sexual predators. Although the issue remains widespread, there are signs that such behavior is now being exposed. In 2018, the Roman Catholic Diocese of San Bernadino, California, publicly named all 34 priests who had served the diocese since 1978 and had been credibly accused of sexual molestation. Some were already dead, and others had been expelled from the church; six had been convicted for their crimes. Although this came as a welcome step forward in terms of bringing the problem to light, a review of the list reveals something disturbing. The list includes the date at which the diocese was made aware of the accusations against each priest and the date on which a report was made to the police. More often than not, the diocese waited some years before reporting these crimes to law enforcement.

A 2019 report issued by the office of the Colorado Attorney General is representative of the scale and longevity of abuse within the state. The investigation spanned almost 70 years of molestation by priests within several dioceses. Shockingly, since 1950, 43 priests had been credibly accused of sexually assaulting a *minimum* of 166 children during that time; the actual number of victims was almost certainly higher. In several cases, the church took 20 years or more to act on reports of sexual abuse once they were made—and "act" typically did not mean reporting such crimes to the police. On the contrary, church officials often took a punitive approach toward those who tried to expose the guilty priests.

Assuming that the Colorado situation is typical of that in other states, it is fair to say that the Catholic Church faces a crisis. As more claims of abuse continue to surface, even the most ardent supporter would find it hard to deny that an epidemic of sexual abuse has corrupted the organization. A slew of multimillion-dollar lawsuits has been levied, costing the Catholic Church an estimated $4 billion in restitution payments to abuse victims—although some estimates place that figure on the low end.

How could men and women of conscience fail to report child abuse to the authorities? One answer can be found in a concept known as "pontifical secrecy," a principle intended to protect the privacy of victims. Throughout the history of the church, clergy have been expelled for violating pontifical secrecy by sharing sensitive information with outsiders. In 2019, Pope Francis removed the pontifical secret as a restriction upon reporting sexual abuse, which many saw as a solid step forward toward reform.

Pope Francis, unlike so many of his predecessors, appears to be interested in changing the church's culture of shielding the predators in their ranks.

Sexual abuse within the church is not restricted to children; investigations have also revealed cases in which nuns have been assaulted. In February of 2019, Pope Francis announced that his predecessor, Pope Benedict XVI, had dissolved a congregation of nuns because they had been kept in a state of "sexual slavery" by male clerics. He went on to claim that the abuse of nuns was still taking place and that the church was "working on it."

What does "working on it" entail? In 2021, Pope Francis declared sexual assault (including the protection of those who do it) and possessing child pornography to be criminal offenses. Although this has long been the case in the world outside, these were not regarded as crimes under Vatican law until the papal proclamation. Also deemed to be a crime is grooming of children with the intent to sexually exploit them.

Prior to this, Pope Francis had already mandated that all cases of suspected abuse must be reported to church authorities, rather than swept under the carpet as they had been so often in the past. He also insisted that in such cases, reports be made to law enforcement agencies outside the church.

There is clearly a long road ahead before the corrupt hierarchy of abusers within the Catholic Church is dismantled and brought to justice—if indeed that ever takes place—but it is encouraging to see what appears to be a shift in the prevailing winds. The changes enacted by Pope Francis may prove to be more temporizing measures than full-fledged solutions, but it cannot be denied that they indicate some of the most significant progress made toward stamping out sexual abuse within the church since it was brought to light in the 1980s.

# The Price of Admission

We all want to do well in life. For some, a key measure of success involves getting into a top university. One reason for this is that the more prestigious the academic institution, the better it looks on a résumé—and therefore, the better the student's chance of getting a top job after graduation. Networking opportunities, too, abound at the Ivy League colleges and other centers of academic excellence.

The competition for admission to such colleges is fierce, and it should come as no surprise that some hopeful applicants prefer to cheat rather than compete. In 2019, however, news emerged of a massive and widespread orchestrated effort to trade cash payments in exchange for entrance into some of those first-rate institutions. The scheme has been publicly dubbed the college admission scandal. To the FBI agents who investigated the case, peeling back layer after layer of corruption and deceit, it was known as Operation Varsity Blues.

The scandal involved student admission to such respected universities as UCLA, Georgetown, Stanford, University of Texas at Austin, Yale, and others. The majority of those charged were not the students themselves but their wealthy parents, who attempted to buy their children's way into college rather than have them succeed or fail on their own merits. Once the scandal broke, it emerged that those parents paid bribes that totaled tens of millions of dollars.

**Grifters, Frauds, and Crooks: True Stories of American Corruption**

Actress Felicity Huffman spent $15,000 to have her daughter's SAT scores falsely inflated.

It goes without saying that the media loves a good scandal, and that is doubly true when celebrities are involved. Two of those charged were famous actresses. Felicity Huffman was perhaps best known for her role on the ABC television show *Desperate Housewives*. Huffman spent $15,000 to have her daughter's SAT scores falsely inflated. The SAT score is a key factor that admissions boards will take into account when considering whether an applicant should be awarded a place at the college. Huffman's husband, the actor William H. Macy, was not charged.

Huffman pleaded guilty in court. The 56-year-old actress was sentenced to 14 days in jail (of which she served 11), fined $30,000, and ordered to complete 250 hours of community service. In a letter written to the judge prior to sentencing, Huffman had requested no jail time. The prosecutor, on the other hand, had pushed for a sentence of four months' incarceration to send a message regarding the severity of the crime.

In the aftermath of the scandal, Huffman's daughter, Sophia, was accepted into college on the basis of her actual SAT scores rather than the fraudulent ones that her mother had paid for. There had been a 400-point difference between the two.

Actress Lori Loughlin, a cast member of the television show *Full House*, was also embroiled in the scandal, along with her husband, the fashion designer Mossimo Giannulli. Loughlin and Giannulli wanted to secure places for both of their daughters at the University of Southern California, or USC. Rather than boost their children's SAT scores, the fraud that they engaged in involved sports—specifically, rowing. The pair paid bribes totaling half a million dollars to maintain the fiction that their daughters qualified for admission on the basis of participating on a crew team. In reality, neither had ever been part of a rowing crew, let alone at the level that would make them competitive prospects for admission to USC.

Large chunks of the $500,000 were paid out in bribes to college administrators and team coaches to support the fiction that the students were recruits for the rowing team.

Loughlin was sentenced to two months in prison, fined $150,000, and made to complete 100 hours of community service. Giannulli was given five months' incarceration. The Hallmark Channel, which had featured Loughlin in many of its made-for-TV movies, publicly severed ties with her over the issue.

> **Huffman, Loughlin, and Giannulli were far from the only wealthy parents who were prepared to pay their kids' way into a top college. They were just exceptionally high-profile ones.**

Huffman, Loughlin, and Giannulli were far from the only wealthy parents who were prepared to pay their kids' way into a top college. They were just exceptionally high-profile ones. Among the other parents who were indicted were venture capitalists, executives, consultants, CEOs, and at least one heiress. All had money to burn in the name of furthering their children's standing in life, and all were willing to break the law to further that goal.

Others, mostly individuals in positions of authority and influence within academia, also were charged once the true extent of the cheating scandal became clear. At the heart of it all was William "Rick" Singer, who operated a business known as The Key and a charity called the Key Worldwide Foundation. The Key's stated purpose was to counsel and coach prospective college applicants, preparing them for the admissions process. In reality, it served as a smokescreen for Singer's criminal activities. Parents such as Huffman made what appeared to be charitable cash donations to the nonprofit Key Worldwide Foundation. These lump sums were actually lining Singer's pockets. The charity was a way for him to collect bribes while making them appear to be legitimate donations.

Much of the college acceptance process depends on SAT scores. To ensure that the children of clients scored highly, Singer ran multiple testing sites at which the exam proctors had been paid to mark the SAT exams so that the students were awarded a much higher final score than they had earned.

When it came to the athletics angle, Singer flexed his creative muscles. To pass off his clients' children as top athletes, he staged photographs of them pretending to compete in the sports in question. He also had some of their faces Photoshopped over those of legitimate competitive athletes.

During meetings with the parents who would purchase his services, Singer pitched himself as giving them a "guaranteed side door" into top colleges. The front door is the honest path, the standard method of scoring highly enough in all areas to gain admittance into one's desired school in the traditional way. The "back door" method involves making significant donations (usually millions of dollars) to an institution in the hope that the institution will then admit one's child. Some might see that method as being morally questionable, but it is not illegal. It also is not a guaranteed way of ensuring admission, though it can significantly boost an applicant's chances.

Rick Singer's admissions shortcut tactics included falsifying sports photos, brokering institutional donations, and outright fixing of test scores.

What Rick Singer offered was a middle ground, a relatively affordable way in—which also happened to be criminal. Somewhat to his credit, he pleaded guilty to all charges that were leveled against him in court, which included money laundering, racketeering, and conspiracy to defraud the United States. In January 2023 he was sentenced to three and a half years in prison and fined $10 million. "I lost my ethical values and have so much regret. To be frank, I'm ashamed of myself," Singer said at his sentencing.

In a move that surprised and infuriated many, Robert "Bob" Zangrillo, CEO of the venture capital investment firm Dragon Global, was given a presidential pardon by Donald J. Trump in the final days of his administration. While it is customary for an outgoing president to issue pardons, the reasons behind this particular case remain unclear. Zangrillo was alleged to have paid bribes so that his daughter could gain admission to USC via the rowing team route, so presumably this was the reason for the pardon.

Zangrillo maintained his innocence and was preparing to go to trial when his pardon came through. Thirty-eight of his fellow defendants were not as fortunate, receiving sentences that ranged from significant fines to 15 months' imprisonment.

# Something for the Pain

Anybody who has ever sustained a fracture or had a heart attack knows that painkilling medications such as oxycodone, morphine, and fentanyl have no substitute. Binding to special receptors in the body's central nervous system, opioids prevent pain impulses from reaching the brain, saving the patient from experiencing severe agony. For millions of chronic pain sufferers, they can be a lifeline, allowing them to function in the face of serious long-term illness and pain.

Unfortunately, this class of narcotic drugs also carries negative side effects. The medicines are extremely addictive and, if taken repeatedly, can easily get the user hooked. Also, when taken in excessive amounts, it is frighteningly easy to overdose. High doses of opioids, particularly when injected directly into a vein, can cause the body to stop breathing. Respiratory arrest soon leads to cardiac arrest, which is often difficult or impossible to reverse.

Every physician knows that prescribing such medications tends to be a double-edged sword. On the one hand, doctors want to treat pain and alleviate suffering. On the other lies the risk of addiction and death. Opioids should never be given lightly or administered at excessive dosages.

Today, the United States faces an opioid crisis of unprecedented proportions. According to the Centers for Disease Control and Prevention in a press release dated November 17, 2021, an estimated 75,673 Americans died of opioid overdoses between April 2020 and April 2021. This tragic number of deaths may have been largely preventable, and it begs the question: Just why is the number of opioid-related deaths so high, and why does it continue to rise?

> The Sacklers are billionaires, and their fortune derives from the profits of controlled substances. They are, in essence, legal narcotics dealers.

Part of the problem involves the aggressive marketing tactics employed by some pharmaceutical companies. One of the biggest offenders was Purdue Pharma, makers of the heavy-duty pain killer OxyContin, the company's brand name for oxycodone. Purdue Pharma is owned and operated by the Sackler family. The Sacklers are billionaires, and their fortune derives from the profits of controlled substances. They are, in essence, legal narcotics dealers. To be fair to them, there is absolutely nothing wrong with manufacturing analgesic medicines, which are used legitimately in hospitals, clinics, and pharmacies throughout the land. Things get murkier when those same drugs are used inappropriately, especially when it's at the behest of those who stand to profit on their improper use.

OxyContin is a relatively new drug, dating back to the mid-1990s. Purdue Pharma developed Oxy (as it is colloquially known) from scratch, put the drug through studies and safety trials, and made it available in 1996. From the outset, there was clear evidence that OxyContin had highly addictive properties. The Sacklers were made aware of this and chose to deliberately downplay the serious risks of addiction and abuse, all in favor of getting the drug out to a wider market—and reaping bigger profits.

At the direction of management executives at the highest levels, Purdue Pharma's sales force painted OxyContin in a much rosier light than it deserved. Far from being highly addictive, they claimed, the reverse was actually true: their new wonder drug was *less* addictive than alternative medications and was therefore safer to prescribe. This was an outright fabrication, and one that came down from the very top of the company.

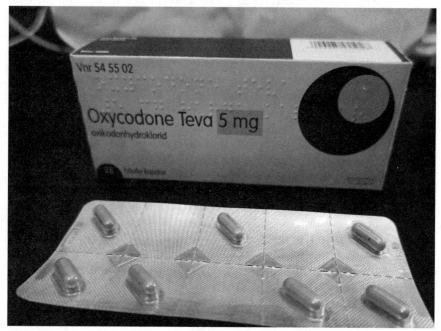

Physicians were led to believe that oxycodone was a weaker (and therefore safer) alternative to morphine, but the reverse is actually true: oxycodone is about 50 percent stronger.

There were also lies concerning the drug's potency. Prescribing physicians were led to believe that OxyContin was a weaker (and therefore safer) alternative to morphine, but the reverse is actually true: Oxy is about 50 percent stronger. Doctors were being intentionally deceived by the drug manufacturer, and it is impossible to say how many unwitting addicts were created as a result or how many lives were lost to accidental overdoses.

As 1999 gave way to 2000, the American opioid crisis was beginning to take hold. Overdose deaths were on the rise, as were cases of narcotic abuse and addiction. Still, Purdue Pharma continued to push an aggressive marketing agenda that centered on OxyContin, for which it alone held the patent. The lion's share of Purdue's profitability (and therefore, that of the Sacklers) is built on the success of that one particular drug.

In addition to their pivotal role with Purdue Pharma, members of the Sackler family are also well known for their efforts in philanthropy. The Sacklers donated tens of millions of dollars to programs benefiting the arts, culture, and scientific research. Prestigious universities, museums, and art galleries accepted huge infusions of cash from the estimated $13 billion family coffers. This bought the Sacklers plenty of influence and goodwill, but all that changed when word of Purdue Pharma's shady dealings became public. An increasing number of institutions and charitable beneficiaries began to turn down the Sacklers' offers of money, uncomfortable with the negative publicity that accompanied being associated with the billionaire family.

To be fair to them, the Sacklers' support for cultural and charitable causes came long before the introduction of OxyContin. When it became clear that their wealth was built on the back of nationwide death and addiction, however, a question arose: Was it ethical for any charity to accept donations from them any longer, or were they offering up tainted blood money?

> Then came the lawsuits—so very many lawsuits—hundreds and hundreds, eventually thousands, from cities and states across the nation.

Then came the lawsuits—so very many lawsuits—hundreds and hundreds, eventually thousands, from cities and states across the nation. There were criminal charges to accompany the civil suits. Several company executives admitted culpability but were given little more than a slap on the wrist—probation and multimillion-dollar fines that they could easily afford. It was a drop in the bucket compared to the damage that had been done in terms of loss of human life, and considering the vast profits Purdue Pharma had raked in.

None of those indicted were members of the Sackler family. They were all employees. The Sacklers themselves maintained their distance, continuing to cash checks and donate money.

Purdue Pharma cannot be held solely responsible for creating the opioid epidemic, but it was undeniably a major player. It must also be noted that not every member of the Sackler family gained monetarily from the success of OxyContin. To this day, neither Purdue

Pharma nor any of those who were associated with the company have accepted responsibility for their role in the opioid epidemic.

The company filed for bankruptcy in the face of an overwhelming volume of lawsuits and claims against it. At the time of writing, attorneys representing a number of the Sacklers were attempting to negotiate protection from all future lawsuits as part of a multibillion-dollar legal settlement. The likelihood was that they would pay out several billion dollars in restitution, some of which would go toward treatment of and compensation for the victims of OxyContin addiction.

# Bro, Please

Developing a new medication is an expensive proposition. It can cost anywhere from hundreds of millions to several billion dollars. Drug manufacturers must make significant investments in time, research, and equipment to realize the potential benefits of bringing a groundbreaking drug to market.

Along the way, there are always missteps and dead ends. Clinical trials that once seemed promising may ultimately go nowhere, meaning that the whole enterprise has to be scrapped and started over anew. After years, if not decades, sometimes it all turns out to have been a massive waste of time.

Small wonder, then, that so few medications survive this long and challenging process to reach the bloodstreams of patients in need. To finance the winnowing out of those drugs that simply won't work, pharmaceutical companies have to recoup the financial expenditures with the proceeds from those medications that do pay off.

Even taking this process into consideration, sometimes the prices charged by manufacturers for life-saving medications are exorbitant. According to a June 2, 2022, article by Hannah McQueen of GoodRx.com, the most expensive drug on sale in the

Martin Shkreli, known by some as the "Pharma Bro," testifies before the House Committee on Oversight and Government Reform in 2016.

United States is Zolgensma, which costs $2.1 million per dose. This particular medication is a gene therapy drug and is prescribed to children afflicted with spinal muscular atrophy.

It's a safe bet that few parents of sick children will have millions of dollars sitting in their bank accounts. Will healthcare insurance companies cover it? In some cases, yes, and in other cases, no. One of the biggest points of contention within the medical field today is the price of care, particularly when much of that cost must be borne out of pocket by the patients and their families.

Enter Martin Shkreli, former head of Turing Pharmaceuticals and a man who earned himself the less-than-affectionate nickname "Pharma Bro." One of Turing's products was a medication named pyrimethamine, released under the brand name of Daraprim. Its primary use is to combat toxoplasmosis, a parasitical infection that can target people with HIV and AIDS, people who eat undercooked food, and people who come in contact with cat feces.

By any definition, toxoplasmosis is an awful way to die. The disease attacks the central nervous system and manifests in a number of unpleasant ways. Drugs such as Daraprim are a genuine boon to ease suffering. At around $13.50 a dose, Daraprim was relatively affordable—at least, until Shkreli increased the price to $750 a pill in 2015. That's a price hike of more than 5,000 percent.

> **At around $13.50 a dose, Daraprim was relatively affordable—at least, until Shkreli increased the price to $750 a pill in 2015.**

When word of what was undeniably price gouging got out, an uproar arose. The price increase for such a valuable drug was considered obscene. Shkreli, for his part, expressed little remorse, retorting that he was simply selling a premium product at a premium cost. Wasn't such an important treatment worth the $750 price tag?

Shkreli began raking in tens of millions of dollars in profits from drug sales. The American public quickly grew to hate him, perceiving him as a profiteer who was making a fortune on the backs of those who were seriously ill. It didn't help that Shkreli often seemed to be smirking whenever somebody put a camera in his face.

Seemingly uncaring of the hate he was getting, Shkreli lavished money on trinkets that were far beyond the means of most people. A one-of-a-kind album by the Wu Tang Clan set him back $2 million. An Enigma machine, used by the Nazi military to encrypt and decrypt secret messages, an original work of art by Pablo Picasso, and a manuscript written and signed by the great scientist Sir Isaac Newton were also added to Shkreli's collection of valuable artifacts.

Many of those artifacts would be claimed and sold off by tax authorities following Shkreli's 2017 conviction of securities fraud. The charges had nothing to do with Daraprim price gouging, relating instead to questionable financial maneuvering Shkreli had committed between 2009 and 2014. He had misrepresented business earnings to investors, for which he was sentenced to seven years' imprisonment, with six months deducted for time already served.

On May 18, 2022, the Pharma Bro was released from prison and transferred to a halfway house to await final release. A smiling Shkreli posted a selfie on Facebook that appeared to have been taken in his car. "Getting out of real prison is easier than getting out of Twitter prison," was the accompanying comment, referring to his banishment from the social media site. On that, at least, Martin Shkreli may have been right.

## Enter Theranos

Conventional wisdom teaches us that nine out of ten startup companies fail before ever gaining traction in the marketplace. Of those that survive the turbulent early years, a significant number fail to make an impact or turn a significant profit.

There are also the shooting stars: startups that blaze a bright trail before falling into obscurity. One such company was Theranos, which in 2014 built its business model around what it claimed was innovative blood-testing technology.

In hospitals, clinics, and even ambulances all around the world, medical professionals draw tubes of blood from their patients so

Elizabeth Holmes, founder of Theranos, is interviewed in 2014 by *TechCrunch* editor Jonathan Shieber.

that doctors can order the appropriate tests. The results of such tests are critical; physicians base their diagnoses and treatment plans on the lab values that are derived from them. To ensure accuracy, it is often the case that a single tube of blood must be used for a single, specific test.

Enter Theranos, which claimed that its product (named the Edison after acclaimed inventor Thomas Edison) could allow *hundreds* of tests to be run from a single sample of blood. Throughout the field of healthcare, the cost savings alone would be enormous. Valuable resources would be conserved and wastage reduced significantly. On the clinical side, the reduction in test times (no more waiting around for multiple lab values to be analyzed) would undoubtedly have had a positive effect on patient care.

What the company promised seemed too good to be true. Unfortunately, that's because it was.

The blood testing technology was the brainchild of Elizabeth Holmes, who had dropped out of the prestigious Stanford University at the age of 19 to found her own company. Holmes had been a precocious child, with aspirations of growing up to be a billionaire. Unlike many childhood dreams, this one would ultimately be realized. Fiercely competitive, the young Holmes was also a hard and diligent student, putting in long hours to master the mathematic and technical disciplines she would eventually put to use in Silicon Valley.

> By her second year at the university, she was already rolling out her business venture, a medical company named Real Time Cures. It would soon be renamed Theranos.

Getting accepted into Stanford was no small achievement. Holmes had put in the effort and earned the grades. By her second year at the university, she was already rolling out her business venture, a medical company named Real Time Cures. It would soon be renamed Theranos. Shortly after, in 2004, she dropped out of Stanford completely so that she could devote all her time to the fledgling startup.

The blood-testing technology seemed such a great innovation that Holmes had no problem attracting venture capitalists with deep pockets to back her idea. There was just one catch: nobody outside the highest echelon of Theranos would be permitted information on how the blood-screening process worked. That highest echelon was Elizabeth Holmes. From the very beginning, she instituted a policy of absolute secrecy within the organization.

Keeping a proprietary technology confidential is sound business practice. Nobody wants to invest hundreds of millions of dollars into an idea only to have it ripped off by a competitor. But that wasn't the reason for Holmes's circumspection. She insisted on keeping the specifics of Theranos's technology out of the public eye because she knew it was

**It simply did not do what Holmes claimed it could.**

nothing but smoke and mirrors. It simply did not do what Holmes claimed it could.

The secret couldn't be kept forever. Perhaps Elizabeth Holmes was trying to stall matters in the hopes that there would be a genuine breakthrough in the company's medical research. However, Theranos employees began to leak information about the troubled technology to the press in 2015, where the rumors reached the ears of *Wall Street Journal* reporter John Carreyrou. Holmes had assiduously cultivated her image as both a business and scientific genius, but the seasoned journalist found the concept of a second-year university dropout revolutionizing the field of medical analysis to be questionable. He began to dig deeper into the goings-on at Theranos. What he found was disturbing, and he wasted no time in going public.

By this point, Theranos had signed deals with major healthcare organizations to supply blood-testing services to their patients.

The Theranos blood-testing machine, the Edison, was so notoriously unreliable that it couldn't be used for the majority of blood tests the company was paid to perform. There were simply too many false results, so Theranos secretly used conventional analysis techniques and ascribed their results to Edison.

> **The Theranos blood-testing machine, the Edison, was so notoriously unreliable that it couldn't be used for the majority of blood tests the company was paid to perform.**

Shockingly, some of the inaccurate Edison-derived test results were factored into the care of real patients by physicians who had been falsely assured of their accuracy. At least one patient was given a false positive HIV test, which understandably upset her deeply. As the number of errors compounded, it became clear that Theranos blood tests might have been relatively inexpensive, but they were equally unreliable.

It took an article in the *Wall Street Journal* and a subsequent government investigation to prove just how bad the situation was at Theranos. Holmes and her colleague, former Theranos president Ramesh "Sunny" Balwani, were formally charged with wire fraud—something she insistently denied—and left the company before its ignominious breakup in 2018. The disgraced CEO lost billions of dollars from her private fortune in the process.

In January of 2022, Holmes was tried in a federal court, where she was found guilty on four counts of fraud. In November, she was sentenced to 11 years and three months in prison.

# Further Reading

Belfort, Jordan. *The Wolf of Wall Street*. New York: Random House, 2007.

Bernstein, Carl, and Bob Woodward. *All the President's Men*. New York: Simon and Schuster, 2022.

Broadwell, Paula. *All In: The Education of General David Petraeus*. New York: Penguin Press, 2012.

Brown, Mick. *Tearing Down the Wall of Sound: The Rise and Fall of Phil Spector*. London: Bloomsbury, 2012.

Chayes, Sarah. *On Corruption in America: And What Is at Stake*. New York: Vintage, 2021.

Collins, Max Allan. *Scarface and the Untouchable: Al Capone, Eliot Ness, and the American Dream*. New York: William Morrow, 2018.

Cuomo, Andrew. *American Crisis: Leadership Lessons from the COVID-19 Pandemic*. New York: Crown, 2021.

Eichenwald, Kurt. *Conspiracy of Fools: A True Story*. New York: Broadway Books, 2005.

Gentry, Curt. *J. Edgar Hoover: The Man and the Secrets*. New York: Norton, 2001.

Golway, Terry. *Machine Made: Tammany Hall and the Creation of Modern American Politics*. New York: Liveright, 2015.

Goodwin, Richard N. *Remembering America: A Voice from the Sixties*. New York: Open Road, 2014.

Henriques, Diana B. *The Wizard of Lies: Bernie Madoff and the Death of Trust*. New York: St. Martin's Griffin, 2017.

Kelley, Jill, and Lura Lee. *Collateral Damage: Petraeus/Power/Politics and the Abuse of Privacy: The Untold Story*. Tampa, FL: Kelley Publishing, 2016.

Knowles, Harry, Paul Cullum, and Mark C. Ebner. *Ain't It Cool? Hollywood's Redheaded Stepchild Speaks Out*. New York: Warner, 2002.

Levitt, Leonard. *NYPD Confidential: Power and Corruption in the Country's Greatest Police Force*. New York: Thomas Dunne/St. Martin's Griffin, 2010.

Maas, Peter. *Serpico*. New York: Bantam Books, 1974.

McCartney, Laton. *The Teapot Dome Scandal: How Big Oil Bought the Harding White House and Tried to Steal the Country*. New York: Random House, 2009.

McDougal, Jim, and Curtis Wilkie. *Arkansas Mischief: The Birth of a National Scandal*. New York: Henry Holt, 1998.

McGowan, Rose. *Brave: Cult Member, Runaway, Captive, Starlet, Victim, Sex Symbol, Justice Seeker*. New York: HarperOne, 2019.

Newfield, Jack. *The Life and Crimes of Don King: The Shame of Boxing in America*. New York: Harbor Electronic, 2003.

O'Reilly, Bill, and Martin Dugard. *Killing the Mob: The Fight against Organized Crime in America*. New York: St. Martin's, 2021.

Posner, Gerald L. *Pharma: Greed, Lies, and the Poisoning of America*. New York: Avid Reader, 2021.

Raab, Selwyn. *Five Families: The Rise, Decline, and Resurgence of America's Most Powerful Mafia Empires.* New York: St Martin's Griffin, 2016.

Schweizer, Peter. *Clinton Cash: The Untold Story of How and Why Foreign Governments and Businesses Helped Make Bill and Hillary Rich.* New York: HarperCollins, 2016.

Spector, Ronnie, and Vince Waldron. *Be My Baby: How I Survived Mascara, Miniskirts, and Madness of My Life as a Fabulous Ronette.* New York: HarperPerennial, 1991.

Toobin, Jeffrey. *A Vast Conspiracy: The Real Story of the Sex Scandal That Nearly Brought Down a President.* New York: Random House, 2020.

Trump, Donald, and Tony Schwartz. *Trump: The Art of the Deal.* London: Random House Business, 2016.

Ward, Vicky. *Devil's Casino: Friendship, Betrayal, and the High-Stakes Games Played Inside Lehman Brothers.* Hoboken, NJ: John Wiley, 2011.

# Image Credits

**Page 2:** Daniel Edgar Sickles portrait: Library of Congress Prints and Photographs Division

**Page 4:** Sickles shooting Philip Barton Key II: *Harper's Bazaar*

**Page 6:** Daniel Edgar Sickles at Gettysburg: via Wikimedia Commons

**Page 10:** President Eisenhower: James Anthony Wills, via Wikimedia Commons

**Page 12:** Cold War; Gorbachev and Reagan signing INF Treaty: White House Photographic Office

**Page 14:** The Pentagon: Touch of Light, via Wikimedia Commons

**Page 18:** Melvyn Paisley: James P. Vineyard, via Wikimedia Commons

**Page 22:** Leonard Glenn Francis wanted poster: U.S. Marshal's Service

**Page 24:** Admiral Gary Roughead: U.S. Navy photo by Mass Communication Specialist 2nd Class Kyle P. Malloy

**Page 28:** General David H. Petraeus: Robert D. Ward, via Wikimedia Commons

**Page 29:** General David Petraeus and Paula Broadwell: U.S. Navy

**Page 32:** Panama Canal, U.S. Army Corps of Engineers: National Geographic Society

**Page 36:** Chicago skyline: Humbledumpty, via Wikimedia Commons

**Page 38:** Michael Madigan: Illinoislawmakers, via Wikimedia Commons

**Page 40:** Al Capone: Federal Bureau of Investigation, Chicago Bureau/World Wide Photos

**Page 43:** Eliot Ness: Public domain

**Page 46:** J. Edgar Hoover: U.S. News & World Report

**Page 48:** Joseph McCarthy: National Archives and Records Administration, Records of the U.S. Information Agency

**Page 50:** J. Edgar Hoover and Clyde Tolson: L.A. Daily News

**Page 53:** James Comey: Official White House Photo by Amanda Lucidon

**Page 56:** Orange County sheriffs dumping illegal booze: Photo courtesy Orange County Archives

**Page 59:** Giuseppe Carlo Bonanno: U.S. Federal Government

**Page 61:** Giuseppe "Joseph" Profaci: Walter Albertin for *World Telegram*

**Page 63:** Joseph Columbo: New York City Police Department

**Page 65:** Carlo Gambino: New York City Police Department

**Page 67:** John Gotti: FBI

**Page 69:** Charles "Lucky" Luciano: New York City Police Department

**Page 71:** Vincent Gigante: U.S. Department of Justice

**Page 76:** Police brutality political cartoon by Eugene Zimmerman: *Judge*, via Wikimedia Commons

**Page 78:** Al Pacino as Frank Serpico: Paramount Pictures

**Grifters, Frauds, and Crooks: True Stories of American Corruption**

**Page 80:** Wayne Newton: Carol M. Highsmith, via Wikimedia Commons

**Page 82:** Abscam investigation: FBI

**Page 84:** John Jenrette: U.S. Government

**Page 86:** William Webster: FBI

**Page 88:** William "Boss" Tweed: Gurney & Son, NY

**Page 90:** "Tammany Ring" cartoon by Thomas Nast: *Harper's Weekly*, via Wikimedia Commons

**Page 95:** Warren G. Harding: Frank Norwell, via Wikimedia Commons

**Page 100:** Richard Nixon swearing-in: Oliver F. Atkins, via Wikimedia Commons

**Page 102:** Richard Nixon departing on Army One: Ollie Atkins, via Wikimedia Commons

**Page 104:** Oliver North: via Wikimedia Commons

**Page 106:** Ronald Reagan and Tower Commission: U.S. National Archives and Records Administration

**Page 110:** Hillary Rodham Clinton and Bill Clinton: White House

**Page 112:** Clintons in front of Air Force One: Jessica M. Fatheree, via Wikimedia Commons

**Page 115:** President Clinton and Monica Lewinsky: White House

**Page 117:** President Clinton television still: Miller Center of Public Affairs

**Page 120:** Hillary Clinton: Voice of America

**Page 122:** Hillary Clinton swearing-in: U.S. Department of State

**Page 126:** Andrew Cuomo: Metropolitan Transportation Authority of the State of New York

**Page 130:** Donald Trump wearing MAGA hat: Gage Skidmore, via Wikimedia Commons

**Page 132:** Trump University parody diploma: Wikipietime, via Wikimedia Commons

**Page 134:** "Report to the House Committee on Ways and Means" about Trump's income tax returns: U.S. Congressional Joint Committee on Taxation

**Page 136:** Stormy Daniels: lukeisback.com, via Wikimedia Commons

**Page 139:** Donald Trump at RNC: Ali Shaker/Voice of America

**Page 141:** Angela Merkel, Jared Kushner, Donald Trump, and Ivanka Trump Kushner: White House

**Page 144:** Bribe money found in freezer: U.S. Attorney's Office

**Page 148:** Charles Van Doren on *Twenty-One*: Macfadden Publications

**Page 152:** Phil Spector with Modern Folk Quartet: Robert W. Young, via Wikimedia Commons

**Page 154:** Phil Spector mug shot: North Kern State Prison, California Department of Corrections and Rehabilitation

**Page 156:** Harry Knowles: Gage Skidmore, via Wikimedia Commons

**Page 158:** Movie screening/AICN: Ground Picture/Shutterstock

**Page 160:** Alamo Drafthouse: blwarren713, via Wikimedia Commons

**Page 164:** Call center: Vitor Castillo, via Wikimedia Commons

**Page 168:** Harvey Weinstein: David Shankbone, via Wikimedia Commons

**Page 170:** #MeToo protest: MandriaPix/Shutterstock

**Page 172:** Twin Towers Jail: Basil D. Soufi, via Wikimedia Commons

**Page 176:** Epstein's island: Navin75, via Wikimedia Commons

**Page 178:** Jeffrey Epstein: State of Florida

**Page 182:** Ethel and Julius Rosenberg: Roger Higgins/*New York World-Telegram and The Sun*

**Page 184:** David and Ruth Greenglass: Department of Justice, Office of the U.S. Attorney for the Southern Judicial District of New York

**Page 186:** U.S. Navy tugboats and submarine, Groton, CT: U.S. Navy photo by Mass Communication Specialist 1st Class Virginia K. Schaefer

**Page 192:** Black Sox players: Underwood & Underwood

**Page 196:** Don King with Roy Jones: mborowick, via Wikimedia Commons

**Page 199:** Don King: Frederick Johnson (Fjohnsonphoto), via Wikimedia Commons

**Page 203:** Salt Lake City skyline: debaird, via Wikimedia Commons

**Page 206:** Lance Armstrong: U.S. Air Force photo/Airman 1st Class Tabitha M. Mans

**Page 209:** Lance Armstrong at Tour de France, 2009: Josh Hallett, via Wikimedia Commons

**Page 212:** Charles Ponzi: Mgreason, via Wikimedia Commons

**Page 214:** Bernie Madoff: U.S. Department of Justice

**Page 218:** Depression-era soup kitchen: U.S. National Archives and Records Administration

**Page 221:** Foreclosed house: Joe DeV/Shutterstock

**Page 224:** Philip Morris ad: Philip Morris/Stanford University

**Page 228:** Jordan Belfort: Tai Lopez, via Wikimedia Commons

**Page 232:** Lion Air Boeing 737 Max 8: PK-REN, via Wikimedia Commons

**Page 235:** Grounded Boeing 737 Max planes: SounderBruce, via Wikimedia Commons

**Page 237:** Boeing 737 flight simulator: Sergei Sobolev, via Wikimedia Commons

**Page 242:** Kenneth Lay: United States Marshals Service

**Page 245:** Jeffrey Skilling: United States Marshals Service

**Page 248:** Mark Zuckerberg of Facebook: Anthony Quintano, via Wikimedia Commons

**Page 250:** Whistleblower Christopher Wylie: jwslubbock, via Wikimedia Commons

**Page 255:** "East and West Shaking Hands at Laying Last Rail," photo by Andrew J. Russell, restoration by Adam Cuerden: Yale University Libraries

**Page 257:** Thomas C. Durant, photo by Mathew Benjamin Brady: U.S. National Archives and Records Administration

**Page 262:** Jimmy Hoffa: John Bottega/*World Telegram and Sun*

**Page 266:** Aimee Semple McPherson: Matthew Sutton, via Wikimedia Commons

**Page 269:** Tammy Faye and Jim Bakker: Peter K. Levy, via Wikimedia Commons

**Page 270:** Jimmy Swaggart: Jntracy75, via Wikimedia Commons

**Page 273:** James Randi: Open Media Ltd., via Wikimedia Commons

**Page 276:** Vatican's Holy See, St. Peter's Basilica: Hunterframe/Shutterstock

**Page 278:** Theodore McCarrick: Andy Mettler/World Economic Forum

**Page 280:** Pope Francis: Pontifica Universidad Católica de Chile

**Page 284:** Felicity Huffman: Angela George, via Wikimedia Commons
**Page 286:** SAT test: smolaw/Shutterstock
**Page 291:** Oxycodone Teva: Praetorian11, via Wikimedia Commons
**Page 296:** Martin Shkreli: House Committee on Oversight and Government Reform
**Page 298:** Elizabeth Holmes interviewed by Jonathan Shieber: Kevin Krejci, via Wikimedia Commons

# Index

Note: (ill.) indicates photos and illustrations.

Rosenberg, Ethel, 181–84,
182 (ill.)
Rosenberg, Julius, 181–84,
182 (ill.)
Rossi, Marco Rosaire, 37
Roughead, Gary, 24, 24
(ill.)
Round Tops, 5–6
Ruddy, Al, 63
"Rumble in the Jungle"
[1974 boxing match],
197
Russia and Russians, 10,
14, 25, 53, 122–23,
181–83, 185. See also
Soviet Union and
Soviets

**S**

Sackler family, 290–93
Sacramento, California,
253
Salt Lake City, Utah,
202–4, 203 (ill.)
Salt Lake Organizing
Committee (SLOC),
202–4
Sam, David, 204
Samoa, 203
San Bernadino, California,
279
San Diego, California, 25
San Francisco, California,
96
Sandinista National
Liberation Front,
104–5
SanDisk, 188
SAT tests, 284–85
Saudi Arabia, 14
Sawyer, Diane, 272
Scarface. See Capone,
Alphonse "Al,"
"Scarface"

Schwartz, Tony, 134
Schwarzenegger, Arnold,
157
Schweizer, Peter, 122
Scorsese, Martin, 74, 171,
229
Scott, Ridley, 159
Seattle, Washington, 95,
235
*Seattle Times* [newspaper],
238
Secret Service, U.S., 45
Securities and Exchange
Commission, U.S.
(SEC), 212, 215, 244
Senate, U.S., 14, 24, 48–49,
84, 117
Serpico, Francesco
"Frank," 75–78
*Serpico* [1973 movie], 77
*Sex, Lies, and Videotape*
[1989 movie], 169
Shieber, Jonathan, 298 (ill.)
Shkreli, Martin "Pharma
Bro," 296 (ill.), 296–97
Sicily, Italy, 58–61, 65,
67–69, 72
Sickles, Daniel Edgar
"Dan," 1–7, 2 (ill.), 4
(ill.), 6 (ill.)
Sickles, Teresa Bagioli, 2–4
Silicon Valley, 298
Sill, Lester, 151
Silver Solution, 270
Simpson, Dick, 37
"Sinclair Consolidated in
Big Oil Deal with U.S.,"
94
Sinclair Oil, 94
Sing Sing Correctional
Facility, 184
Singapore, 21
Singer, William "Rick,"
285–86

Sipe, Richard, 276–77
Siskel, Gene, 155
*Siskel and Ebert at the Movies*
[1986 TV show], 155
Skilling, Jeffrey, 242–45,
245 (ill.)
Skorupa, John A.,
112 (ill.)
SLOC (Salt Lake
Organizing
Committee), 202–4
Snipes, Wesley, 159
Society of St. Tammany,
87
Soderbergh, Steven, 169
Sons of St. Tammany, 87
Sony Pictures, 158
*The Sopranos* [1999 TV
show], 74
Sorvino, Mira, 170, 172
South Carolina,
83–84
South Korea, 14
South Side, Chicago, 41
Southeast Asia, 12
Southwest Airlines, 237
Soviet Union and Soviets,
9–11, 103–4, 185–86.
See also Russia and
Russians
Spain, 91
Spector, Harvey Phillip
"Phil," 151–54, 152
(ill.), 154 (ill.)
Spector, Veronica
"Ronnie" Bennett,
151–53
Spielberg, Steven, 156
St. Valentine's Day
Massacre, 42
Stalin, Joseph, 10
Stallone, Sylvester, 197
Stanford University, 283,
298–99